STARTING IN LIFE

THEODORE ROOSEVELT

Twenty-sixth President of the United States; born in New York City, 1858; graduate Harvard College, 1880; member of the New York State legislature, 1882–4; resided on a ranch in North Dakota, 1884–6; unsuccessful Republican candidate for mayor of New York, 1886; United States Civil Service Commissioner, 1889–95; president New York Police Board, 1895–7; assistant secretary United States Navy, 1897–8; resigned to organize with Surgeon (now Maj. Gen.) Leonard Wood, the 1st U. S. Cavalry Volunteers (" Rough Riders "); promoted colonel for gallantry at the battle of Las Guasimas; Governor New York, elected 1899; Vice-President United States, 1900; succeeded President McKinley, 1901; elected President, 1904; big game shooting in East Africa, 1909–10

STARTING IN LIFE

A Turn-of-the-Century Career Handbook

BY
NATHANIEL C. FOWLER, Jr.

ILLUSTRATED BY
CHARLES COPELAND

THE LYONS PRESS
Guilford, Connecticut
An imprint of The Globe Pequot Press

The Lyons Press is an imprint of The Globe Pequot Press.

Printed in the United States of America

10 9 8 7 6 5 4 3 2 1

ISBN 1-58574-813-7

Library of Congress Cataloging-in-Publication data is available on file.

Luck is the result of chance
Success is the product of intention

The Truth I give you as It came to me, undraped by painted tapestries, untouched by flowery rouges.   Right or wrong, there is reason to believe that I am right, for every word was fired in others' crucibles until the flavor of fancy burned out of it.

N. C. F.

EXPLANATORY

BECAUSE practically every boy, if he lives, will eventually become an active participant in some trade, business, or profession, an advance knowledge of what each class of pursuits offers — its advantages and disadvantages — is axiomatically of very great consequence.

The success of the man is dependent upon the start of the boy.

A majority of the failures is due to the wrong start, which, in many cases, permanently leads the boy in the wrong direction, where he never meets with the opportunity to use his real self.

The advice of a biased adviser may be worse than none at all. The circle of personal knowledge, for most of us, is of small circumference, because it may not more than surround our environment. Honest and unbiased personal opinion is seldom possible. The optimistic lawyer naturally advises in favor of the law; the pessimistic doctor cannot see why any one should wish to become a physician; the millionaire manufacturer looks upon his business as the greatest of all trades; the unsuccessful merchant thinks well of every calling save his own.

Just a word about myself:

I would not have written this book, or have assumed the distribution of advice, if fortunate conditions and environment had not made me into a clearing-house of experience.

Over twenty years ago I originated and established a business-profession, in the practice of which I was brought into direct contact with the methods pursued in the leading trades, businesses, and professions. I was given continuous opportunity of personally seeing the very heart-workings of their machinery. I was permitted to observe the manner of action, and to view, at close range, the causes which led to success or failure. This information I received at first hand.

I acted only in an advisory capacity, and, therefore, I was removed entirely from the prejudice of self-interest.

That I might reduce the opportunity for error to the minimum, raise the probability of correctness to the maximum, and guard against the over-use of my personal opinion, I submitted the first draught of the manuscript of each chapter to two or more authoritative representatives of the calling treated. These men read it with painstaking care and returned it to me with their suggestions and criticisms.

I then rewrote each chapter, accepting the criticisms or suggestions made in so far as they could be verified and did not represent the purely personal opinion of the critics. Where the authorities differed materially, others were consulted, until a more unanimous position was reached.

To further remove the work from personal opinion, and to make it truly composite, I requested two or more prominent representatives of each calling to give brief outlines of the advantages and disadvantages of their respective trades, businesses, and professions as seen from their individual points of view. At the close of the chapters these expressions are printed as they were written, having been subjected only to proofreaders' corrections.

As a rule the manuscript of each chapter was approved by others than those whose printed words appear at the close. Every effort has been made to present facts instead of opinion, and every precaution has been taken against material error.

I hope that I have succeeded in preserving a compromise between depressing pessimism and a too highly magnified optimism. To have done otherwise, or to have allowed personal bias to influence my writing, would have been unfair to the young reader, or to any one who may seek to benefit from the facts contained in this book.

It is obvious that no book of reasonable size could contain information about more than a limited number of callings. I selected only those lines of work which represent distinct classes; for example, the stage is peculiar to itself, and so is the practice of medicine, and neither can be treated other than individually. The manufacturer is distinct from the merchant, and there is little in common between the storekeeper and the sailor. But there is not a sufficient difference between the keeping of a hardware store and the running of a market to justify a separate chapter for each.

N. C. F.

CONTENTS

CONTENTS

CONTENTS

CONTENTS

Gifford, pastor of the Delaware Avenue Baptist Church, of Buffalo. Arthur T. Hadley, LL.D. president of Yale University. Joseph Alden Shaw, A.M., principal of the Highland Military Academy, of Worcester. The Rev. Amory H. Bradford, D.D., associate editor of the *Outlook*. Mr. Josephus M. Larned, ex-president of the American Library Association, late superintendent of education of Buffalo. The Hon. Carroll Curtis Boggs, justice of the Supreme Court of Illinois. Henry T. Byford, M.D., of Chicago. The Hon. Charles D. Hine, of the Connecticut State Board of Education. William E. Huntington, Ph.D., president of Boston University. Mr. John Thomson, librarian of the Free Library of Philadelphia. Harry Pratt Judson, A.M., LL.D., head professor of political science, dean of the faculties of arts, literature, and science, and acting president, University of Chicago. Professor William Libbey, Sc.D., of Princeton University. Mr. Philip E. Howard, president, Sunday School Times Company. Professor Joseph W. Richards, A.M., M.S., Ph.D., of Lehigh University. The Hon. Carroll D. Wright, Ph.D., president of Clark University. Mr. Charles Gallaudet Trumbull, editor of the *Sunday School Times*. Charles Franklin Thwing, D.D., LL.D., President of Western Reserve University.

INDEX TO CHAPTERS

INDEX TO COLLABORATORS

Starting in Life

THE PHYSICIAN

THE physician is one of the noblest products of civilization. His associates are of the highest grade; his surroundings are refined, broad, progressive, and civilized. He lives both under the sunshine of life and under the shadow of death; and, by day and by night, he feels the pulse of humanity, and continually listens to the beating of the public heart.

Practically every doctor in good and regular standing is a man of ability and a credit to his community.

The brainless man of inactive goodness may be tolerated in the pulpit, the man of "wind" may be allowed to practise at the bar, but the regular physician cannot maintain his position unless he gives proof of his competency. True, there are in the medical profession some practitioners who would make better blacksmiths than doctors; some are better fitted for other callings; but the rank and file of regular physicians are men of much education, careful training, strong character, and pronounced ability. Comparatively few mediocre men are attracted toward the medical profession, because efficiency in it, and financial success resulting from its practice, not only demand long and hard study, but require willing and continual sacrifices.

In speaking of the medical profession, I am referring to the regular physician, the graduate of one of the two great schools of medicine, allopathic or homœopathic, and a member of one of the two recognized and standard medical societies. I am not referring to the quacks, charlatans, and other uneducated and untrained practitioners, who certainly ought to be sent to jail, and would be, if the majority of our people exercised the full prerogative of citizenship.

No man can occupy a more honorable, a more respected, and a more responsible position than does the regular doctor. In the actions of his brain, and in the skill of his hands, he often holds the control of life. He is our friend at birth, and he remains with us until we die. He is a necessity, for without him we could not be properly born, nor could we properly live.

To become a physician, one must pass through the longest and hardest courses of study, where favoritism is unknown, and where each student must depend upon himself or fall by the wayside.

Not one boy in ten thousand has the natural abilities to make him fitted for the medical profession, no matter how many there may be who think they want to become doctors; and the parent who pushes his son in this direction, unless the boy shows marked characteristics which point to this profession, not only wrongs the boy, but the community as well.

The boy most likely to succeed as a doctor is one who takes life seriously, and yet is not morose; for successful seriousness sees the bright side of life as often as it does the cloudy side.

While it is true that some frivolous boys have later acquired great sobriety of demeanor and thought, and have become eminent physicians, yet the majority of good physicians have developed from thoughtful and serious lads, who early realized that life had its responsibilities, and that there was something in it besides chance and pleasure.

The embryo physician is likely to be a student, almost always an experimenter, an early seeker after truth, a natural reasoner, and one who does not readily accept any statement unless it is backed by probability. He is seldom, if ever, superstitious. The miraculous is to him the natural law of God, and the working of God's Nature.

Such a boy loves Nature, and in his crude way is an evolutionist, and a believer in cause and effect. He feels the growth of life, and becomes familiar with its different forms. Physiology is his favorite study, and he may even acquire a fair knowledge of anatomy. He may faint at the first sight of blood, and become unnerved in the presence of suffering, so that his parents may conclude that because the boy does not seem to have the strongest of nerves, therefore, he is unfitted for the

medical profession. The physician has nerves. No
man without nerves, and no man without feeling, is
fitted to be a physician. The greater the physician,
the greater the amount of feeling he possesses. But he
also has the power of nerve concentration, which allows
him to cut in mercy and to seem not to care while in
action ; but no man of fine intellect, no man of consum-
mate skill, can idly stand unmoved beside the bed of
suffering. Good butchers are not good doctors, and
the man without tender feeling never made a good
surgeon.

The wild boy, the thoughtless boy, the boy who does
not possess the characteristics of manliness, and who is
not willingly a student, will never become more than a
mediocre doctor.

One of the first indications of ability in this direction
is the perceptible enjoyment which the boy shows at
the visits of the family physician, and the earnestness
with which he listens to all that the doctor says. As
he grows older, he associates with medical men, and
probably borrows medical books, and studies them earnestly. The chances are that he does not display
marked money-making ability, and he probably thinks
more about becoming a man, and a useful member of
society, than of being a mere money-getter. He does
not necessarily despise money, but his inner thoughts,
his higher ideals, are along the ethical, scientific, and
professional sides of life. His first aim, his first ambition, is to become proficient in some special line of work,
to actually do something worth the doing, something for
the benefit of humanity. His secondary aim may
be to make money; but he does not allow money-getting to interfere with the development of his better
talents.

The ordinary boy, the boy who has no particular ambition, who does not know what he wants to do, and does not seem to care what he does, is not fit to enter the medical profession, and any attempt to force him in that direction is criminal. Thus it is the exceptional boy, not the average boy, who is fit to become a doctor.

The physician is reasonably sure of a livelihood, but he must not expect to be self-supporting during the first year, and perhaps not during his second and third years of practice. His chances are much better in the country than in the city, unless he possesses remarkable skill or has strong social influence. A very few physicians, in large cities, enjoy incomes of about twenty-five thousand dollars a year, and possibly there are some whose receipts exceed this amount. The average physician, in large cities, receives probably from twenty-five hundred to five thousand dollars a year, and comparatively few established city doctors have annual incomes of less than fifteen hundred dollars. There are, in large cities, quite a number of family physicians, who are not specialists, yet have practices worth from five thousand to ten thousand dollars a year.

The average annual income of the physician established in some country centre is from two thousand to three thousand dollars, the minimum probably being not over one thousand dollars, and the maximum not in excess of from six thousand to seven thousand dollars, comparatively few receiving more than the larger amount. Well-established country physicians earn from eight hundred to twenty-five hundred dollars a year.

The physician must deduct from his income the cost of maintaining his practice, which consists chiefly in keeping a horse and carriage, and a man or boy to care for them, and the sums paid out for medicines, dressings, and instruments. The majority of physicians maintain their offices at their residence, consequently office expense is likely to be merely nominal.

Unless a physician is fortunate enough to acquire an extended practice and stands well socially, he probably cannot become self-supporting in a large city inside of four or five years.

The country-centre physican is not likely to find himself upon a self-supporting basis in less than a year, and in many cases his income will not be sufficient to support him in ordinary comfort until he has practised three or more years. The country town physician may have uphill work, for there is likely to be much competition, and even opposition, in his field. It is exceedingly difficult to usurp the older physician, who is the friend, as well as the physician, of the whole community. Some of his patients may be afraid of young physicians. If there is little competition, the country physician may begin to earn his living in less than a year.

Many young physicians find an opening in the country by succeeding some old doctor, who either has become too old to practise, or who removes to the city.

The so-called specialist is a regular physician, who, after years of practice, devotes his time to some one disease or class of diseases.

The specialist, except the one who gives his attention to the eye, ear, or nose, seldom begins as a specialist. He usually does not attempt to act as a specialist until he has succeeded in a general way. If he is successful to a marked degree, his income, if he is located in a large city or at a country-centre, is likely to be considerably in excess of the amount obtained by the regular family physician. Comparatively few physicians, even good ones, have the peculiar ability necessary for becoming successful specialists. The majority of physicians will do better, in every way, especially financially, to continue their family practice, than to attempt to become specialists.

Regular family physicians, who are not specialists, and who practise in large cities, usually receive from one to three dollars per office call, the majority of such fees being one dollar; and from two to three dollars for outside calls, the two-dollar rate being the usual one. The country-centre physician seldom receives more than a dollar for office calls, nor more than two dollars for outside calls, although the most successful may command three dollars for outside visits. In some of the smaller places the office fee is as low as fifty cents, and the outside call rate not higher than a dollar or a dollar and a quarter.

Nearly every doctor of ability can earn his living. The specialist, if extremely skilful in diagnosis or in surgery, receives very large fees, often running into the hundreds or even thousands of dollars. Yet few specialists are wealthy men, because it is an unwritten law that the specialist shall give of his time to cases where there is little or no hope of more than ordinary remuneration; and he must often be present, either actively or otherwise, at numerous operations, where there is no possibility of compensation.

Comparatively few young men are specialists, because to become a specialist one must have spent many years in study and practice; consequently, the specialist of large fees receives comparatively little in the aggregate, if he reckons his receipts from the time he began to practise.

There are few pauper physicians. The competent

doctor, whether located in the city or in the country, is, in time, reasonably sure of a livelihood. The kind of stamina that makes the good doctor is that of the nature to insure independence. But the medical profession is not, and never will be, a money-making business. He who loves money better than his fellow-men, he who loves business better than study, and he who cares more for bodily comfort than for making the mighty sacrifices which help to push progress and to relieve the suffering of humanity, is unfitted for the medical profession, and has no business to give it any consideration as a calling.

There is no profession, and there are few callings, either of trade or of business, which make such demands upon their practitioners as does the medical profession. The practising physican is the slave of his work; he has little or no time for diversion or recreation; he is liable to be called at any hour of the day or night, in rain or in blizzard. The little time he has at his disposal he must use for study, for without continual study he cannot keep up with the progress of his profession.

The boy who sincerely wants to become a doctor, and who has the necessary ability, cannot be turned away from it. But the boy who says he wants to be a doctor, or who wants to be a doctor because some of his friends are going to be doctors, and who can be talked out of it as well as into it, is not likely to make a good physician, and probably will never more than moderately succeed in any direction.

No one unfitted for the medical profession should attempt to enter it, — first, because he cannot legitimately make a success of it; secondly, because he is not likely to earn more than a moderate living; and thirdly, because he will be a positive menace to the community.

Adaptability is absolutely essential to any kind of medical success. Any one can learn the elements of the technique of medicine and surgery, almost any one can become a " book-doctor," and any well-read book-doctor can successfully treat a case when he knows exactly what is the matter with the patient and what the patient's constitution requires. In the skill at diagnosing lies the physician's real success and his real value. Without this proficiency, he is little better than a medical book.

Unless the boy, some time during his common-school career, shows indications of a diagnostic instinct, he is not likely to become a good physician, and should not be allowed to enter the profession.

Mere scholarship is not an indication of adaptability. The successful physician is more than a scholar. While he must have a fundamental education, and must have passed through the courses of medical study, and have answered questions put to him by the severest examiners, he must also have had actual experience, hospital and laboratory practice, and know, from observation and from instinct, much that no book, or any amount of theory, can teach him.

It is impossible to state with any degree of accuracy the proportion of college-educated physicians and those whose higher education began with the medical school, but it is said at a venture, that probably sixty per cent of our leading physicians are college graduates, and that about one-third, or a little more, of the rank and file of doctors are college bred.

A college education will prove of great value to the physician, not because he will practise the classics, but because he needs the discipline, and the more general knowledge which is not obtainable in the common schools. It is true that many of our most successful practitioners never entered college; but few, if any, of them would refuse a college education if they could start again.

The discipline of the higher education, with its environment, fits a man the better to grasp the perplexities of life.

The business man can get along without the college, and sometimes he may be better off without it. The doctor, or other professional man, can succeed without the higher education, but he will feel the lack of it constantly. It is not so easy to reach the pinnacle of success without it. He must pass through the training of an immense amount of study. If he does not do it in his youth, he must do it afterward; and it is much more economical and satisfactory to build the general educational framework of success before one has established himself in any professional calling.

The medical-school course is from four to six years, and must be taken before one is permitted to practise as a regular physician (M.D.).

George M. Gould, A.M., M.D., of Philadelphia, editor of *American Medicine*, and author of standard medical works, in a letter to the author, says:

" The choice of a profession is rarely made by a young man's own free will, and still more infrequently by a due consideration of his peculiar fitness for the special work. Whim, accident, and circumstances usually rule. Physicians seldom advise their sons to become physicians, since, by the time of the son's majority, life has demonstrated to the forty- or fifty-year-old father that the world has little thanks and thought for the true doctor or his work.

" If the father is of that enviable type that learns to

lightly love and deftly scorn the motives of his sentimental youth-time, — the hunger for fame, for gratitude, etc., — he is likely to discourage his boy from taking up the physician's hard life. If he is of a different type, and sees in his son a character that will love truth and duty more than ambition and selfishness, the boy may be quietly encouraged to study medicine.

"Any young man of good stock and mental structure can succeed in our country, fairly well, at least, in whatever calling he may take up. The test of exceptional success of a genuine and desirable kind, however, will come with the clearness of recognition and the intensity of the motive of altruism and truth-seeking.

"For the sake of decency, humanity, and medical art and science, do not allow a young man whose character is of the commercial or politician, ambitious, selfish type, to choose the medical calling. In other callings, the cunning may have their place, they can be watched by the more cunning — egotism and astuteness are expected, planned for; but among the doctors, the politicians are already our curse, the traitors that make up one-third or one-half the army. Do not increase the afflictions of the profession of the next fifty years by adding a single Mephistopheles; for, while to a magnanimous man the medical life brings rewards of exceeding satisfaction, to the hunter after success, LL.D. degrees, popularity, and leadership, the gratuities are likely to be superficially brilliant; but long before the end of the play the plot fails, and the tragedy rings the farcical curtain down in disgust.

"None know the secret shame and pitiful plight of the medical 'leader,' who has achieved success and power by collusion with the daily papers, who has intrigued and wriggled himself to fame by every device of posing and subtle chicane. It is a pretty safe rule with us that the more a physician is in the newspapers, the more he is honored, 'degreed,' banqueted, the higher his fees, the more he is president and chairman, the more useless he is as a physician, the more contemptible his private character, and the methods whereby he has gained his vogue. There may be exceptions, but the wise will not err in putting them down as few indeed. On the other hand, the rewards of the modest and unselfish lover of men and of science are of the highest and most satisfactory kind.

" In no other calling, not even in pure science, is there such an opportunity to make great discoveries of tremendous value. And these discoveries are for all men, for the whole world, and for all time. Moreover they are practical, affect the very warp and woof of life, reaching into the daily and hourly well-being — or ill-being — of the lowest and the highest. There is a peculiar reason for this, consisting in the fact that no two men's diseases or ' cases ' are exactly alike. The cause and nature of every one's illness differs from that of every other that has been or may be. This gives an individuality to practice, and supplies the basis of the art of healing, which is unlike that of any other calling. The great ' case,' the unique experience, the illuminating discovery, may just as well come in the country town to the ' unknown ' family doctor as to the most erudite in the city laboratory.

" In another way the modest, silent worker has an advantage over the schemer, who slyly gives his photograph to the assistant, who in turn hands it to the reporter ; and that is the intimate and affectionate relation in which he stands to patients in their personal and social life. The calling which removes one farthest from the real feelings, sufferings, hopes, and joys of men, is most to be suspected ; it breeds most superficiality and self-seeking, and encourages coldness and cruelty.

" The physician who grows callous to the needs, wants, and woes of his patients, and of the community, should be ' Oslerized.' He is out of place, and should have been directed, when young, toward some other calling.

" As in every profession, the real discoverer of medical truth is ignored and even hated, not only by the leaders, but by the rank and file. Physicians are human beings, and humanity has never had anything but martyrdom for the light-bringer and the truth-shower. Luckily, when one is so fortunate or unfortunate as to be a discoverer, he has probably learned that there is no human reward he can or is likely to get that avails him aught. His true reward is to see his truth wrought into the lives of his contemporaries. That can rarely happen in any calling. But if he loves his fellow-men, his far away and unknown fellow-sufferers, he is reasonably content to know that they will profit by the work of the unknown discoverer, who loved them although unknown to him.

" And after all, when we view the ill-success of the vast majority in self-seeking (and not finding), the material rewards of the conscientious physician average well with those of the others. His calling is not unhealthful, in spite of the fact that he handles infection and disease. He has, as a rule, good food, warm clothing, a roof over him, wife and little ones, and a position of trust and honor among his fellow-workmen. These things ' pay ' no man for his highest work — and higher work is not rewarded ; and the coveted excess of food, clothing, and roofs, one learns to believe, like all excesses, brings — well, they do not bring happiness and well-being."

Jay W. Seaver, A.M., M.D., of New Haven, for twenty years at Yale University, and president of the Chautauqua School of Physical Education, in a letter to the author, says:

" If I advised a young man to study medicine, it would be because I found that he was a man of sympathetic nature, and had a mind that was quick and resourceful in meeting the emergencies of life, and a body that was strong and able to bear all the possible hardships, and that was under such

control that it could be depended on to do the bidding of the
mind in the most exact and easy manner.

"He must possess both mental and physical accuracy and
a fund of patience and optimism that will carry him through
all the experiences of a physician's life without letting him
drop into pessimism or cynicism, for the physician must
believe in man as well as in God and have an enthusiasm
for service.

"If I advised a man not to study medicine, it would be
because I knew him to be unhealthy morally, mentally, or
physically.

"If a man has an ambition to gain wealth, or notoriety,
or influence, or social prestige, I would advise him to seek
some other avenue to his goal.

"The lack of certain necessary qualities, such as have
been indicated above, would also lead me to advise a young
man not to become a physician."

John H. Kellogg, M.D., superintendent of Battle
Creek Sanatorium, editor of *Modern Medicine* and *Good
Health*, president of International Medical Missionary and
Benevolent Association, International Health Associa-
tion, and American Medical Missionary College, author
and lecturer, in a letter to the author, says:

"The study of medicine is the study of man and of his
relations to his environment. It is the broadest and most
useful of all the professions. A skilful physician can find
opportunity for the employment of his highest skill in a
hovel as well as in a palace. He is alike welcomed by the
king and by the peasant.

"A man is not prepared to take care of himself, or to
render the most necessary and most helpful service to his fellows, without possessing at least a large part of the knowledge which is gained in the study and practice of rational
medicine.

"The exactions of the physician's calling are more severe

than those of any other profession. The burden of knowledge to tax his brain, and of anxieties to weigh upon his
heart, exceed those of any other profession. His life must
be irregular. He must constantly unload great masses of
stored facts, which have become obsolete, and learn new.
He must be content to hold all his personal plans for pleasure, profit, or recreation subject to the exigencies of many
other lives as well as of his own, so that his life must be less
regular than that of other men. He belongs to the social fire
department. He must often imperil his health, even his life,
to save the health and lives of others. He must be content
with a short life. But all these disadvantages are inducements to the man who desires to live up to the highest and
noblest ideals."

THE DEPARTMENT STORE

THE modern and apparently irresistible tendency toward trade centralization and business consolidation gave birth to what is popularly known as the department store.

A department store, broadly defined, is a store of departments, a combination of what may be considered distinct stores, yet all under one roof, and managed by one general head.

The department store grew from the dry goods store. Substantially all of those department stores which have been in existence more than a dozen years were at one time dry goods establishments.

The dry goods business for some reason seems to offer basic opportunity for enlargement and division. The dry goods store is, in every sense, a family store, catering to family trade; and as substantially every department of the department store carries goods for family consumption, it was but natural that the dry goods store should be divided and sub-divided to meet conditions.

There is no limit to what a department store may sell, although comparatively few of them carry other than household goods. Some stores, however, sell everything from carriages and harnesses to meats and provisions. Commercially speaking, a dry goods store, which sells other than dry goods, may be considered a department store, although its number of departments may be limited. If this classification be allowed, then substantially all dry goods stores are now department stores, for there are few such stores selling only dry goods.

The country village store, or what is known as a cross-roads store, is virtually a department store, in that it sells everything; and the great city department store is an outgrowth of these country stores. Here the country has led the city, or rather the methods of country storekeeping have been followed by the city neighbors.

The great department store is a city in itself. It employs from one thousand to six thousand persons, of whom by far the most are women.

The organization of a great department store is almost military in its discipline, and is one of the best examples of what organization can accomplish. The proprietor is commander-in-chief, and under him are a number of assistants who are what might be considered district supervisors. Below them are the heads of departments, who are responsible to their district chief or to some other head. The floor-walker, the man who is so much in evidence, because he spends his time in the aisles, is, in fact, a superintendent or foreman in charge of a department or series of departments.

Each counter is under the general supervision of what is known as a head salesman, but this head salesman is subject to the direction of the floor-walker. Of

the rank and file of employees, probably more than ninety
per cent are salesmen and saleswomen, — counter-folks,
whose places are behind the counter, and whose duty
it is to sell goods from the counter, none of them being
what is known as travelling salesmen or drummers.
These great stores maintain extensive bookkeeping
and cashiers' departments, and a well-organized buying
department.

The so-called cash boy or cash girl has largely dis-
appeared, the mechanical contrivances having usurped
them; but there still remain bundle girls, whose duty
it is to receive the goods from the mechanical carriers,
to wrap them properly, and return them to the counters
from which they came. In some department stores the
clerks wrap up the goods, but in most cases the work
is done by bundle girls, who are placed at the termi-
nals of the mechanical bundle carriers, or sometimes
there is a bundle girl to each counter, who sits usually
above the shelves.

As this book is devoted to the interest of boys and
not of girls, it will hardly be fair to consider the
relation of girls and women to the department store
further than to say that about seventy-five per cent of
the clerks are women, who are paid anywhere from four
to twelve dollars a week. Head clerks or head saleswomen receive from twelve to twenty dollars a week;
but comparatively few, even of the fitters in " ready-
made " departments, draw salaries of over twenty-five
dollars a week.

Some of the higher-grade department stores employ
men exclusively in certain departments, paying them
more than women receive for the same work. First-
class, experienced salesmen, in the larger stores, seldom
receive less than twelve dollars a week, or more than

JOHN WANAMAKER

Merchant prince; born in Philadelphia, 1838; educated in public schools until 1852; errand boy in bookstore at 14; retail clothing salesman, 1856–61; established, with Nathan Brown, clothing house in Philadelphia in 1861; established department store, 1876; purchased business of A. T. Stewart, New York, 1896; active in anti-machine Republican politics; postmaster-general, 1889–93; ardent religious worker; superintendent Bethany Sunday School, probably the largest in the United States

twenty-five dollars a week, although occasionally as much as thirty dollars are paid ; but this latter sum almost invariably goes to the head salesman or to one in charge of a department. Junior clerks, that is, green clerks, are paid from six dollars to eight dollars a week at the start. The floor-walker is generally well paid, his minimum salary being not far from twenty dollars a week, and his maximum in excess of fifty dollars, with an average of about twenty-five dollars. Buyers for large stores occasionally enjoy incomes of ten thousand dollars a year, and from that down to a thousand dollars a year; and the average first-class buyer for a large department store probably does not receive less than thirty-five hundred dollars a year.

Does the great city department store offer good opportunities to the young man who desires to take up this business for a livelihood?

I answer yes and no. The ambitious and capable department store salesman has more apparent than real competition. The apparent competition is due to the large number of persons working along his lines. When it is considered that not one department store salesman in a hundred has more than ordinary ambition, has more than ordinary capacity, or more than moderate willingness to earn promotion by hard work, it would appear that the boy of ability and ambition, from this very fact alone, has a greater opportunity for advancement than he could have if there were less numerical and stronger mental competition.

Because the customer comes to the salesman, and because the salesman does not have to go to the customer, the department store salesman need not possess so high a grade of salesmanship as is necessary to the success of the travelling salesman or drummer. Consequently, less capacity or ability is necessary to fair success behind the counter than to success upon the road. For this reason, many young men, who do not know what they want to do, who have little ambition, and who are not particularly industrious, enter the department store, where they are reasonably sure of a livelihood.

Comparatively few of these young men ever get more than a few dollars' increase in their salaries. At the end of ten or twenty years they are not far from where they were at the start. But the ambitious young man, the one with ability, industry, and ambition, is sure to rise in the department store as rapidly as he would under many other environments, and to reach in time his proper place; although the department store may not give the young man of much ability as wide an opportunity for advancement, nor for as rapid advancement, as is presented to him in the wholesale house or upon the road.

Certainly, the department store is the best place for a young man to enter if he is without active ambition and is reasonably industrious and of ordinary capacity. If he is much more than these, it may be well for him to consider some other entrance into business, not with prejudice to the department store, but with a preference, perhaps, in some other direction.

I have been referring to the city boy, not to the country boy.

I would not advise the country boy to go to the great city to enter one of its department stores unless there is positive evidence that there is no opportunity in the town of his birth or in some nearby towns.

The country store, which in many cases is a department store, offers the average country boy a better opportunity than does the great city department store. True, the country store, whether it be a department store or not, will never pay the salaries paid to the managers and heads of departments of great city department stores. The city department store, financially, is way above that of the country store; but half-way to the top, and almost anywhere between near the top and the bottom, the country store offers more to the country boy, everything considered, than does the city department store, or any other city store, for that matter.

A boy of ordinary ambition, with ordinary industry, is more likely to find his proper place in the country than he is in the city. The boy of tremendous capacity, and with unlimited ambition, may be better off in the city department store, for there he will quickly rise to the top or close to the top, and become a business giant, a commander of men and things; but while this same ability, and this same ambition, if allowed to develop in the country, does not bring the young man so large an amount of money, they will bring him money enough and far more of solid comfort together with those things which make men men.

I therefore would not advise the country boy to come to the great city with the intention of entering the department store, or any other city store, unless he has exhausted the opportunities of his home-town and of the neighboring towns. Then, if there be nothing for him at home, or near home, he may have reasonable excuse for coming to the city; and when in the city, the department store certainly offers him some opportunities, and more than most other kinds of retail stores, and less, probably, than some other classes of business.

The city department store is a great machine, run by machine methods; and each clerk, yes, even the head clerk, is but a screw, or bolt, or wheel, or spring of that gigantic engine. For this reason, one's individuality is not much in evidence, and it may take a long time for ability to be recognized.

This is both an advantage and a disadvantage to the boy just starting into business life. To be a part of a great machine gives him the most strenuous kind of discipline, the grade of discipline which is likely to be fair and which plays few favorites. This discipline may be of inestimable value to the boy, and no other place offers this discipline in larger quantity or better quality than does the department store. Then, even if the boy is only a mediocre, he will probably remain a self-supporting part of the machine just so long as he desires to stay; but if he has more than ordinary capacity, his ability will sooner or later be recognized, and he will become an officer in the firm, a head salesman, a department manager, a buyer, or will occupy some other official and executive position.

I have no sympathy with the hue and cry which is continually rising from the counter, and which has for years been but one wail of dissatisfaction. The claim that the department store clerk has no opportunity rests upon the basest misrepresentation. No great business machine, no matter how large and how complicated, can refuse to recognize, sooner or later, that which is out of the ordinary and of commanding quality. This recognition may come more slowly to the department store clerk than it does to the travelling salesman or drummer; it may not be so prompt as in some other lines of trade. But the boy of capacity is sure of a recognition of his ability, whether he begins behind the counter in the department store or takes to the road as a seller at wholesale. Just as sure as water finds its level, just so sure business ability, with fair opportunity, will not fall below the fulfilment of its deserts.

The department store clerk has a chance, and a far better opportunity than he thinks he has. True, favoritism may count against him, and so it may everywhere else. That is something which he must expect to meet. But where there is the most discipline, there is the least favoritism. In the great department store, where it is business and nothing but business, clear, sheer ability is likely to be allowed to move in its own road, and to go as far up that road as the capacity of its possessor can push it.

The department store has come to stay. It began in the country centuries ago; and now it is one of our great city institutions. Whether or not it would be better if there were fewer large stores and more small ones, whether or not it would be better if the dry goods man sold only dry goods, and the shoe man only shoes, and the market man only meat and provisions, and the grocer only groceries, need not be considered, because the conditions of trade and of competition, whether merciful or cruel, are under but one law, and that is the survival of the fittest. Consequently men of enormous capacity and of great ability will gradually spread out their business and bring unto themselves everything within their reach which will pay them a profit commensurate to their labor.

The department store is expanding, becoming greater and greater, as the days go by, to the sacrifice of the small merchant, of the small grocer, and even of the small market man. This gigantic institution, overwhelming in its power, is recognized as a permanent business institution, and therefore it is worthy of the consideration of every young man about to enter business.

Perhaps the best advice that I can give to the young

man is to enter the department store unless he knows of something better suited to his ability, or to his inclination. There is opportunity here for him, and there is lack of opportunity; and these conditions prevail in every line of business, in every store, in every office, in every town, and in every city.

The best way to take up the business as a permanent calling is to go right into the department store and begin at the bottom. The application may be made by personal call or by letter. Many of the department stores advertise for clerks, bookkeepers, salesmen, and other workers. From a few to several of these advertisements appear in the want columns of the daily newspapers. The would-be department store employee should follow carefully the want columns of the newspapers, and answer the advertisements by letter or by call.

In regard to the school education necessary for success in the department store: a common school education is essential; the graduate of a high school has a better opportunity than have those whose school education ceased with a lower grade. While upon general principles I believe it is rather difficult for one to have too much school education, — for one can never tell when this education will come into profitable play, — I hardly feel disposed to recommend the expect-to-be department store employee to enter, or to graduate from, a college or institute of technology or other technical school. It would appear, if one judges by results, that a general education beyond the high school can hardly be considered more than advantageous. However, I should advise any boy, whether he intends to enter a department store or not, to graduate from a college if he can do so without too great a sacrifice. I should advise most emphatically the boy who intends to enter a profession to become a college graduate, even at heavy sacrifice; but I would not recommend more than ordinary sacrifice if one is to take up a purely commercial business, like that of the department store.

The hiring of salesmen, and other help, in all of the department stores, is done by one of the partners or by a superintendent. They are men of large experience, and thoroughly understand their business. Usually, they are willing to give advice, and their advice is generally good. I would advise any boy who intends to enter this business to call at several department stores, and talk with the men who engage the help. By seeing several of them, he may obtain many valuable points, and be better able to judge as to whether or not he is fitted for the work, and to find out if his preference for it is merely a passing fancy or if it has the stronger foundation of real aptitude and love.

Mr. John Shepard, president of the Shepard-Norwell Company, of Boston, in a letter to the author, says :

"My advice would depend, first, very much upon the boy. In order to grasp the advantages, he should have a preference for mercantile life. Then, if he has courage, application, and industry, is ordinarily intelligent, has good health, is absolutely truthful, is ambitious, and determined to get ahead in the world, the department store offers him unbounded opportunities. He may enter the store as an errand boy, bundle boy, or attend to other rudiments of the business; but if he has an eye always to the future, and is determined to get into the firm, or occupy a position as buyer, or rise to some other prominent position in the store, the opportunity exists. The crowd at the bottom is large, and those who are indifferent to success or without ambition generally stay there. But the young man with strong characteristics and plenty of pluck finds an opportunity for advancement always open to him.

"I have stated the advantages and described the necessary characteristics. Now to speak of the disadvantages — these would apply to the young man himself. If he is without courage, if his health is not vigorous, if he does not take to mercantile business and is not ambitious and energetic, and endeavors to pass the time away with the least effort possible, and requires continual stimulating by those in authority, the department store is no place for him. Any one of these reasons is sufficient to disqualify him from succeeding. And above all else, the distaste for mercantile life would prove a quantity of failure."

Mr. Isidor Straus, member of the firms of R. H. Macy and Company, of New York City, and Abraham and Straus, of Brooklyn, in a letter to the author, says:

"No enterprise can succeed unless the public supports it and the steady growth of well-managed department stores is indicative that they fill a popular need and want.

"The objection to them as monopolies has no basis in fact; they are the very antithesis of so-called trusts, with which they are sometimes confused, as the sharp competition between them keeps prices at a minimum.

"They are, therefore, not only a great convenience, which is recognized even by the fiercest enemies, but are also a tremendous factor for economy in the household.

"The buyers and managers of department stores average salaries which will compare most favorably with the incomes of ordinary storekeepers. This dissipates another mistaken argument of the uninformed in their diatribes.

"Concentration of effort is the order of the day, and when it does not lead to combinations for controlling output or prices, can only rebound to the welfare of the public at large.

"I know of no drawback, excepting that in a large business all employees are a part of a big machine. If the boy has the capacity or equipment to build a machine of his own, that is a question which each can best decide for himself."

THE ARCHITECT

HE germ of architecture began with the conception of the first prehistoric building, and took no account of its size, of its character, and of what it was made.

The age of the world is timed by its architectural ages. Architecture is a component part of all history, both modern and ancient. Nations, even of the twilight ages, were known by their architecture, and some of them have left nothing else to history.

The architect is a professionalist; the practice of his calling demands the full exercise of the intellect, at some sacrifice of business capacity. The architect is a creator of originality. He is not a mere plan-drawer and a specification-writer. He actually does something. He is not an artist in a painting or sketching sense, yet he has the artistic temperament, without which he could not be more than a successful draftsman or copier. The architect possesses something which is not a part of the man of business, — a sense of harmony, an artistic mental attainment, a creative ability, — yet he must have some of the qualities of the successful business man;

an appreciation of the importance of detail and the ability to handle men and things.

The boy who cares little for art, who is in no sense creative, and who possesses only ordinary talent, can never hope to succeed at architecture. He may become a draftsman, or even more than a plain builder, but he cannot become an architect.

Architecture may be considered a city profession. At any rate, nearly all of the architects reside in the city or in the larger country-centres; and few, if any, of them, are found in the smaller towns.

The architect, like the doctor and the lawyer, is seldom self-supporting at the start, and frequently cannot maintain himself in even moderate comfort, unless he has an outside income, for a few or several years after he begins the practice of his profession. Notwithstanding the high and enviable position occupied by the architect, comparatively few, except those at the architectural top, or close to it, enjoy more than moderate incomes. There are probably not over a dozen American architects who receive upwards of fifty thousand dollars a year, and not more than twenty-five earn as much as twenty thousand dollars a year. Good, first-class architects, with the artistic sense, who are thoroughly competent to plan and superintend the erection of nearly every class of building, earn, on an average, from five thousand to ten thousand dollars, and from that figure, the yearly incomes run as low as a thousand dollars for ordinary architects.

The architect's receipts, unless he is working on a salary, are variable, being subject to the rise and fall of the building business, which, in its turn, is affected by the state of general business. His income is also largely dependent upon the class of contracts he receives, and not so much upon the number of contracts. Yet all, or nearly all, architects manage to earn a living. Many great architects devote a year's time, or perhaps more, to the planning of one building, the erection of which they usually superintend, receiving for this double work their entire year's remuneration. The architect, after he has acquired a reputation, is reasonably sure of a comfortable income, although the size of it varies materially. At one time he is likely to have more work offered him than he can conveniently attend to, and again he may suffer from idleness for an extended period.

The architect's fees vary, but the average fee, and the most usual one, is from two to three per cent for plans and specifications, and about five per cent for plans, specifications, and superintendence. By superintendence, I mean that the architect becomes the actual superintendent of the erection of the building which he has planned. Although he may not sign the building contract, no contract is made without his approval. He, or his assistants, visit the ground daily during the process of construction; and if the building be of much consequence, one or more of them are continually upon the premises. The contractor or builder virtually works for the architect; he cannot receive any payment on account, and no final payment, without the architect's approval. The fee for the planning of small buildings is seldom less than a hundred dollars, and the architect of a great edifice, like a city block, hotel, or public building, receives from three thousand to twenty-five thousand dollars, his duties including superintendence.

Many of our best architects work under the partnership arrangement; that is to say, two or more of them associate themselves, occupy the same office, and practise their profession as a firm, not as individuals. This combination is a profitable one, because there are specialties in architecture; therefore, a combination of architects, each an expert in some line, can render better service than could any one by himself.

The architect employs assistants, who do the mechanical part of the work, the architect originating the ideas, which are worked out by these assistants, or draftsmen, as they are commonly called.

The embryo architect often displays at an early age artistic and creative capacity. He is at least original, and his spare moments are often spent in building or planning something to make. Perhaps he erects a hen-house, a toy house, or something else within his limited range of opportunity. His method of accomplishment indicates a natural though crude respect for harmony. He is not likely to do awkwardly anything that he attempts to do. If he makes a box, he gives some character to it, and his method of putting it together shows more than ordinary attention. If he starts a garden, the arrangement of the beds follows some well-conceived plan, and there is a harmonious grouping of the plants. If he arranges the furniture in a room, he does it to the furniture's advantage.

The architect is born; he cannot be made. If the boy does not show some creative skill, even while in his teens, there is not one chance in a thousand that he will ever become a successful architect. The copier is not an architect. The architect may copy, but he does something besides copying. He mixes his own ideas with those of others, and nothing that he does is devoid of his personality. The boy who can draw a plan geometrically correct may be entirely without the artistic temperament necessary for success in architecture.

I am well aware that there are thousands of mere
builders who label themselves architects, and who, with
the help of ready-made plans, are able to give satisfaction. But these men are not architects; they are simply expert builders. It is also true that these builders
and so-called architects at times give as good service
as does the true architect, and they certainly enjoy better incomes than the mediocre architects, who confine
themselves to the practice of the professional and artistic side of architecture.

As a rule, architects are not developed from builders,
although some of the best of this profession were at one
time builders and even carpenters. Generally the tendencies which show that the boy is fitted to become a
carpenter or builder are not in the same class with those
which foretell the architect. The carpenter or builder is
a mechanic, and occasionally a business man also, but he
is not a professionalist; while the work of the architect
is in every sense professional, requiring a different capacity from that which makes a success of business,
mechanics, or trade.

Because the great architect often receives both fame
and fortune, and because the profession is honorable and
recognized as one of the highest of human attainment,
an over-ambitious parent may attempt to force his boy
into architecture, without the slightest excuse for so doing. If the boy at an early age shows constructive ability, and is able to plan something on paper or in his
mind, and afterwards make it with his hands, the parent imagines that his son possesses the abilities necessary for the practice of architecture. It is true that
the boy who cannot construct " in advance " plans,
either in his mind or upon paper, has not the foundation qualities necessary to the architect; but unless

these creations in their earliest or crudest state give evidence of more than ordinary ability, the chances are the boy is better fitted for the building trade than for architecture.

Mere mechanical ingenuity and ability to construct properly in themselves do not furnish more than an indication of architectural quality. Correctly, the parent should not urge the boy to study architecture unless the boy gives reasonable evidence of much more than mechanical capacity.

Not only the ability to construct, but also that quality of ability which creates in advance the plans of construction, is essential to the proper practice of architecture. The successful architect is both a nature-made and a self-made man, — nature-made in that he possesses the natural ability necessary to success, and self-made because he has thoroughly trained this natural ability. The most pronounced natural capacity without special training is likely to fall short of the goal; while all the education that all the world can give will not make more than a mechanical architect out of the man who does not possess natural aptitude for this work.

A college course can hardly be considered essential, although it is to be recommended to those who can afford the time and money for its accomplishment.

A thorough training in an architectural school, or in the architectural department of a technical school, is generally considered indispensable for the proper making of an architect.

I would not advise any boy, even though he gives many evidences of architectural powers, to consider architecture as a profession, unless he is able to obtain the proper special education necessary to his ripest development, or unless he can study directly under some thoroughly competent architect. To attempt to branch out into architecture without this special training is likely to result in failure or to materially retard one's progress.

The architectural school, at the start, is much to be preferred to actual experience in an architect's office, because the school will teach the broad principles, while working experience is likely to be limited to one class, or to a few classes, of work.

While love for the profession accompanies the ability to successfully practise it, the mere desire to become an architect, in itself, is not to be considered a sufficient reason for entering that profession.

No boy should begin to prepare himself to enter this calling until some competent and reliable architect, after he has examined him, will, without bias, advise him to select this profession.

Unless the boy can present prospective ability to one competent to judge, his own desire, and the opinion of his parents and friends, are unworthy of consideration.

If the boy has any doubts, and those competent to judge do not feel reasonably certain of his success, he had better consider some other calling.

Mr. John M. Carrere, of the firm of Carrere and Hastings, of New York City, architects of the Ponce de Léon and Alcazar hotels, at St. Augustine, and of the New York Public Library, in a letter to the author, says:

"In my judgment, the advantages offered to a young man in the field of architecture greatly outweigh any possible disadvantages. The work is intensely interesting and full of variety and opportunity. It affords ample scope for specialization, according to the temperament, ranging from the purely practical to the highly artistic. The work is educational and broadening in the extreme, and is intimately related to all of the other arts, and with these the architect is bound to be brought into contact.

"The architect's relations, whether with his client or with those who are working for him, as well as with the artists and the public generally, can always be made pleasant and sympathetic. He is sure of a competency, of social position, and an opportunity to earn fame; besides finding happiness in his work and being enabled to contribute to the happiness of those with whom he comes in contact professionally.

"The only disadvantages, so far as I know, consist in the fact that an architect cannot make a fortune by the practice of his profession, and that he frequently fails to command the appreciation and encouragement which his work deserves, and which is given more frequently in other professions.

"The greatest hardship with which an architect has to contend is due to the fact that the very nature of his work, combining as it does the practical with the artistic, prevents the average man from distinguishing between real merit and mediocrity. This is true to an extent hardly possible in any other profession, so that the architect's recognition as an artist comes mostly from other architects and artists, and seldom from the public. But even this disadvantage is a stimulus to the architect never to halt in his efforts to do his best. It maintains his enthusiasm, and therefore keeps him young and active."

Mr. Allen B. Pond, of Chicago, the architect of many of the noted buildings in Chicago, and the author of several architectural papers, in a letter to the author, says:

"It is to be assumed that the young man who is planning to become an architect has some natural qualifications, and intends to achieve success by honorable means and without the sacrifice of his self-respect.

"The advantages offered by this profession are not to be

despised. Its product is concrete and visible, and it directly reaches with its impress a large number of persons beyond the circles of the immediate client, and by the wide circulation of photographs and sketches, indirectly reaches a vastly greater number. In this respect architecture affords a wider field than that offered, for instance, by the professions of law, medicine, and teaching, or by most lines of commercial enterprise.

"In common with the arts of sculpture, painting, and music, its product has a relative individual permanence enjoyed by few industrial and by no commercial pursuits. Its product is far less ephemeral than the work of the actor, or the musical virtuoso, or the ordinary littérateur, is not so easily thrust aside and forgotten as the work of the musical composer, and not so easily obliterated as the work of the sculptor or painter.

"The work offers scope for an exceptionally high degree of creative and imaginative faculty, ranking herein with the higher forms of literature and music, excelling sculpture and painting, and wholly surpassing the range of any scientific, technical, industrial, or commercial pursuit.

"It imposes the necessity of solving puzzling mechanical problems, of devising ingenious expedients, and of coping with emergencies.

"It presents, in an exceptional degree, a field for the exercise of knowledge of human nature, of tact, of wisdom, and of foresight.

"It involves close contact with a wide range of activities and situations, and brings one into close and often intimate relations with individuals of exceedingly varied occupations, positions, and points of view.

"It offers the opportunity to aid signally in making an environment that shall contribute to the health, comfort, charm, and distinction of human life.

"To one who appreciates its scope and opportunities, and who measurably meets its demands, it yields a deep satisfaction and a keen sense of useful achievements quite independent of financial return.

" To the few it brings a considerable financial return.

" It has some disadvantages: The status of the profession is not well established in the United States. The work of the architect is to develop creatively and critically the plan and design, to perfect the drawings and specifications, and faithfully supervise the construction of a desired building. The degree of technical skill, the breadth of accurate information, the painstaking foresight, the intelligent coordination, the amount of sheer labor required for the work in the case of buildings adapted to the complex requirements of modern life, are wholly beyond the conception of the building public.

"The compensation for work of ordinary size, such as must make up the bulk of the output of the average practitioner, is wholly inadequate, if the work be intelligently and thoroughly done. The conscientious, hard-working architect, endowed with a fair degree of talent, usually gets from his profession an income less than the earnings of a small contractor. At the minimum rates, established by the American Institute of Architects, few architects to-day acquire a competency for old age. Yet the public regards these absurdly low rates as exorbitantly high.

" Not only is the remuneration inadequate to the skill required and the actual labor expended, but it is totally inadequate to the responsibility placed on the architect — to what may be called the moral risk involved; for, in a sense, an architect should be morally, if not legally, a guarantor of the technical quality of his work. And such a guarantee is absurd, when the man on whom rests the responsibility for both plan and execution gets a bare pittance for his pains.

" The public, having only a vague comprehension of the skill and training required to cope with technical difficulties, and being unable to judge intelligently of artistic quality, makes scant distinction between the work of the able, conscientious architect and that of the bungler and fakir.

"Necessarily family connections, social position, friendship, and the like, play a considerable part in securing business for a professional man. It frequently results from the confusion in the public mind, noted above, that the selection of an architect quite lacking in professional merit is made merely because he is an acquaintance, or is a good fellow, or is in one's set, or has 'a pull.' From this fact, also, it follows that an undue premium is placed on such adventitious qualities as 'personal magnetism,' and ability 'to hustle,' at the expense of the man who either cannot or will not 'work' people and who depends for recognition solely on professional merit. It therefore not infrequently happens that a first-class man has a reputation among his confreres wholly out of proportion to the extent of his practice, and that he may, in fact, have an absurdly small income.

"This lack of status and of adequate public comprehension leads people to demand of architects, without remuneration, sketches that largely solve the plan problem and determine the main lines of the design; and similarly to expect architects to compete without pay save to the one who chances to please. If the self-respecting architect accedes to the demand for an unpaid, catch-as-catch-can competition, not judged by experts, he is handicapped by being placed in competition with those who make catchy meretricious designs, or who wilfully deceive as to probable cost, and who thereby seem to offer more for the money.

"The complexity of modern life as echoed in modern buildings is so great that the work of the conscientious architect is arduous and wearing in the extreme, if he faithfully tries to be and to continue reasonably well posted on the technical processes that enter into the buildings he is called upon to erect. His leisure will be proportioned to his neglect of things he ought to know and to do, — an unfortunate situation for a conscientious man, but inherent in the situation of the smaller architect, whose compensation does not permit the employment of specialized departmental heads."

THE MANUFACTURER

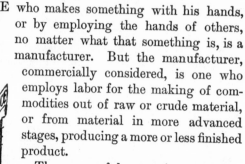

HE who makes something with his hands, or by employing the hands of others, no matter what that something is, is a manufacturer. But the manufacturer, commercially considered, is one who employs labor for the making of commodities out of raw or crude material, or from material in more advanced stages, producing a more or less finished product.

The successful managing manufacturer, or working head, of a concern, is a business man, who, in conjunction with his knowledge of business and his trade-training, understands the practice if not the detail of manufacturing.

Occasionally one sees evidence that mechanical proficiency is not, or does not seem to be, an essential requirement for success. There are some successful manufacturers who are apparently devoid of mechanical capacity, and who do not appear to be able to comprehend anything of a mechanical nature. These men, although at the heads of manufacturing businesses, are not true manufacturers. They are business giants, long-range manipulators, with the exceptional power of making up their deficiencies by proxy, by engaging those who understand what they do not or cannot comprehend. They are too much the exception to be the occasion for general consideration.

The manufacturer is distinct from the merchant, or purely business man, in that he both makes and sells. The exclusive mercantile or business man sells without making.

The successful merchant must know how to buy and how to sell, to buy at a price sufficiently below the selling point to produce a profit. The manufacturer goes further than this. He must know, first, how to buy material; and, secondly, how to make something from the material; and, thirdly, how to sell the finished production at a profitable price above all costs.

The successful manufacturer, then, is more than a business man, for he combines with his buying and selling a knowledge of the methods of production. Like the business man, he must be proficient in organization and able in management; otherwise he cannot profitably handle his employees, upon whom he is dependent. True, a large manufacturer is not, and should not be, his own superintendent or foreman, nor does he work at the bench; but if he is a pronounced success, he probably has either come up from the shop or has otherwise mastered every material detail of manufacturing. He knows how to properly handle his workmen, because he can do the workmen's work himself.

If the manufacturer's son enters the trade, he often begins at the bottom as a common workman, and works up step by step, receiving few privileges beyond those granted to the rank and file in the factory. This is as it should be.

One of the great laws of success-making prohibits one from telling others to do what he cannot do himself; and this principle, broadly interpreted, seems to be fundamentally and commercially acceptable.

Large manufacturers are usually wealthy, and many of our richest men are manufacturers.

Manufacturing is one of the best and safest of businesses, although the manufacturer occasionally takes heavy risks, which cannot be avoided.

Notwithstanding the fact that a manufacturer can earn a fortune in a year, and lose it in the next, manufacturing is one of the most stable of commercial institutions, and is recognized as one of the foundation stones of commerce.

If the boy hopes some day to be a manufacturer, he should begin by learning manufacturing. He should start at the bottom of the ladder and master every round as he climbs upward, always moving cautiously and carefully, and not attempting to forge ahead by jumps. Unless he begins at the bottom, and works at the bench or machine, he will not be properly equipped to master management.

An important part of a manufacturer's work is not only the directorship of the making of finished products from raw material, but the handling of his employees, — one of the most difficult problems, and one which tries the nerve of our strongest and best equipped men.

Unless the manufacturer has actually worked with the men, unless he knows from experience the details of manufacture, he is at a disadvantage. He cannot understand the situation from the view-point of the employee; and because he cannot understand it, he cannot successfully deal with the complications which are constantly arising.

A common school education is absolutely necessary, and a technical education is of the greatest value, to

the young man who is ambitious to become a manufacturer. The graduate of an institute of technology or mechanical school has a far better opportunity for ultimate
success than others not thus equipped educationally.

The few extra years spent at school are not wasted.
They are often the most profitable years of all. True,
the boy equipped with a higher education must start
three or four years behind others of his age, who enter
the factory from the common school; but at the end
of half a dozen or more years, the broadly and specially educated man will surely outstrip the others, all
things being equal.

I consider a higher education in mechanics of considerable importance; in fact, I may say it is well-nigh indispensable to "top" success. Experience in the factory
itself will never give to the boy that general knowledge
of mechanics which is imparted to him in the high-grade
technical school.

When he enters the factory, his work will be confined,
to a large extent, to one process or to a few processes;
and his education from this point will be narrow instead
of broad. Consequently, unless he has obtained this general mechanical education at some school, he will find
it difficult to become more than an expert along some
exclusive line.

The question may be asked: Should a boy who
intends to give his life to shoe manufacturing, for instance, have a mechanical education and know about
things with which he is not likely to come in contact?

The answer is simple. Yes, by all means, yes.

The mechanic best able to handle any one class of
mechanics is he who understands mechanics in general.
It is the same in the sciences. The best eye-specialist
springs from the general physician, who was a family

doctor before he became an eye-expert. No one is fully equipped to do any mechanical part who does not understand the mechanical whole. The man educated by experience along only one line of mechanics, with little general mechanical knowledge, may not see beyond the boundary of that which he is doing, and therefore cannot easily connect the broad with the narrow, and is unable to get the most out of his machines or the most out of his employees.

But let it be understood that education, even in the best institute of technology, does not, and cannot, make a mechanic; and does not, and cannot, fit one to become a manufacturer; neither can it produce the skilled workman. There must be natural ability in the first place, otherwise the education will be like good seed sown on bad soil.

I would not advise any boy who has not a decided mechanical bent, who is not handy with his hands, who does not possess a creative mind, and who does not know how to produce something or to improve upon something already made, to consider the possibility of becoming a manufacturer. He need not necessarily be an inventor, but he should not be utterly lacking in inventive propensities.

The boy who cannot make anything, who cannot do anything mechanical, who cannot properly hang a door, or drive a nail, or saw a board straight, is not likely to have in him the essentials of the manufacturer.

I do not mean to say that it is necessary for a boy to be mechanically expert to succeed in manufacturing; but the boy who has no mechanical skill had better keep away from manufacturing.

If he has the mechanical ability he will succeed, even though his success be confined to the purely factory side; but if he develops, with mechanical ability, business sagacity and the power to properly handle men, he will sooner or later become a superintendent or a managing head, and perhaps an owner in the business.

To become a manufacturer, in a commercial sense, one must have business ability as well as mechanical skill.

The boy who is simply mechanical, and who has no head for business, who simply makes something for the sake of making it, without any regard to its practical value, may or may not be a mechanical genius; but he is not adapted to manufacturing. In other words, the successful manufacturer must have a love for the mechanical, and some skill in mechanics, and in addition to this he must possess a general business capacity, which will enable him to profitably sell what he makes.

I cannot too forcibly impress upon the boy, and upon his parents, the tremendous advantage of a liberal education. This education will do one of two things: It will either show the boy that he is unfitted for manufacturing — and it is worth a great deal to know what one cannot do — or it will acquaint him with a rating of his capacity.

The graduate of a technical school seldom remains at the bottom. He is generally found, in later years, at least half-way towards the top, and is quite often near the top or at the top.

The combined processes of making a manufacturer appear to be about as follows: first, the right kind of a boy, one with both a mechanical and a business brain; secondly, a common school education; thirdly, a technical education is some institute of technology or polytechnic school; fourthly, a beginning at the very bottom of the factory end and working up until he has mastered

ANDREW CARNEGIE

Capitalist, financier and philanthropist; born in Dunfermline, Scotland, 1837; came with his family to Pittsburg, 1848; first worked as weaver's assistant, Alleghany; became telegraph messenger boy, Pittsburg; then telegraph operator, Pennsylvania R. R.; gained nucleus of his fortune in Woodruff Sleeping Car Co.; after war developed iron works, introducing in this country Bessemer process of making steel, 1868; in 1901 sold out to United States Steel Corporation and retired; total benefactions exceed $150,000,000, including 1500 libraries

most of the details and all of the principles of manufacturing.

When the boy or young man has become thus equipped, he will be in a position to grasp opportunity and even to assist in making opportunity.

Mr. David M. Parry, president of the Parry Manufacturing Company, of Indianapolis, ex-president of the National Association of Manufacturers of the United States, and president of the Carriage Builders' National Association, in a letter to the author, says:

"What are the principal advantages offered by the business of manufacturing?

"Manufacturing offers a very attractive field to those desiring to participate in a large way in the activities of the times.

"The manufacturer deals with many men, his sphere of life is usually broader than that of men in many other pursuits, and his influence is often called into service in shaping large public questions.

"The possible rewards of manufacturing are attractive, and one's success is limited only by one's strength, determination, application, and brains. While your workshop is only local, your field of operation may be the whole world.

"What are the principal disadvantages in the business of manufacturing?

"The manufacturer is often brought face to face with conditions in the market which arise suddenly, and which he could not foresee. The broader the market, the more susceptible is his business to the chances of trade. Then, too, the manufacturer has often to face serious and unpleasant problems in dealing with his employees, which problems are made the more difficult by the fact that he is necessarily dependent, in good measure, upon his foremen and chiefs of departments in the handling of men. Furthermore, the processes of manufacturing are constantly changing through invention, and often requiring good but 'old' machinery to be thrown aside and new machinery to be substituted at a big expense.

" Success or failure may depend on quick decisions."

Mr. Alanson D. Brown, president of the Hamilton-Brown Shoe Company, of St. Louis, in a letter to the author, says:

" If I were to advise a young man to go into the business of manufacturing, what would be my reason for so doing?

" My reason would be that the young man, whom I recommended, had a good business head, was ambitious, honest, and of good habits, and was going into the manufacturing of some article of necessity for man or beast, which would insure a steady and continuous running of his factory through good times and bad. He would also be a man who could concentrate his mind entirely upon his business and allow nothing else to interfere with it.

" If I were to advise a young man against going into the business of manufacturing, what would be my reason for so doing?

" My reason would be that the young man lacked in business judgment, that he preferred a profession, or that he found his greatest pleasure in music, travel, or something else that would detract from his business; or that his habits were such as would prevent his making a success in the manufacturing business."

THE AGRICULTURIST

IN the world's dictionary, the farmer is defined as a plain tiller of soil, and the agriculturist or planter as one who has lifted the farm on to the plane of business.

The term "farmer," however, covers that vast company of workers, who, by the planting of the seed, raise any kind of a harvest, or who breed and raise cattle and other stock.

The planter of the South, and the agriculturist of the West, are both farmers, but, by right of courtesy, are described by other titles, because they carry farming into business, or rather apply methods of business to planting and harvesting.

The railroad may cease running, and things will continue to live. The stock-board may board up its doors, and the world will continue to move as it has been moving for centuries, subject only to transient financial cloudiness. Most businesses may go out of business, and the professionalist may no longer continue to practise, yet people will continue to live and to propagate. But when there is no longer any farmer, there will be no longer any people, for the world will have starved to death.

The farm, with what the farm stands for, is the essential factor of human maintenance.

The farm, then, is an indispensable necessity, without which the nations would never have begun their existence.

The wealth of the world is not in its business, is not even in its mineral resources, but consists in the cultivation of the earth's surface — in the farm.

The farmer is the original producer of that which makes life possible, and without which no life can be maintained.

The fundamental corner-stone of all physical progress was originally placed upon the farm, and there it will remain so long as we have physical natures and require material food.

Farming is our greatest industry, the industry preservative of all industries.

Notwithstanding the existence of hundreds of abandoned farms, and the constant exodus from the farm to the city, the farm, in its numerical and financial strength, is to-day the greatest power in the whole civilized world.

The farmer is not recognized as he should be, because he seeks neither notoriety nor prominence, but quietly does his work, allowing others to play at society and to receive its shallow reward.

Here, however, has been made a grievous mistake. The farmer, like the lawyer, should be proud of his profession, sufficiently appreciative of it to contribute to it the full measure of his self-respect. Because he does not do so, he has lost both the social and business prominence which really belongs to his calling.

To be in love with our work does not fully suffice. It is necessary to have the love for the work so appear before men that they may honor us, and, by respecting us, be more willing to become of us or to help us.

Some farms do not pay, partly because some farms cannot be made to pay. The barren farm is a worthless piece of property. The sooner it is abandoned the better.

Probably not more than one-half of our fertile farms pay as well as they would pay if the right effort was made to make them pay. It is but a common remark that a great majority of farms are unprofitable because of the indifference on the part of the owners.

Altogether too many farmers, instead of working their farms, allow their farms to work them. The situation, or rather the farm, is their master, instead of their being master of the situation.

The principles of business, the laws of progressive economy, are not applied to the farm as they are to other trades or businesses; consequently, the farmer is not always financially well-to-do; and usually, through no fault of the farm, but because he does not exact what he should from it.

The tendency to-day is unmistakably away from the farm. The farmer's boy, partly because he wants a change, but largely because the great unknown shines with a light apparently brighter than all the lights he has ever seen, desires to leave the farm and to earn his living under entirely different conditions, away from Nature as he had experienced it, where he may lead a life diametrically different from that of his childhood.

But the farmer's boy is not altogether to blame for leaving the farm. The fault, in more than half the cases, is due to the farmer himself and to the way the farm is

conducted. The boy brought up upon the farm which is
not properly cultivated, and where most of the work
is drudgery, or is made to be drudgery, where intellectual growth is stunted, naturally, in the ignorance
of his youth, assumes that all farms are like the farm of
his childhood, and that the opportunities of life must
be elsewhere. Therefore, he gravitates to the city, not
so much because he loves the city, but because he feels
that that which he knows nothing about, although he
may think he does, is better than that which he does
know about from actual boyhood experience.

The farmer, rather than the farm, is driving the boy
to the city, and the boy is going to the city simply because in a negative way he has been forced cityward.

If the average farmer works harder than does the
business man, it is not always because he has to, but
generally because he thinks he must.

I do not deny that there is much of drudgery in farm
labor — there is. So there is in almost any other calling
or work. But the excess of drudgery is often the fault
of the drudge, not of the work itself.

So far as the long farm hours are concerned, they are
no longer than those required of the majority of men in
business for themselves and of members of all professions. The farmer has as much time on his hands, and
generally more, than does the city business man or professional man. It may seem to him that he works longer,
but he does not. As a matter of fact, the chances are that
he works fewer hours than does his city neighbor.

Lack of success in farming, unless the farm be unmistakably barren, generally comes from lack of intelligent application. Altogether too many farmers imagine
that success is wholly due to hard and laborious labor.
Labor is necessary to any successful result, but the labor

in which the mind acts the part of partner is the kind which pays and which does not wear men out. As hard as farming is, and as small as is the compensation it usually brings, it gives the farmer more than is received by the average city dweller, — more, even, of actual dollars and cents.

The average city clerk, at the end of the year, has less money, and less ready money, than has the farmer; and the chances are that the city man has worked harder, although he may have enjoyed stated holidays and vacations.

Although the average city business man may take in more money than the farmer can possibly gain under the most favorable circumstances, he pays a greater penalty for what he obtains, and in the majority of cases is worse off than is the farmer.

If the farmer treated his work as he should, and applied to it the intelligence that is given to other trades, he would reduce the drudgery to a minimum, and ready money would not be a stranger to him.

Nearly all farmers make a living. Comparatively few, of course, grow rich from the proceeds of the farm; but more than half of the farmers, whether located on the rocky hills of Maine or on the rapidly producing Western soil, not only make expenses, but are able to save something every year.

The farmer is seldom found in the poorhouse.

From farmers' children have sprung the majority of our great men, both of business and of the professions.

Many a man, who does not know anything about it, and therefore speaks with positiveness, claims that the farmer's life is narrower than most others, and that the farmer has little opportunity to better civilization. As a matter of fact, the farmer, unless he is located miles

from the heart of progress, has a better opportunity to
learn what he should know than has the artificially-
living cityite, whose broadness consists not so much in
the good things, but to an alarming extent in the bad
things, of life.

The city clerk or city business man, working in a
block and housed in a flat, does not have one-half as
much opportunity to progress, in the truest sense of the
word, as does the farmer on a fairly fertile farm, working
as his own master on his own property.

The farmer, above all other men, is independent.
His vocation is the only self-supporting business on
earth.

The successful farmer is a man of education, although
he may not have been book-taught. He is well equipped,
so far as general knowledge is concerned, and, further,
he is a man of business.

With the modern periodicals, and the distribution of
every class of reading matter, the farmer has much
opportunity for mental development.

There always will be some poor and half-starved men
among farmers, but this class is far less prominent upon
the farm than in the marts of business; and there are
ten times more impecunious city workers than there are
farmers in actual want. But right here let it be said
that even the poorest farmers are better off than are the
average strugglers of the great city.

Should the farm boy remain upon the farm? Upon
general principles I say, yes, and emphatically, yes.
There are exceptions. There are many boys who have
no business to stay upon the farm, because they are
destined for something, not necessarily better, but something entirely different from farming; but, generally
speaking, I would advise the farmer's boy to remain on

the farm, unless he can give legitimate, sensible, and positive reasons for a change.

Where we are is, in most cases, where we should remain. Where Nature placed us would appear to be our natural field of action, subject only to exceptions.

Therefore, the boy born upon the farm should consider the farm the place for his life work, unless there are reasons why a change of base should be made.

For any reason, save a good reason, many a farmer's boy despises the farm, when he should be proud of his agricultural heritage. He is of the nobility of the soil — a nobility not of many dollars, but descendant from the parent of dollars.

The boy who would leave the farm, and who gives no good reason for leaving, may as well go as stay, for he will undoubtedly be a failure anywhere.

The boy who dislikes the farm because he does not like work will not be a success anywhere. If he is not willing to work as hard upon the farm as he would have to away from the farm, he will not work hard enough anywhere else to earn more than a mere livelihood.

The boy who does not like farming, who dislikes it from his very soul, who has absolutely no love for planting or harvesting, and yet is not a loafer, is not likely to become a good farmer, and forcing him to remain there indefinitely • is certainly bad judgment and will prove unprofitable.

Any boy has a right to dislike the farm if his dislike is sensible; but many boys, perhaps the majority of them, who leave the farm to go to the city, do so because they look upon farming as inferior labor and believe that the farm offers little opportunity. This is all too often the farmer's fault, not the fault of the farm itself. Thousands of boys, failures in great cities, might have been successful citizens upon the farm.

The drudging farmer, the ne'er-do-weel digger of the soil, with weedy garden and shabby house, cannot expect his boy to respect the farm or to love the farm; and this boy, unless he is broad enough and intelligent enough to see beyond his father's farm, will probably leave it even if he has to run away.

Should the city boy leave the city to become a farmer? Yes, if he wants to. If he goes, the chances are that he will become a happier man, a healthier man, and a better citizen; but if he does not want to go, do not force or even urge him.

Probably a great many more city boys might go to the country if they only knew the meaning of life in the country. However, there are comparatively few city boys who turn farmers, and it may be a long time before the sense of the city will be strong enough and broad enough to see beyond its brick walls and towering buildings.

But we have no right to force the city boy into the country. We may assume that because he is born in the city, he has a right to give the city first consideration.

The truly sensible city parent, the one who really loves his son, may give the city the preference; but he should suggest to his city-born and city-loving boy that he consider the country; and the chances are that if the country is given the consideration it deserves, many a city-bred boy will turn to the open fields and forsake man's city for God's country.

But the country boy, born and reared upon the farm, should give the farm the preference. Instead of despising his home surroundings, because his father did not make a success of farming, he would better use his father's failures as stepping-stones to success. Let him consider it thoroughly and intelligently and without prejudice, and if this consideration be given, there will be comparatively little migration from the farm to the large city; and those who do go will be more likely to succeed, because they have a good reason for going.

The farm, which gives the father a mere living, may give the son a competency.

The farmer's boy should realize that success is not so much how much one earns in a year, as how much one gets out of a year, both in experience, money, and opportunity, to enjoy life. A few hundred dollars earned on a good farm may leave at the end of the year much more in actual money than five times the amount of earnings will leave to the boy or man in the city.

True, the city boy may say that, although it costs more to live in the city, one gets more that is worth while, and therefore city life is worth what is paid for it. There never was a greater mistake made. While the city may give more than does the country, even in some things worth having, the city charges more for what it gives, even when intrinsic value is considered, ounce by ounce and pound by pound. Many of the things which city people think they want they neither want nor need. Our comforts depend largely upon the difference between what we earn and what we need to spend.

There are unhealthy farms, but there is little reason why they should be so. There are farmers who live in illy ventilated rooms, and who feed upon indigestible food, and are less healthy than the city dwellers; but the majority of farmers are better off physically and mentally than are the men of our great cities, and they have double the opportunity of living healthful and contented lives.

The farmer may receive the minimum amount of income, but he also has the minimum amount of worry and expense.

What the world needs to-day is more, and not less farms, and more intelligent and scientific farming, and more business farmers.

The farm may offer the farmer's boy more health, more real contentment, more solid comfort, and more money, in the aggregate, than does any business or profession which the great city is likely to allow the farmer's boy to enjoy.

I would not ask the farmer's boy to remain on his father's farm if it is improperly cultivated and is a mere place of drudgery; nor would I ask him to remain upon a barren farm, where every product is literally forced from an unwilling soil. I would simply say, because you are a farmer's boy, give the farm the preference. If your father's farm is not suitable to your ambition, and to your capacity, go to some larger and better farm. Consider your father's farm first. If there be evidence that this is not best for you, then consider some other farm. Give the farm the first choice, consider it from every standpoint and without prejudice, even though your farm experiences may have been unfortunate and disagreeable.

After you have placed all the advantages of farming in one column, and all the objections in another, study each advantage and disadvantage by itself and collectively; then, if the disadvantages greatly outweigh the advantages, you have every sensible, moral, and business right to forsake the farm, either for a mercantile life in the city or in the country. But do not leave the country or the country town, even if you leave the farm, until you have intelligently exhausted its opportunities. The country needs you; the city may not want you. Do not make a radical change without a high motive, and be sure that your motive is not a mistaken preference. Do not go from outdoors to indoors unless tested reason leads the way.

What kind, and how much, school education can the farmer use to advantage? To specify is well-nigh impossible. Upon general principles, however, it may be said that there is little likelihood of the farmer, or the would-be farmer, acquiring too much book-knowledge. Practically every one is exempt from this danger.

In this country there are many successful farmers who are graduates of colleges, and this broad education has not injured them, although it may not, in every case, have been of financial benefit.

If I were forced to answer this question specifically, I would advise the boy who intends to follow agriculture to obtain at least a high school education. I would not advise against a college course, but I find it impossible to consider this higher education essential.

I recommend most emphatically and enthusiastically the boy to attend, and graduate from, an agricultural college. These institutions, teaching as they do the very essentials of fundamental agriculture, are rapidly increasing, and their grade is growing higher, and they are more carefully covering this broad occupation.

If the boy and his parents are not familiar with the location, scope, and requirements of these agricultural institutions, information can be obtained from the editor of the local newspaper, the minister, the lawyer, the doctor, or the teacher; or, a letter addressed to the secretary of state, of any state, at the state capitol, would either bring full information or would inform the writer where he can obtain it.

Professor John F. Duggar, M. S., director of the experiment station at Auburn, Ala., and professor of agriculture at the Alabama Polytechnic Institute, in a letter to the author, says:

" While I am unable, at this time, to prepare a complete and condensed discussion as to the advantages and disadvantages of farm life, I would say that I am thoroughly convinced that many a boy overlooks rich opportunities for a useful and prosperous life in the country.

" The country has been made unattractive to the farmer's children on account of isolation, on account of the farmer's uncomplimentary talk about his own vocation, and on account of the failure of the average boy to understand the fascinating operations of Nature with which he is surrounded.

" Fortunately, every condition of urban life is improving at a rate much more rapid than is generally appreciated. Awakened public sentiment in favor of improved rural schools and better roads is already noticeable, and will result in partially overcoming the isolation of such a life.

" Among the considerations which should be weighed by the young man investigating the advantages of rural life are the following: First, land is advancing in value, and unless one gets a foothold in this generation, its acquirement in the next may be far more difficult. Secondly, the highest degree of health and independence and happiness are obtainable in the country. The returns from agriculture are more certain, even though less in gross amount, than in most other occupations, and the opportunities for saving are far greater than in the city. Moreover, increased knowledge of the sciences on which agriculture is based, brings increased profits, and affords the inestimable satisfaction of pursuing a vocation congenial and fascinating.

" About ninety-nine per cent of city men, as they advance in life, cherish the ambition to own a farm, and most of them desire to spend their latter days upon it. While the gratification of this desire is possible for the relatively small number who amass fortunes in the city, it is not usually possible for the average city man."

Mr. Frederic Grundy, of "The Orchards," Morrisonville, Ill., in a letter to the author, says:

"Among the principal advantages which agriculture offers to young men is complete independence. The farmer who owns his farm is, if he understands his art, the most independent man on earth. He is in partnership with Nature, and, with her assistance, produces what all the world must have — food.

"There is a never-ending demand for his products. Then, his home is truly his castle, and he may, if he will, make it a haven of comfort and contentment. His hand is his own, and no petty boss or party chief can hold any rod over him that he need fear in the least.

"Agriculture does not hold forth to the young man the promise of great wealth, but of independence, comfort, peace, and full enjoyment of life.

"The disadvantages are not numerous. The young man who begins with only his hands and fair health has before him a struggle which will test his mettle. The price of land is high, and only the most skilful management can make an acre pay for itself in what may be termed a reasonable number of years. Skill counts for more than muscle now. If a man is content to be only a common hand, progress toward the ownership of a farm and home will be very slow. More than likely his hopes will never be realized. But if he makes of himself a really skilful farmer (which any bright young man may do) he will not long remain a hired man."

The Hon. O. B. Stevens, late Commissioner, Department of Agriculture, State of Georgia, in a letter to the author, says:

" Boys, stick to the farm!

"It is an independent profession; it produces bone, muscle, and a strong constitution, and these develop the brain. The daily duties of the farm prepare one for the realities of life.

" No profession brings as much revenue from the amount invested as that of farming. No profession gives wider scope for the practical application of the various sciences, — chemistry, geology, botany, entomology, engineering, — consequently, the ideal farmer is an accomplished scientist.

" Lastly, no profession brings a man closer to Nature.

" Avoid politics."

THE SALESMAN

HE salesman was born at the birth of trade, and ever since their dual creation he has been in increasing evidence.

Selling has become an art. Its practice is universal. It is one of the two fundamental elements of business.

It may be said with absolute truth that there is not a wholesale, or a retail, or a manufacturing house of any kind without a greater or less number of selling representatives.

The tradesman may know what he wants, and he doubtless is aware that he cannot do the maximum of business without the proper goods, and yet for some reason, which has not yet been fully explained, the chances are that he will seldom order these goods by mail, or go after them, but will wait until some travelling salesman has called upon him and solicited his trade.

It would appear to be an unnatural condition of trade that makes it necessary for the buyer to be told what he should buy; but whether it be unnatural or not, it remains a fact.

The selling of practically everything, except a part of that which is sold over the counter, is the direct result of solicitation, or of what is known as drumming; and this occupation of solicitor or drummer is one of the foundation stones of commercialism.

The travelling salesman, or drummer, as he is commonly called, is one who solicits outside of the office or store. He usually earns a higher salary than is paid the counter-man, who handles the trade which comes to his store or office; and while to be successful the latter must possess the abilities of the solicitor, yet it is not necessary that he be so alert and aggressive as the drummer, who goes from place to place for orders.

The real difference between the outside and the inside salesman is this: the outside salesman takes the initiative, while the customer, to some extent, makes the first move when buying goods from the inside salesman.

It has been claimed, and with a sufficient degree of truth to make it almost indisputable, that no man can direct the selling of any commodity unless he has actually sold goods himself. I do not recall a single successful merchant or storekeeper who has not, at some time in his career, actually met his trade face to face and personally sold goods.

Probably seventy-five per cent of the successful merchants and storekeepers began as salesmen, and nearly every prominent wholesaler was at one time a drummer.

It is certainly common sense to assume that few men can successfully direct the movements of others unless they have actually done what their employees are called upon to do. True, a man may be an expert at selling, and not make a good manager of salesmen or a good merchant, for some men's selling ability needs the direction of a broader and greater mind. It is also true that some sales managers have little actual selling capacity, and cannot successfully meet a customer.

All, or nearly all, of our merchants and storekeepers entered a mercantile life through office work or through the selling department. They began either as office boys or as store boys, and after one or more years of menial work, of little value to any one except to themselves, they became clerks or salesmen. Many boys, particularly the bright ones, jump directly from this boyship into subordinate salesmanship.

The average boy, working in an office or in a store, receives anywhere from two to six dollars a week, four dollars being a fair average.

The young salesman, even at the start, seldom receives less than eight dollars a week, and occasionally he is paid as much as ten or twelve dollars a week. From the twelve-dollar mark his advance depends upon his proven ability and the conditions under which he is working.

Ability without the assistance of an encouraging environment will hinder the boy's advancement sometimes; however, not so much as will less ability with a good opportunity. It is therefore extremely important that the boy should start right; that is to say, that he should connect himself with some business which he will not outgrow.

For the first few years the boy will be learning, and really accomplishing very little. This is his apprenticeship, and during these initial years he cannot hope to receive more than a few dollars a week. When he becomes a salesman, then he begins to rise, and if he has the right kind of stuff in him, and the conditions are right, his advance may be rapid.

The rank and file of country store salesmen, that is inside men, do not receive, on the average, more than ten or twelve dollars a week, even after they have be-

come thoroughly experienced; and the maximum pay
has probably never exceeded twenty-five dollars a week.
Department store salesmen in large cities draw salaries
of from eight to thirty dollars a week, the average paid
to a good salesman of experience being from eighteen
to twenty dollars. The average salesman in small city
stores, and even in those located in large cities, receives
anywhere from eight to twenty dollars a week, comparatively few drawing the latter salary.

There are two reasons why the inside salesman cannot expect to draw more than a moderate salary; first,
the customer comes to him, and he does not have to go
after the customer; and secondly, fully ninety per cent
of inside sellers are women, who are willing to do work
for much less than the amounts paid to men. The merchant, in business for gain and not for philanthropy,
buys his salesmen in the market and pays market prices,
although to the credit of business it must be said that
there are a few merchants who invariably pay more than
market rates, and in return maintain an unusually high
grade of business, which is permanent in character.

The demand for bargains and for cheap goods of every
class is a mighty factor in the maintenance of low salaries. The customer, more than the storekeeper, controls the situation. So long as the majority of our
shoppers are demanding bargains and goods at cut prices,
it is evident that a grade of salesmanship suggestive of
high salaries cannot always be maintained.

Resident salesmen of experience, in wholesale houses,
command salaries as high as three thousand dollars a
year, and a few enjoy incomes of ten thousand dollars
a year; but the average annual salary paid to the first-
class resident salesman is probably not more than twelve
hundred dollars.

The travelling salesman usually begins at ten dollars a week, and the average salary of a good salesman is less than fifteen hundred dollars a year.

First-class travelling salesmen seldom receive less than two thousand dollars a year. Those of long experience, and of exceptional proficiency, may enjoy annual incomes of as much as five thousand dollars. Comparatively few reach this latter figure, and a very few exceed it, although there are now " on the road " a number of travelling salesmen drawing salaries as high as ten thousand dollars a year, and probably there are some whose annual incomes are not far from double this amount; but these men are great exceptions.

Unless the travelling salesman sells upon commission, all of his necessary travelling expenses are paid by the firm for which he sells.

The salesman on commission is really in business for himself, and his income almost always exceeds what he would receive on salary. Some salesmen have a dual arrangement with their employers, by which they sell upon both salary and commission; that is to say, they are guaranteed a certain amount every year, whether or not their commissions reach it. But it is obvious that no concern will continue to pay a stated sum if the amounts that it would pay in commissions long continued to be below such sum.

The store salesman is confined to narrower limits, and unless he possesses aggressive or other exceptional ability, he stands little chance of rising above the position of head of his department. The travelling salesman has a much better opportunity for advancement. His work is more difficult, and requires closer attention and greater energy. If he makes a success of it, he is likely to be recognized and to be promoted. If he is particularly successful, and has built up a large clientele, it occasionally happens that he is given an opportunity to enter the firm, or he may form a business partnership with other salesmen of his capacity.

As substantially all merchants and storekeepers were at one time salesmen, we must draw the conclusion that the selling department of business offers the greatest opportunities for advancement to the boy who wishes to enter a mercantile business life.

I have said that the inside salesman does not find so good an opportunity for advancement as does the drummer. While this is true, and while I would advise the boy to go " on the road " in preference to remaining inside, I do not wish to give the impression that there is no opportunity behind the counter. There are many men of strong selling ability who do not seem to possess the aggressiveness necessary for outside drumming. They are natural salesmen, know how to impress the buyer, and understand the goods, but, for some reason which they themselves cannot explain, they lack the ability to get out into the open to fight trade face to face. These men are not adapted to outside selling. Their place is inside. Their ability is sure of recognition, although they may have to wait longer for it. Sooner or later, unless conditions are very much against them, they will be promoted to responsible positions, and occasionally they may combine with others in establishing a business of their own.

The first-class inside salesman frequently becomes a buyer, and thus he may or may not remain a salesman.

The travelling salesman is without a home; he lives on trains and in sleepers and at hotels. He is obliged to put up with every kind of accommodation, and is exposed to sickness and to accident. Every form of temptation is presented. But there is temptation everywhere, and the boy of well-formed character, who is conscientious and faithful, can safely take to the road. Travelling may facilitate the distribution of the bad, but the bad is sure to come out, whether one remains at home or travels. The boy of loose habits, who has little stability, who is easily influenced, and who cannot be trusted, will immediately yield to temptation, and will sacrifice his morals and undermine his health. But if this boy is so weak in character that the road will ruin him, is it not logical to assume that he might just as well be ruined rapidly on the road as to stay at home and undergo a similar but slower process?

While it is true that many salesmen do not rise above the lower grade of ordinary success, the same is also true of almost any other trade, business, or profession; for most of us are ordinary mortals, and few of us can hope to become extraordinary. Many a boy longs to become a salesman, in order that he may travel and see the world. He looks forward to the excitement and the novelty of continuous journeying. All this wears off, and very quickly; and the necessity of continually visiting the same towns soon dispels the novelty, and the boy finds that the weariness of the road is far more disagreeable than the monotony of the home store.

Selling on the road is hard work, travelling is tiresome, and a continuous hotel life is not conducive to pleasure.

At the very start, the boy, in deciding to become a drummer, should not allow himself to be governed by the thought of the pleasures of travel, or by any thought save that he has his place to make in the world, and that this furnishes a means of making it. If he goes on the road, he should go simply because the road is his road to success. The road to him should be a means to an end, something disagreeable, something to be endured, but something which he must not allow to master him.

The salesman should be impressed with this one great fact, — that the amount of remuneration one receives during the first few years, whether indoors or on the road, is of little consequence so long as it is sufficient for his actual needs. What the position will lead to is of more consequence.

Small pay with good opportunity is far better for the boy than more pay with less opportunity. The boy during the first years of his salesmanship is a student of business. No matter how hard his work is, and no matter how little he may be paid, he is receiving more than he gives.

A word about the storekeeping salesman, and by storekeeping salesman I mean the salesman in the country store. While his salary is likely to be less than that of the city salesman, and while the top is not so high, yet I verily believe that the average boy stands a better opportunity for success in life in the country store than he does in the city store. Only our brightest boys will reach the tiptop, and under any circumstances there is only room for a certain number of boys at the top, and the great majority must be contented to remain in the lower positions.

The country store salesman, even though he may work every other night, is near his home, enjoys a local atmosphere, has a chance to become known, and has the opportunity of amounting to something. Certainly, his worry and expenses are very much less.

I am aware that the country store does not offer very great opportunities for monied success,— - neither does the city store. Competition is greater to-day than ever before, and greatly lessens the chance of advance of other than the most proficient. The probability is that the average salesman, whether in the country or in the city, will not rise very high in his calling, nor is the member of any other business or profession likely to. There must always be more soldiers than officers. I am simply comparing the opportunities offered the country store salesman with those enjoyed by the city store salesman. I believe that if one is satisfied with an ordinary degree of financial success, and cares more about himself, his family, his neighbors, and his citizenship than he does about his actual money income, then he is far better off in the country than in the city.

Not one inside salesman in a dozen is a good salesman, and most inside salesmen possess little real selling ability; consequently it must be assumed that one can earn a living behind the counter even if he cannot develop more than the rudiments of salesmanship.

The ordinary salesman seldom shows any marked characteristics while a boy. He is simply an ordinary boy, travelling along as ordinary boys do, and he will go in the direction that his parents point out or his playmates happen to suggest.

But the first-class salesman develops from the boy who has himself well in hand, who understands men and things, and who is a leader of boys, who generally has his own way, not by force but by persuasion, and who governs his playmates simply because he knows how to handle them.

Such a boy knows how to buy his own clothes, and does it.

Even if the parents object to his buying his own clothes, and attending to his own affairs, yet, in so far as he does do business as a boy, he may prove to his parents that he is really competent to do what they would not allow him to do. He is a trader, and knows how to place a value upon things, and above all, knows how to impress others with their value.

While a good talker does not necessarily mean a good salesman, the good salesman is almost always a good talker. Either he talks much and well, or else he talks less and very well. There are some salesmen who have little to say, and who seem to possess the ability of saying much in little. But nearly all successful salesmen are fluent talkers; in other words, they know how to represent that which they have to sell. They know how to present the good points of their goods, so that the buyer will want to buy; and, further, they possess the power of persuasion, — that power which enables them to make the buyer feel as they feel, and want to do as they want him to do. This is not mesmeric power or anything supernatural. It is simply a natural ability, born of nature and developed by experience.

The successful salesman must understand human nature. He must know how to approach a customer. He must anticipate his customer's wants, and he must be genial, meeting people easily, and be himself easy to approach.

The crabbed boy, the conservative boy, the boy who is not popular with his fellows, is not likely to make a good salesman.

The salesman is pre-eminently a business man. Selling is permanently removed from anything savoring of professionalism. The fact that selling is pure business, and even cold-blooded business, offers no excuse for lack of school training.

A liberal school education, even in the higher branches, is reasonably sure to be of material assistance to the salesman. While I would not recommend a classical college course, I see no objection to it. It can in no way interfere with his success, although it must be admitted that, perhaps in some cases, the four years of college-spent time can be used to better advantage. At any rate, the salesman's school education should carry him through the higher grades of the common schools.

If one is to devote his life to the selling or management of mechanical articles, like machinery or electricity, graduation from an institution of technology is to be highly recommended.

The more the salesman knows about what he sells, the better able he is to sell it. If his goods be of a scientific or mechanical nature, a liberal training in a scientific or mechanical institution is next to essential to complete success.

The salesman, above all, should be well posted on the common topics of the day and be able to converse intelligently upon popular subjects. A reasonable amount of talk is necessary for the consummation of trade, a proportion of it being of general and social import. To successfully carry on an animated and interesting conversation, a salesman must be a well-informed man, his knowledge encompassing men and things in general.

Mr. Charles F. Abbott, general manager of The Warner Brothers Company, of New York City, in a letter to the author, says:

"I would not advise any one to become a travelling salesman unless his character was well formed and he had himself well in hand. The temptations of the road are unlimited, and only those of strict integrity and of strong character can hope to maintain their equilibrium. The travelling salesman is away from home, lives on sleepers and at hotels, and his tendency is toward dissipation, not because he naturally desires to become dissipated, but because of lonesomeness and of nothing else to do after the day's work is over.

" I would not advise any one to go upon the road who is not a natural seller, and who is not willing to work hard and stand any amount of opposition and disappointment. The young man without ambition, and who has little control of himself, who has not a set and definite character, would better go behind the counter and stay there.

" Perhaps the travelling salesman has the best opportunity, because he has the chance of developing in himself all that there is in him, so far as business is concerned. If he knows how to sell, and sells, he is sure of recognition. Without this selling experience, which is obtainable only upon the road, he will never be in a position to properly direct salesmen or to handle the distributing side of a business.

" The successful business man usually springs from the travelling salesman who on the road was a successful seller of goods. Occasionally an unsuccessful salesman becomes a successful inside man; but as a rule, a failure on the road is a failure at home.

" Comparatively few men who are without selling capacity have the ability to succeed in ordinary business.

" Most of our successful men, even though they may not have sold a bill of goods, could have sold had it been necessary for them to do so. In fact, the salesman's work on the road is but an apprenticeship for better things."

Mr. Charles W. Rice, Supreme Travelling Representative of the Order of United Commercial Travellers of America, in a letter to the author, says:

" The principal advantages offered by commercial travelling as a business :

" (1) Travelling broadens a man's ideas and makes him a student of human nature. There is a continual variety in the life of a travelling salesman that makes the work fascinating. (2) Larger remuneration for the same ability than in any other line of salesmanship. There is some financial advantage from having one's living expenses paid while on the road. The salary named means 'and board,' although one must not lose sight of the fact that it is necessary for the travelling salesman to earn his expense money as well as his salary. (3) There is better chance to demonstrate one's value to his employer than a house or retail salesman has. The travelling salesman has the opportunity of going out after his customers, while the house salesman must wait for the customer to come to him. This might seem in favor of the house salesman, but the employer sets a higher value on the services and results of the man who can go out and get the business. It takes less ability to sell to the man who comes to you, for the fact that his coming indicates that he wants to buy. The personality of the travelling salesman gives him individual recognition that house salesmen cannot win. He is the representative, the 'House.' He holds a responsible position, because he must decide many questions that the house salesman can refer to his superiors. He gains, in time, a joint proprietorship in the trade, and becomes more or less indispensable, because he can often take his trade with him to another house.

"The principal disadvantages offered by commercial travelling as a business:

"(1) The travelling man is deprived of home influence and association; indeed, of many social advantages. If a married man, the separation from wife and family is a hardship; if a church man, he is deprived of the privilege of worshipping with his family; if a lodge or club man, who might be chosen to fill important offices, he cannot accept them because of being so much away from home. (2) He is compelled at times to put up with extremely poor accommodations at hotels and on railroad trains and at small junction points. (3) The travelling salesman is sometimes misjudged or misunderstood by the head of his house or department, because he comes in contact with them mostly by correspondence, seldom visiting the home office for a personal interview. (4) Often the employer wishes to promote to a more responsible and lucrative position a travelling salesman of ability, but the latter fails to get the promotion because the house can find no one to send on the road who can hold up the well-established trade of the traveller. (5) The travelling salesman who tries to do his best does or can work harder than the house salesman, or perhaps we might say, that the same hours are more taxing. After travelling a few years, the man often becomes more or less unfit for any other business."

THE LITTERATEUR

BROADLY considered, literature is a class of writing, including poetry, fiction, and belles-lettres, of the highest grade. But here in our definition we confront a difficulty. What constitutes the highest grade? What one editor or one critic may consider real literature, another equally distinguished individual may refuse to so label. Even the lexicographers dislike to definitely define literature, and certainly they do not do so with harmonious accord. Generally speaking, however, and commercially speaking, at least, literature may consist of about every class of writing save newspaper news and advertising matter.

The writer, then, of any book, whether it be poetry, prose, fiction, history, or science, may consider himself a littérateur, although the terms "literary man," "literary woman," or "littérateur" are generally applied only to the authors of books and magazine articles and to the writers of general fiction or matter that is not technical or scientific.

Other writers or authors usually come under a special classification; for instance, the editorial scribe, while a literary man, is known as a journalist or editor; the writer of scientific works is classified as a scientist; the writer of essays is known as an essayist; and the poets enjoy a somewhat exclusive grouping. But all of these, practically considered, are literati, and members of the great literary clan, — that army of people who either write for a living or write because they love to write, for money, or for fame, or for both.

The lines of society are zigzag, elastic, and uncertain when compared with the self-made boundaries of literary workers. Here, caste is cast in the deepest die. Many a writer is placed, either by himself or his friends, or by both himself and his friends, upon a pinnacle of his own; yet his position may not be secure, for he may have as many dissenters as advocates.

There are, however, a few great authors, most of whom are dead, who, by common consent, are grouped in the Hall of Literary Fame. Their position is "fixed" both in and out of the literary world; but outside of these "Standards" there are comparatively few living authors who are universally recognized as being at the apex of their profession.

One reason for this is that there is not, and never can be, a scale which will correctly weigh literary values, nor is there ever likely to be an accurate separator which will properly label and classify literary quality.

There are as many grades of literary successes as there are apparent classes of literary work. The writer of literature of the higher grade may not receive more than a small proportion of the credit due him, during his life, at least. It may be years before he is "discovered," and sometimes the "finding" does not occur until half-centuries or centuries have elapsed. It has been said that if the immortal Shakespeare were born upon earth now, he would have to be a hundred years dead before a new set of Shakespearian dramas would be universally recognized.

The literary market is overstocked. The road to literary fame is double-paved with the dry bones of failures. More people who cannot write think they can write than think they can do anything else that they cannot do.

To many people there is no apparent necessity for training for a literary life. Equipped with a pen and a pad of paper, the would-be writer starts in and writes, and continues to write, whether he really says anything or not. A half-fool, with half an education, and with an antiquated dictionary, can patchwork words and juggle sentences.

Probably not one story-writer in a thousand meets with any real success, and comparatively few authors of fiction earn a comfortable livelihood.

Historians and scientists, and all others who enter the field of special writing, are usually well-trained for their work, the general author, without special education and knowledge, having sense enough to realize that he must not attempt to compete with specialists; therefore this literary, or would-be literary, class confines itself to fiction, to articles of moral or alleged moral import, and to the more or less promulgation of every class of reform, and usually of popular reform.

In America alone there are upwards of half a million men and women who seriously believe that they have literary talent. They mistake inclination for real ability; and, with the help of flattering friends, enter, or attempt to enter, the literary field. Most of them will work for nothing, and some of them are willing to pay to have their contributions published. Nearly all of them are prolific, even to the swarming point. They write upon every subject, and assail everything with the boldness of ignorance. If they have never been to France, they write a French novel. If they have spent their lives among the trees, near to Nature's heart, they plot their story within city walls, that they may write about that which they have never seen, and therefore know little about.

The average magazine and literary periodical receives every month, in addition to other matter supposed by the writers to be literature, from five hundred to a thousand manuscripts, which vary in length from a yard to half a mile. When it is remembered that there are comparatively few publications which pay really high prices for stories and other productions, and that these periodicals cannot use, on an average, more than a dozen a month, it would appear that the supply is not far from fifty times greater than the demand.

Not one boy, or man, or girl, or woman in ten thousand can write, or can learn to write, good fiction. Because of the fame which a very few reap, the public sees the successes, and either does not see, or forgets, the failures. The prominence given to the one in many thousands attracts multitudes of men and women who more or less honestly believe that the undeveloped germ of authorship is within them; and, in their ignorance, they expect the maximum of fame and fortune for the minimum of effort or ability.

No one jumps into authorship. If he has not the natural talent, he fails at the start, or fails somewhere along the line of struggle. If he has the right capacity, even then success is impossible without long-continued study and the hardest kind of training. Without this study and this training, ability is worthless. Even the greatest Nature-endowed author-to-be may have to begin at the bottom, or, at any rate, not far from the bottom, and work for years before he can hope to see, even in the far distance, the open door of success.

Occasionally we hear of authors who have apparently leaped into fame. I do not deny that this has occurred, although I have never actually known of such a case. An author may become famous in a night, but his prominence comes only after years of preparation in something other than book-writing.

The desire to write often develops into a conceited belief in one's own literary capacity. A story is begun, and finished. It is read to the author's friends, who honestly or dishonestly praise it. It is then sent to a magazine or other periodical, or to a book publisher. The editor-in-chief, or other editor, seldom sees it. Together with a dozen, or perhaps a thousand, unsolicited contributions, it is handed to what is known as the first reader; and this reader, or critic, may or may not have the time, and perhaps may not have the inclination, to read it thoroughly; and it is even possible that he is incompetent to determine its value. Generally, the first few pages are sufficient to show that the manuscript is, or is not, worth further attention. The professional first reader may not go beyond the opening pages. If they strike him favorably, he proceeds; if not, he may read no further. Because in the majority of cases the quality of the opening pages may be considered as fairly representing the value of the manuscript, the author usually receives his deserts. Occasionally, however, a manuscript is turned down on account of what is, or appears to be, a lack of quality at its beginning.

The first readers, connected with the better grade of

book and magazine publishers, are almost invariably
high-class and competent literary men and women, of
natural and trained discrimination, and they seldom
slight a manuscript. They read it from start to finish,
or until they discover unmistakable proof of worthless-
ness or unavailability.

But it must be admitted that correctly diagnosing a
manuscript is one of the most difficult things to accomplish. The man does not live who can correctly forecast
the degree of success or of failure of any book or article.
There are many recorded instances where a several
times turned down manuscript has exceeded all expecta-
tions, and has become an overwhelming success; and
on the other hand, many a manuscript which has favorably passed the critics and has been looked upon as a
winner has met with no more than indifferent success.

Thus, the unknown writer may long be a victim of
chance, his fate depending at the start upon the judgment or caprice of some first reader, or upon public
opinion, which is often fickle, and which at times
appears to run amuck.

The first reader does not exercise any more than the
right of opinion. If he reports very unfavorably upon
a manuscript, the chances are that it will be returned
immediately to its author. If his report is favorable,
or partially so, the manuscript will be read by some
other reader, or an editor, or by the editor-in-chief of
the publishing house. The recommendation of the
editor-in-chief of the book-publishing house is likely
to assure the publication of a manuscript, although
he must pass it to the final tribunal, which may consist of one or more of the partners or officers, or all of
them.

But genius, real genius, can seldom be either dwarfed

or killed. It will develop under any condition and will be improved by hardships.

Financially speaking, story writing, or, for that matter, almost every kind of authorship, seldom brings more than a moderate profit.

Our greatest authors cannot produce more than a limited amount of work a year, and even at the highest prices paid, their annual incomes are not likely to exceed a few thousand dollars, except where a great and often accidental hit is made; and even then comparatively few writers can hope to receive from any one book a profit exceeding ten thousand or fifteen thousand dollars. A very fortunate few may obtain double that amount, and perhaps more; but literary hits are scarce, always have been, and probably always will be.

The majority of authors do not depend entirely upon their literary work for maintenance, many of them occupying salaried positions. They are, for the most part, professional men and woman, teachers or editors, or are in charge of departments of periodicals, and the recipients of comfortable salaries; and they consider writing, financially speaking, a side issue.

The introduction of the literary syndicate has raised the price and decreased the demand for short stories and articles. The syndicate story or article is one which appears simultaneously in several publications. The syndicate buys a story or article, paying for it at the rate of from four to twenty-five dollars per ordinary newspaper column. The matter is put in type, and proofs are sent to the newspapers in the syndicate, only one newspaper in a town or city being a member of the syndicate. By this arrangement, the expense is distributed among several publishers, and the author is likely to receive more than he would from any one publication.

It is, however, extremely difficult for an unknown author to sell his work to a syndicate, for the chances are that the syndicate, solely for business reasons, will be obliged to consider a manuscript more with regard to its author's name than to its intrinsic merit.

The publishing of a novel or short story, or of any other kind of literary production, is cold, financial business. The publisher, whether he issues a periodical or books, is in the business for profit. From a business point of view he can have no sympathy with the author. He buys a manuscript just as the butter man buys his tub of butter, to sell it at a profit. The enormous supply allows him to purchase really good matter at a price very much less than what it would be if there were less competition.

The average short story by an unknown author, or by an author not generally known, seldom brings more than two cents a word, and perhaps not over one cent a word. Comparatively few magazines pay over ten cents a word, even to well-known authors ; and the average rate does not exceed five cents a word. A few high-class magazines pay as much as thirty cents a word. Occasionally a prominent author, or one who is temporarily conspicuous in the public eye, will receive for his work, whether it be a story or a series of articles, a sum all out of proportion to the current prices. For instance, I have reason to believe that a certain great English story writer was paid, by one American publisher alone, as much as sixty cents a word for a series of stories. I have also been informed that this same author received a dollar a word for his stories. I am inclined to believe that this is possibly if not probably true. The periodical, however, did not have to pay the entire expense, because, after it had printed the

SAMUEL L. CLEMENS

Author and lecturer, and America's foremost humorist; born in Florida, Mo., 1835; educated in common schools; apprenticed to printer at 12; became successively Mississippi River pilot, soldier, miner, reporter, editor, and publisher. Best known as a story-teller and author of "Innocents Abroad," "Adventures of Tom Sawyer," and "The Adventures of Huckleberry Finn," etc. Died, beloved by all, at Redding, Conn., April 21, 1910

stories, they were syndicated to the daily newspapers which materially reduced the original cost.

Magazines or periodical short stories or articles seldom contain less than one thousand words, and run up to five thousand words, thirty-five hundred to four thousand words being considered a fair average. Serial stories usually contain more than twenty-five thousand words, and quite often run above one hundred thousand words, and occasionally number one hundred and fifty thousand. Books of fiction are seldom less than fifty thousand words in length, and the average is not far from one hundred thousand, although some novels run to more than one hundred and fifty thousand words.

The writers of book fiction are not usually paid by the word, nor do they often receive an outright cash payment.

Almost universally they are given a royalty, usually ten per cent of the retail price of the book; that is, the publisher pays the author, if the publisher takes the financial risk, ten per cent, and sometimes more or less of the retail price of the book, irrespective of what the wholesale price may be, the wholesale price being from twenty-five to fifty per cent less than the retail price.

When the author takes the risk, and the publisher acts as his agent, the author pays all expenses, and in addition gives the publisher a commission of fifteen per cent or more for his services.

More than ninety per cent of all the books are published on a royalty basis, the publisher assuming all costs and financial risks.

Comparatively few books enjoy a sale of exceeding five thousand copies; in fact, the average sale of any book, barring the few "hits," do not exceed two thousand copies. Publishers can afford to handle any well-written work, if they feel assured of a net sale of two thousand copies. This gives them a fair profit, and they take reasonable business chances of the book's selling beyond expectation.

The average retail price of a book is a dollar and a half. The royalty to the author, if he receives ten per cent, is fifteen cents a copy. One thousand copies, then, will bring him one hundred and fifty dollars; two thousand copies, three hundred dollars; three thousand copies four hundred and fifty dollars.

Unless the author is a well-known writer, whose name is a household word, he cannot expect his book to bring him more than a few hundred dollars, but he may hope for the unexpected, which sometimes occurs.

Popular novels occasionally have sales exceeding several hundred thousand, and there are a few books which have become sufficiently popular to run close to the million mark.

A novel of fair popularity, however, not infrequently sells beyond twenty-five thousand copies.

Some authors succeed better financially by confining their writings to periodicals, while others do much better through their books. Still others write both for periodicals and for book publishers, and occasionally a novel first appears in some magazine, and later in book form.

Right here I want to sound a note of warning. Never deal with other than a reputable publisher. If you are unfamiliar with the publishing business, consult any school-teacher or local editor. He will give you the names and addresses of a dozen or more first-class and honorable publishing houses.

The eagerness, I might say insanity, to write, has made possible the establishment of irresponsible publishing houses, who prey upon authors. By advertising, and in other ways, they become known to unknown authors, who are persuaded to present their manuscripts to them. Invariably the author receives a flattering letter, which, in most cases, he believes is genuine encouragement. The publisher makes the author what appears, on its face, to be a very liberal proposition. He suggests that he, the publisher, and the author, become partners, so to speak, the author to pay the mechanical cost of publication, the publisher to undertake all other expenses. As a matter of fact, there are no other expenses, and the bill sent the author for mechanical cost is generally double the real cost.

This, then, is a printing proposition, not a publishing one, the publisher receiving one hundred per cent more than any printer has a right to charge. If the author is inexperienced and has money, or can borrow it, he is likely to bite at this bait, which is apparently a most alluring one. The book is printed, but never really published, the publisher making no effort whatever to sell the book, except a few copies for form's sake.

The rapid growth of these illegitimate publishers has made the book-dealer suspicious, and many of them refuse to purchase any book except from a responsible publisher.

Authorship may be ethical or professional, but publishing is business; and, unfortunately, the publisher, if he be a business man, cannot well be a philanthropist, except to a limited extent. As a publisher he is obliged to publish that which will sell. He keeps a finger on the pulse of public desire. This is something that the authors seldom do, for most of them write only what they want to write. The publisher must publish what the public wants, or what he believes the public wants. If he did not do this, he could not be in the publishing business, unless he conducted a philanthropic concern.

Success in authorship depends, in the first place, upon quality; but it must be admitted that, while the name or reputation is built upon intrinsic merit, the salability of a manuscript often depends more upon the author's name or reputation than upon its real worth. This may seem to be unfair,— and so it is; yet it is natural, to some extent at least. The author, with a remarkable name or reputation, obtained that name or reputation by furnishing intrinsic values, consequently the public has reason to consider the author's name or reputation a part of the value of the book, and it does.

Every reader has one favorite author, or several, and he reads everything that that writer writes; therefore the author of reputation has a clientele in advance of the publication of his book.

The publisher knows that a book by an author of reputation will sell. He does not know whether or not it will make a "hit," but he knows that a reasonable number of copies will be sold; therefore the publisher takes the minimum of risk.

Seldom does an author of reputation produce an entirely worthless work. That which made his reputation refuses to allow him to do anything poorly, although there may be many degrees of quality in his writing.

There is no more honorable, noble, and good-doing profession than that of authorship. To this profession, as much as to any one cause, civilization owes her progress. The writer of good literature, whether he be a novelist, a poet, an historian, or a producer of scientific matter, is a true philanthropist and one of the greatest and noblest products of the times.

While every author is entitled to a comfortable living,

not one in one hundred receives it from literature. He is the subject of conditions as they are, not as he wants them to be. Authorship is one of the poorest paid of professions. Only those of much ability and of great proficiency can expect to make a living at it, and comparatively few of them earn more than that. There is no profession so overcrowded, or so filled with failures.

This condition is largely due to the fact that so many people want to write, and that so many people write whether they can write or not. This gluts the market, and enables the parsimonious publisher to obtain all that he needs, and of every grade of material except the highest, for nothing or at a merely nominal cost. Ninety per cent of our writers to-day, whether they have ability or not, would rather write for nothing than not to write.

I would not advise any one to attempt to become an author if he must depend upon his pen for his bread and butter. He would better take up some other profession, and give his spare time to writing, depending upon his salary or income for his livelihood. If he has great ability, and gains a name or reputation, his writings may eventually make him self-supporting; but he cannot, no matter what his ability, expect to earn his living with his pen until several years after the publication of his first production.

The author cannot be made. Success in authorship is impossible unless there be actual capacity. All the colleges, and all the other institutions in the world combined, and all the books read, and all the learning possible for one brain to hold, cannot produce a genuine author or an author capable of writing any work of originality or any work with real soul and color to it.

Even with education and experience, I doubt if one could ever become able to produce historical or scientific

works, and do his subjects full justice, unless he is first
of all a natural writer. His work, although mechanically
correct, will not have that life in it, that something
which makes it live, that something which appeals to
the reader and shows to the reader the character of the
author.

Embryonic literary ability is harder to discover than
almost any other kind of proficiency. If the child
wants to write, let him write. It may do him good,
even if he never becomes an author. It will either
develop him along literary lines or it will show him
that he is unfitted for authorship.

The " business " boy is not likely to blossom into the
littérateur.

The boy who does not think, who is very matter-of-
fact, who cares little for books or for study, who never
dreams, who is without any pronounced ambition, is
not destined to travel, nor will he want to travel, literary
paths. The mere dreamer, who is seldom on earth, will
doubtless remain a failure in literature.

The successful author is usually a composite individual, one who both dreams and works, one who ignores
neither sky nor earth, but who weaves his fabrics from
the webs of fact and theory.

The author is both a man of vision and a man of
action; a man of vision, in that he knows how to read
and to see beyond the present; a man of fact, in that he
can utilize what he thinks and what he feels, combining
the real and the unreal into a substantial whole.

The author, or would-be author, is seldom a wor-
shipper of money. He may love money, but the getting
of it is not his chief endeavor. He seems to have a
mission, and he is sure to have an ambition. He thinks.
He studies. He is looking for experience; his experi-

ences leave deep impressions upon him. He is a student of character. He finds something in everything he sees. Yet, with all these apparent prerequisites, many a boy may have no literary talent whatever, and may lack that power of using what he has accumulated.

One condition is reasonably certain: if the child has literary ability he will show it before he is out of his teens, and he will write against all obstacles.

Experience, as well as actual capacity, is a necessary requirement. No one can write properly about that of which he knows nothing. Any attempt to write without experience invites failure.

The boy's compositions at school may or may not be indications of literary promise. The "smart" composition, and even the bright one, may show no indications of those essentials which are necessary to permanent literary quality. Merely smart writers, like smart doers in anything else, are as apt to fail as to succeed.

Originality is an essential to fiction writing. The scientific and historical writer may or may not possess originality. If he does, so much the better for his work; but without originality, the novelist cannot hope to climb above the first round of the ladder.

Every author of note, both past and present, has shown in his works, from the first page to the last, unmistakable evidence of pure originality, — originality not only in plot, but in construction and treatment. But let it be understood that originality, in itself, does not necessarily point to authorship. Many an original boy, a genius at repartee, cannot become a great author, because he does not possess that something which permits him to assemble his original ideas. His originality, to an extent, is but a flash in the pan, without much heat under it.

A broad, yes, a very broad, education, even if not collegiate, is considered essential to literary success. Without more than a common-school training, the greatest literary genius will seldom be able to handle language advantageously, and is likely to fall far short of what would be the result of his developed capacity.

I would advise most emphatically the would-be literary writer to obtain a college education, and I would suggest a post-graduate course. The more education he obtains, provided it is not purely technical, the better equipped he is for general literary work. Without the broadest and most liberal education, he is handicapped at the start, and is liable to work at a continuous disadvantage.

Graduation from an institution of technology or a polytechnic school is necessary to the scientific writer. Unless he understands broad science, that is, science in general, he cannot become proficient in any of its branches. The expert in astronomy, for instance, began his education, not as an astronomer, but as a scientist, and he mastered all the known essentials of science. After he had obtained this broad education, this general knowledge of all things scientific, he made a specialty of astronomy, and succeeded.

The scientist, however, is a scientist first, and a writer afterwards, his writing generally being the result of his investigations.

The author, like the painter, is an artist — an artist in words.

The author, filled with real earnestness and with the love for his work which breeds success, is willing to wait, — not to wait at a standstill, because he is always busy, but willing to wait for results. He appreciates the value of time, and he knows that without it success is impossible. He improves himself along every line necessary to the ripest result.

Many men are what is known as leisure-time writers. They write between working hours, or they are wealthy and take up writing as a recreation or to gratify a desire to do something, or to be somebody; but none of them have succeeded unless they have made serious work of it.

Whether one writes a part of the time or all of the time, his best work is a production of concentration and application. The real author has a mission, and that mission he will fulfil if he lives.

Authorship offers the widest possible field, for the whole world is at command. Literature is one of progression's tallest monuments, and upon its top burns one of the blazing lights of civilization.

Mr. Edward J. Wheeler, editor of *Current Literature*, and late editor of *The Literary Digest*, in a letter to the author, says:

" Some of the principal advantages offered by literature as a profession, to one who is passionately fond of literature (and to any one else the advantages it offers are not worth considering) are as follows :

"(1) A chance to live by the work one loves to do. A man must get happiness out of his work if he expects to get much of it in this life.

" (2) A chance to express one's self, his thoughts, his feelings, his whole personality. This expression of our personality is what we are all striving after in the homes we build, the business institutions we develop, the professional records we make. To the extent that they express our personality we rejoice in them. The opportunities for this expression are greater in the literary profession than in any other.

" (3) Constant association with the best minds in the world. One cannot pursue the literary profession successfully without familiarity with the best that is said and done in the particular field he is cultivating. It goes without saying that such contact is ennobling and stimulating.

" All these advantages are what might be called subjective. Some of the objective advantages are as follows :

" (1) The scope and inherent importance of the profession are almost boundless. Printer's ink has become the mode of communication in most civilized countries. Literature, in its broad sense, has become a necessity of the race, not a luxury. The literary profession has a stability which is at least equal to that of any other profession.

" (2) It presents also a wide variety of specialties from which to choose. Religion, science, politics, sociology, the fine arts, any or more of these one may make a specialty of, as suits his bent.

" (3) Then the tangible rewards for literary success never were so great as now. Writers of fiction not infrequently earn tens of thousands of dollars on a novel. Five cents a word is not an unusual rate for the payment of stories, sketches, and essays. The editor of a certain "yellow journal" made a contract, a few weeks ago, whereby he receives a salary of a hundred thousand dollars a year. Even in a pecuniary way, therefore, the prizes for the literary profession are by no means meagre.

" The disadvantages of the literary profession may also be divided, for convenience, into subjective and objective.

" Literary pursuits are apt to develop a certain aloofness from life. This is by no means an inevitable consequence, but it is one often to be observed. The social faculties are not encouraged by such pursuits as they are encouraged in most other professions. Literary men and women are apt to appear very far from their best in personal intercourse. The social importance of the successful literary man or woman is not equal to that of the successful lawyer, preacher, or doctor. The work of the former does not dovetail so closely into the social life of the community. This is less true to-day than a generation ago, but it is still true in large measure.

" As a money-making profession, literary pursuits, despite the increase in number and value of prizes won by the most successful, are still more uncertain and hazardous than the other leading professions. Public favor is a flighty thing, and upon it the writer is constantly dependent. The ease with which the profession is entered, too, is inviting to many who fail to dignify it either by their worth or character. There are no barriers to entrance, as in the case of other professions. This lowers the general tone, and increases the amount of competition in the lower grades.

" Aside from journalism, where there is a reasonably steady demand for workmen, and a reasonably steady recompense, the literary profession is the most hazardous of all professions for a young man or woman who is dependent upon his or her labors for a living."

Mr. William V. Alexander, managing editor of the *Ladies' Home Journal*, in a letter to the author, says:

" What are the principal advantages offered by literature as a profession ?

" Great opportunities to do good; to cheer, uplift, and help in divers ways.

" For a successful writer, the making of innumerable friends. With this should be coupled the pleasure an author derives from meeting, or receiving letters from, readers whose admiration is sincere.

" The possibility of winning enduring fame.

" As fair a chance to make a fortune as other professions offer. Sometimes a single book, perhaps only a year's toil, means that an author need work no more.

" In short, it seems to me that there is a larger proportion of sunshine in literature than in many other professions.

" What are the principal disadvantages in literature as a profession?

" Before taking up some professions one must prove one's fitness. Anybody may adopt literature; hence too many people do.

" Poor work is turned out. It wearies and discourages publishers. Thus many a new writer, who really can do good work, is badly handicapped, and as some trash commands a ready market, he may soon be strongly tempted to forsake his ideals. So he is unlikely to win what is worth having, to be truly successful in the finest sense, unless he has high aims and possesses patience, courage, tenacity, faith in himself — all in a large degree."

THE BOOKKEEPER

THE bookkeeper is, as his name implies, the keeper of the books of business, primarily of those devoted to debit and credit. While the bookkeeper is required to exercise intelligence, and the expert bookkeeper must possess more than ordinary skilfulness, the work is to a considerable extent clerical, and in some degree mechanical. His mind is by no means at a standstill, but the routine of his work has a retarding influence on its development, and tends to mechanical methods of thought. This condition presents a contrast to the callings in life where men are required to mingle with their fellow-men, and where they stand or fall on the merits of their ability to quickly meet kaleidoscopic conditions as they transpire.

The profession or business of bookkeeping brings a man into contact with the inside of business-doing, and puts him in possession of most valuable facts on which to base sound conclusions about the particular business in which he is working. Bookkeeping should, therefore, train a man to step up into ownership of a business.

But history shows that, as a rule, bookkeepers do not graduate into owners or partners.

The rank and file of bookkeepers are clerks, and will remain as such, unless they become head-bookkeepers or have some other duties in connection with their book-keeping. Their position is subordinate ; usually they do not seize the opportunity for exercising more than clerical judgment.

Understand that I am referring here wholly to book-keepers who do nothing but keep books, not to those who have other duties, or who are office managers, superintending or head-bookkeepers, and thus occupy, in connection with their bookkeeping, some executive or advisory position.

Two fundamental business branches open up from the office boy ; one leads towards the selling or active side, the other towards the bookkeeping or clerical side.

Unusual talent is sure to show itself. No matter how it starts, the seed of ability will grow, even in sterile soil, and will sprout at the mere suggestion of fertility. But great ability is exceptional. The boy with average ability, and most of our youth are not above the ordinary grade, is very dependent upon his start. If he starts in as a bookkeeper, a bookkeeper he is likely to remain, subject to limited advancement. If he chooses the sell-ing or active side of business, and has as much as ordinary capacity, he will undoubtedly rise higher and accomplish more than he will in purely clerical lines, simply because this active side of business broadens him, develops him, and gives more opportunity than the exclusively indoor and more closely confined position presents.

But a knowledge of bookkeeping has its advantages, and a few months of training in this department may not injure the boy of better parts, and may do him good, even if he does not intend to remain a bookkeeper. But if he starts in this way purely for the experience that clerical work will give him, he must keep his true object in life before him, and practice bookkeeping and other clerical work simply as a means to another end.

Upon general principles, however, I would not advise a boy of more than ordinary ability to take up book-keeping even for its experience, unless he intends to perfect himself in that art, for sometimes it is quite difficult to turn from the road on which one has started. Many a boy becomes a bookkeeper, with his ambitions aimed far above clerical work, and seeks a bookkeeping experience simply as a means to a higher end. But he succeeds as a bookkeeper, and is able to earn a comfort-able livelihood. Depression in business, marriage, or other things may take place, which will suggest that he would better remain where he is, instead of giving up a certainty for an uncertainty.

Thus, this boy who did not intend to become a perma-nent bookkeeper never leaves the clerical ranks; and although he may eventually become a head-bookkeeper, or manager of some department, it is probable that he will never reach as high a position as his normal capacity would permit him to fill.

It is therefore much safer for a boy to begin with that work which he intends to continue through life, and not to diverge from this line more than necessity compels.

The good bookkeeper must have a natural liking for figures. He must be methodical and exact, and have a strong, well-trained memory, and he must be a good penman.

General business ability and capacity for financiering and salesmanship are not essential qualifications ; in fact, these are seldom possessed by the good clerical worker.

Expert accountants are bookkeepers of extraordinary ability, men who make the very minimum of errors and are able to grasp the most intricate situation and work it out to a successful finish.

Expert bookkeepers or accountants, who travel from office to office and from store to store, examining books and correcting the mistakes of the regular bookkeepers, occasionally earn from two thousand to four thousand dollars a year, but the rank and file probably do not receive more than two thousand dollars a year.

No one bookkeeper in a thousand can ever become an expert accountant, and if there were many more expert accountants than there are now in practice, they would find extreme difficulty in obtaining engagements, for only the largest concerns employ them.

Auditors are expert accountants who possess much more than clerical ability, and are able to size up a general situation and successfully handle it. While their work is not entirely removed from the bookkeeping side, still they are not accountants in a clerical sense, and they rank commercially with secretaries, treasurers, and general managers. In fact, the first-class auditor, although his training may have been chiefly clerical, is a commanding officer, and is so recognized in business circles. The auditor is really a business man, who would have been a success in many other lines aside from the clerical.

Auditors' salaries or incomes are substantially the same as those received by heads of departments, general managers, and the higher officers, varying from two thousand dollars a year to about twenty thousand, although the average salary does not probably exceed three thousand dollars.

Ordinary bookkeepers' salaries vary materially. Comparatively few are paid less than five or six dollars a week, and six dollars may be said to be about the average salary for beginners. Good, all-around, experienced bookkeepers, in large city offices or stores, receive from five hundred to twelve hundred dollars a year, and from four hundred to one thousand dollars a year in the smaller places.

First-class head-bookkeepers sometimes command salaries in excess of two thousand dollars, but any sum above fifteen hundred dollars is paid only to those of high grade, and to men who are able to manage bookkeeping departments or to successfully attend to outside duties.

A few top-notch bookkeepers may enjoy salaries of from four thousand to five thousand dollars a year ; but if they do, it is for executive abilities of some sort and not because they are bookkeepers.

The average bookkeeper is given little opportunity for promotion, except an annual raise of salary, which is sure to stop after a certain point is reached. He has little opportunity to exercise other qualities than those of correctness and faithfulness. He is for the most part away from the active line of business, and therefore can bring little business to his employer ; consequently, his services are not usually looked upon as worth more than ordinary pay, and he is seldom in a position to demand a material increase of salary.

Bookkeepers have, perhaps, less opportunity for advancement than any other class of store or office employees. Occasionally a bookkeeper becomes a partner.

Sometimes he combines his ability with that of an expert salesman, and if he is a good financier the combination is likely to succeed; but he has then become something more than a bookkeeper. He is a manager, a financier, and a partner.

The better grade of bookkeepers may sometimes obtain positions of trust in banks and other corporations; but here, again, they have become something more than bookkeepers.

Bookkeeping offers attractions to the boy or man fitted for it, and who is apparently not so well adapted to do anything else; and likewise offers much to the man who can sift out the advantages and lessons that he inadvertently learns, and then strike out for himself and make use of them. It is not the best occupation for the man who is capable of meeting the world and of successfully struggling against competition, and who is able aggressively and successfully to handle responsibilities.

The bookkeeper's position is, perhaps, the most permanent of any of the salaried vocations. He is likely to be less affected by depression in business and outside complications than any of his fellow-workers. If he is content to remain a bookkeeper, is not particularly ambitious, and is satisfied with a moderate and reasonably permanent income, there are few lines of work which offer him more than does professional bookkeeping. Certainly the bookkeeper has the minimum of business worry.

The boy of good habits, who is quick at figures and possesses a ready memory, and who is methodically correct, will make a good bookkeeper; and it may be well for him to turn his ambition in this direction, provided he has not more than ordinary ability and does not possess the energy for more aggressive work.

Perhaps the best advice that I can give to the boy about ready to enter upon his business career, and who is seriously considering bookkeeping, is to caution him not to become a professional bookkeeper if he has good reason to believe that he is better adapted to do something else, and particularly something closer to the activities of business, which will give him more opportunity to develop and utilize the ability that is within him.

This advice is based upon the supposition that his ability is above the ordinary; but ordinary capacity is also often likely to have a better chance for advancement outside of the conservative lines of this purely clerical calling.

A common-school education is essential to bookkeeping success. I would advise the would-be bookkeeper to graduate from the high school. Some of our public schools effectively teach the rudiments or foundations of bookkeeping; but few, if any, of them go far enough to perfect one for this calling. In every large city or town there is at least one well-equipped and reliable commercial or business school making a specialty of the practical science of bookkeeping.

While I am aware that some expert accountants and head-bookkeepers prefer to take a boy right from the public school, and to personally train him in bookkeeping, I think that the consensus of bookkeepers' opinion is decidedly in favor of a course in a commercial school.

As some of these commercial schools are run for revenue only, and are owned and managed by avaricious and incompetent men, I would suggest that the boy carefully investigate the claims made by the schools before making a selection.

Mr. Erwin W. Thompson, chief auditor of The Southern Cotton Oil Company, of New York City, in a letter to the author, says:

" What are the advantages offered by bookkeeping as a business?

" Blacksmithing as a business offers a livelihood; as an occupation it offers the opportunity to advance to better things.

" Bookkeeping is not unlike blacksmithing. The man who enters either as a life business does so with the certainty that he will derive nothing beyond an ordinary living.

" The man who takes up bookkeeping as a stepping-stone to higher things, but with the determination to do his daily work as well as if it were his final goal in life, is on the surest road to commercial success. Nothing can keep him from it, except individual unfitness and lack of ambition.

" What are the principal disadvantages to bookkeeping as a business?

" Atrophy of ambition is always standing at the door (sometimes on the inside) of the confirmed bookkeeper.

" Nowhere is there a better opportunity to learn the methods and secrets of a business than at the bookkeeper's desk, and nowhere is the opportunity so systematically disregarded.

" In the natural course of events the bookkeeper automatically and unconsciously acquires the habit of mistaking the body for the soul. In his wholly praiseworthy zeal to have his figures correct and his books in balance, he ceases to think of their meaning."

Mr. F. S. Hayward, office manager and general auditor of all of the offices of Swift and Company, at Chicago and other cities, in a letter to the author, says:

" I would not advise a boy to take up bookkeeping as a means of livelihood.

" A knowledge of bookkeeping is valuable to a man in almost any position in life, and I would advise a boy to get that knowledge as a stepping-stone to something better, but not to become a bookkeeper with the idea of following it for a living, for the reason that the field for a bookkeeper is comparatively limited, and that much greater progress can be made, after the knowledge of bookkeeping is obtained, by getting into a manufacturing or selling line.

" The percentage of bookkeepers who attain to any considerable position, as compared to the percentage of men that rise in other lines, is very small."

THE LAWYER

ECAUSE about one-half, if not a larger proportion, of our statesmen and other public characters have practised at the Bar, and because the attorney-at-law, or the lawyer, as he is commonly called, is apt to acquire some prominence, and seems to be closely associated with political office, the legal profession is looked upon as the leader of all professions, and as offering the best opportunity for local, state, or national advancement and fame. Certainly the successful lawyer is universally recognized and respected, and no doubt his calling offers to him greater opportunity for general advancement in almost every branch of public life and office-holding honor than is presented, all things being equal, to members of any other vocation.

The training of the law school, and the experience before the Bar, will usually make a good speaker out of any one who has a fair amount of capacity for delivery.

The lawyer in the practice of his profession is obliged to think quickly, and to think upon his feet. It is but natural, then, that he should become a good speaker, if he has any ability in that direction, and it is obvious that good speaking is an essential part of public life.

Granting that the Bar unquestionably presents the greatest opportunity for "noticeable" success, and admitting that more than one-half of the men who have been, and are, in the public eye are lawyers, yet the law in itself does not, and cannot, make the man; nor can it, of itself, give to any one any prominence, honor, notoriety, or intrinsic benefit which the man himself does not deserve.

It is the man behind the law which makes the man and is responsible for his advancement. The law and the man are distinct propositions.

The mediocre lawyer is not respected. He is invariably looked down upon and despised; and his profession offers to him absolutely no opportunity for more than subordinate advancement.

The great lawyer would be a great man in another calling, because he has in him the stuff which makes greatness. He is great anyway — fundamently great, great in himself. The law may have made it easier for him to realize his greatness and to attain an honorable position. The law simply offered an opportunity for the right kind of man to help himself.

Almost any one of ordinary ability can become a lawyer; that is to say, he can, by close study, pass the necessary examinations and become a member of the Bar. The law school does not, and cannot, go further than to require a written or oral examination; and if the candidate passes this examination, by correctly answering technical questions, the school must necessarily present him with a diploma, and the state and national Bar will likewise admit him to practice. But a knowledge of the law does not make a lawyer any more than a knowledge of theology fits a man to become a clergyman. Unless the legal knowledge is accompanied by the ability to use that acquirement, its possessor has no attainments of any value to himself or to any one else.

Knowledge stored in a mind incapable of distributing it is like so much unavailable junk, not worthy its storage room.

It has been derisively said that there is a lawyer to every case; but this is exaggeration. It is a fact, nevertheless, that the supply of lawyers, and even of good lawyers, much exceeds the demand; and that seventy-five per cent of them, not excepting those of any class or grade save the highest, might easily be excused from practising their profession. There is room, and plenty of room, at the top. The top never has been, and never will be, crowded in the law or in anything else.

There is also much room a few steps from the top, for even the upper rungs have not been fully filled. To reach the top, or to get near the top, with the superabundance of judicial minds now before the public, — successfully meeting this terrific competition, — is almost as difficult as shovelling water uphill.

There are few geniuses to-day, although there are more geniuses now than there were yesterday. But we must look at things as the averages run, not as the exceptions flash.

Only the genius, the great genius, can be at the top of the law, or at the top of any other profession, or business, or trade.

Therefore, the boy must picture his prospects in the light of the average, not as they may appear in the flashes

MELVILLE W. FULLER

Chief Justice of the United States Supreme Court; born Augusta, Me., 1833; graduate Bowdoin College, 1853; attended lectures at Harvard Law School; admitted to bar, 1855; practiced in Augusta until 1856, then went to Chicago, where he practiced until 1888, when he was appointed Chief Justice

of the exception, and he must consider each prospective calling as it appears from the results shown by the average persons who have entered it.

The lawyer at the top is at the very apex of eminence. The lawyer near the top occupies a prominent position. The lawyer at the middle of the ladder is a man of recognized success. The lawyer at the bottom, if he stays there, is the laughing stock of his friends, if he has any; is recognized nowhere, and practically amounts to nothing.

There is no other profession which offers so much and so little in the way of prominence and fame.

There is no easy road to legal eminence. The goal cannot be reached by a series of jumps. It is hard work at the start, and hard work all along the line. It is work, work, work, and grind, grind, grind, ever working and ever grinding; and many a law student falls by the wayside, never to pull himself together again.

The graduate of the law school, even if possessed of ability, will travel uphill for a year, probably for two years, not unlikely for three years, and perhaps for longer, before he reaches any kind of a plane upon which he can firmly plant his feet and successfully market his learning and ability.

Unless the young lawyer occupies a high social position, and enjoys the close friendship and confidence of many leading business men and capitalists, he will probably not be self-supporting inside of five years, if he is located in a large city; and it may take from two to three or more years before he can earn anything more than a fair living in the country.

The maximum annual income of our greatest lawyers exceeds a hundred thousand dollars a year. I can vouch for the correctness of the statement that a leading metropolitan attorney earned, or at least received, not less than a quarter of a million dollars for six months' services. It is possible that his success has been duplicated, but if so, it has not been done many times.

Many city lawyers annually receive from ten thousand to twenty thousand dollars. The average income of the city lawyer is, however, not over three thousand dollars a year. The maximum income of a leading country centre lawyer is not far from five thousand dollars a year; although a few, and a very few, earn twice this amount, and a limited number may exceed it, if they have metropolitan connections or have occupied some high government position, or have been in other ways prominent in the public eye. The average amount earned is about two thousand dollars a year.

The lawyer in a small country town seldom receives from his practice more than eight hundred to one thousand dollars a year, which amount is, with economy, sufficient to maintain him in reasonable comfort.

Where one lawyer gains fame and fortune, ninety-nine are not much more than self-supporting; and comparatively few, including those of considerable, and even of marked, ability, rise beyond the winning of a moderate competency.

One of the highest of the lawyer's ambitions is to become a judge. There is no position more honorable, nor is there any of greater responsibility. The judge is respected and honored everywhere, because he deserves to be.

While there are disreputable characters in every profession, I think it may be safely stated that, with rare exceptions, our judges, whether municipal or state or national, are true representatives of our civilization. In their hands is the nation's security, the nation's credit, and the nation's stability.

The higher court judges devote themselves exclusively to the Bench, but those of some of the district and municipal courts are allowed to practise, and therefore derive ·incomes otherwise than from their salaries. The justices of the state supreme courts receive salaries ranging from seventeen thousand five hundred dollars down to much smaller sums, depending on the size of the state and its wealth. New York State pays the judges of the Appellate Division of her Supreme Court seventeen thousand five hundred dollars a year, which is the largest salary paid in the United States to any judge. All of the salaries paid by New York State and New York City to judges, counsel, and other official lawyers, are the highest paid by any state; the Surrogate of New York receiving fifteen thousand dollars; the judge of the city court, ten thousand dollars; the judge of General Sessions, twelve thousand dollars; while the judges of the municipal courts are paid six thousand dollars each. In other states, these salaries are seldom as much as ten thousand dollars, and on the average are less than five thousand dollars.

The justices of the United States Supreme Court are paid twelve thousand five hundred dollars a year, except the Chief Justice, who enjoys a yearly salary of thirteen thousand dollars.

No grade of ability and adaptability is elsewhere so poorly paid as in the case of our justices and judges. Practically all judges are paid less than one-half of what the duties of the office would seem to warrant.

No man is fitted to be a judge, and few men ever become judges, who have not given years to the closest study of law, and who have not developed natural judicial ability. Why they should be underpaid is one of the unanswerable questions of American political economy.

The judge, however, has one advantage over other professional men, for, with few exceptions, he cannot be removed from office except for misbehavior; that is to say, he is appointed for life, and his salary is paid to him as long as he lives, whether or not he continues on the Bench.

A man may be a good lawyer and make a very poor judge. A man may be well fitted for the Bench and be less adapted for the Bar. The judge, however, must be first a lawyer. He must have also a judicial mind, one capable of sifting evidence and of getting at the truth ; and he must not only know the law, but must know how to apply it. Not one lawyer in a thousand is fitted for the Bench.

The legal profession is divided into several sections, classes, or branches.

These are represented by the following :

(1) The regular practitioner, who is familiar with the law in general, and with every kind of law except the so-called technical law, like the law of patents.

(2) The office or desk lawyer, who confines his practice to the drawing up of documents and to giving advice on general law matters, and who seldom appears before the court.

(3) The corporation lawyer, who is attorney for the great corporations, like railroads and other consolidations of capital. This class of lawyers enjoys the largest incomes, but only the most skilful can hope to successfully meet the requirements.

(4) The patent lawyer, who confines his work to obtaining patents and to patent litigations. He is

distinct from the patent solicitor, who may or may not be a member of the Bar. Although both perform the same duties in obtaining patents, the solicitor's work ends when the patent has been obtained; the lawyer's duties go beyond, and cover litigations. The patent lawyer must have mechanical ability, and, to be successful, must also possess unusual general understanding. He must be a business man as well as a professional man.

(5) The real estate or land lawyer, who handles real estate cases and whose chief work concerns land titles.

(6) The divorce lawyer, who confines his work to divorce cases, in and out of court.

(7) The collection lawyer, who practises little law save that pertaining to debts and indebtedness, and who is usually connected with a collection agency.

(8) The criminal lawyer, whose practice is confined to defending criminals before the court. Comparatively few lawyers are fitted for criminal cases. The successful criminal lawyer is keen and smart, whether or not he is great. He must be a good pleader, a convincing speaker, and able to make much out of little; a reader of human nature, and a manipulator of the human mind, which he must handle as the potter moulds his clay, shaping it the way he wants it to set.

The court lawyer, whether a criminal lawyer or not, is not, as a rule, a good desk lawyer; that is to say, his knowledge of the manipulation of the law is greater than actual knowledge of the law itself. He is, to an extent, the " wind " of the law; and I say this in no disparaging sense, because the " wind " of the law may be as necessary to success in law as is the real substance of law. Most so-called court lawyers are connected with law firms, so that their lack of ability in one direction will be balanced by the capacity of their partners, one or more of whom are indoor or desk lawyers, the other attending to the court business.

Very few men are able to handle successfully more than one class of law cases.

The successful lawyer, specialist or not, is, however, proficient in fundamental or general law. Without this knowledge he could not practise any branch of it. He learns first to be a lawyer, and afterwards to be a specialist.

As in all professions, there is much money, much satisfaction, much honor, for the man at the top, and enough of reasonable satisfaction for the man in the middle; but, in law, particularly, it is extremely hard to reach the top, and not one lawyer in five thousand comes anywhere near realizing his ambition, even though it is placed several rungs below the top of the ladder.

In every business centre there are one or more lawyers of considerable ability; and there are, in America, upwards of ten thousand practitioners of sufficient capacity to handle other than ordinary cases. Below this grade there are many men who are by no means deficient, and who are thoroughly trustworthy and of natural and developed ability, who receive fair incomes, and who live comfortably, but whose prominence, if they have acquired any, has not been necessarily dependent upon their chosen profession. They are good citizens, public spirited, and, to an extent, receive their deserts.

The young lawyer cannot reach prominence, nor can he hope to advance more than a step or two from the ranks, until he has successfully pitted himself against long established and successful attorneys. Alone he must enter the battle, and he must fight personally against terrible odds. In the law there is the hardest kind of competition — competition so fierce that it breaks down the ordinary man, and strains its heroes to the breaking point. Yet in this competition lies only a fair remuneration to the man of considerable ability.

The lawyer, unlike the business man, is not tied down to working hours. He does not work with any degree of evenness. He overworks and underworks, and studies and rests between the "heats."

The ordinary boy has no business to think of becoming a lawyer. Parental pride and desire should not be allowed to count in making a decision.

Many a parent has irrevocably ruined his boy, and made a failure out of what might have been a success, by forcing him into the law for some other than a good reason.

Of course, an ordinary boy may study law, and eventually be admitted to the Bar. He may put out his sign, and sooner or later have some sort of a clientele; but unless he is adapted for the profession, he will not be able successfully to assume responsibility, and the few cases given him will be of an unimportant character. He will not be so much respected, nor so successful, as he would have been had he not attempted to enter a calling above his capacity.

Of course, the desire to become a lawyer is the first requisite, but the desire is worth nothing in itself.

The successful lawyer must be equipped with a peculiar mind, a special mind such as Nature only occasionally gives. This equipment cannot be acquired and cannot be taught. It cannot be borrowed. It cannot be grafted into the boy. He must have it in the first place. Without it, he cannot become more than a book-practitioner, and all the study, pushing, and crowding will be useless.

The boy likely to become a good lawyer, and likely to make any kind of success of himself in that profession, not only possesses, but gives evidence of, reasoning qualities, and has a pronounced power of analysis. These may be crude and undeveloped, but they are there; and if examination will not discover them in the boy, they will not come out in the man.

At an early age, the boy fitted to enter the law can reason out probable results from circumstantial data. To a certain extent he knows how to produce apparent fact from probability, and even from possibility. He invariably enjoys discussion. He presents reasons, or apparent reasons, for every stand he takes. He may or may not be more than an ordinary student at school, although the bright lawyer usually develops from the bright scholar.

The boy who will make a good lawyer desires with his whole heart to be a lawyer, and nothing but force of circumstances can keep him from practising. He cannot be discouraged by ordinary discouragements: a lawyer he will be if he has one-tenth of a chance. Hardly without exception, the boy destined to shine before the Bar, or to make even a fair success at law, in early life expresses a strong desire for the profession. He reads intelligently reports of prominent trials and visits the court-room as often as he can. Before he has finished his common-school education he has probably read one or more law books, and very likely has been a leader among his fellows at mock trials and debates on complicated subjects.

No boy ever made a successful lawyer who did not

early show the characteristics which go to make the successful attorney-at-law.

It is useless to say that a boy may be restraining these characteristics, and that one cannot tell accurately whether or not he is predestined for the legal profession. It may be true in a few cases, but the exceptions are too few to be worthy of any consideration.

Boys, do not become poor lawyers. Better be fair or good at something else. If you are Bar-bent, somebody besides yourself will have observed the curve of your destiny. If you think you want to be a lawyer, first find out whether or not you really want to be one; and when you have decided that question in the affirmative, examine yourself and let others examine you. Look into yourself with your whole mind and your whole soul; probe yourself to your very depths; hunt with the microscope of all your acuteness for the characteristics which point law-ward, and ask others to discover what you are good for; talk with lawyers and other clear-headed and able advisers, and ask their advice.

If you and your parents are in favor of your entering the law, and other persons who are of fair discriminating capacity are opposed to it, I advise you to consider for many days before you plunge into a pool which is more likely to drown you than to float you.

A very large proportion of our young attorneys-at-law, and those who began to practise at the Bar within twenty years, are graduates of law schools. Many of our older lawyers read law in law offices, and neither attended nor graduated from a law school. This so-called law office education prevails to-day, but to a much less extent than in the past.

A college education cannot be considered essential,

but it is to be most strongly advised. The graduate of a college has a great advantage over the man whose school education is limited. The discipline of college work, and the environment of college life, irrespective of what the college actually teaches, are of fundamental advantage to the would-be lawyer. Even if it could be said truthfully that the college teaches nothing, and that the graduate of the college obtained little so far as mere learning is concerned, I would enthusiastically recommend a college education to any one who intends to enter the legal profession. The associations begun at college will be of ever-present value to him.

I don't mean to say that the lack of a college education prejudices his legal success. The right kind of man will become a successful lawyer with or without a college education. The college, however, helps, and helps mightily.

I would therefore advise any one who intends to study law to enter college and graduate from it, even at great personal sacrifice. I would recommend the law school, as the well-equipped law school is in every respect a better preparation than reading law in a lawyer's office, although many of our most eminent attorneys did not graduate from law schools.

The Hon. Edward Lauterbach, of the New York Bar, in a letter to the author, says:

" If I advised the young man to enter the law, it would be only in the event that I knew him to be possessed of unusual and exceptional qualifications for the profession, and especially because I believed him to be possessed of the attributes necessary to enable him to be an advocate in the courts. There is an unusual scarcity of lawyers fully equipped for the actual trial of important cases. There is,

JOSEPH H. CHOATE

Lawyer and diplomat; born in Salem, Mass., 1832; graduate Harvard College, 1852; Harvard Law School, 1854; admitted to Massachusetts Bar, 1855; New York Bar, 1856; assisted in breaking up the Tweed ring, 1871; ambassador to Great Britain, 1899–1905. Noted as a public and after-dinner speaker

and will be for years to come, a glut in all other branches of the profession.

"The qualifications referred to would consist in part of a good presence, a studious temperament, a knowledge of human nature, and a gift of eloquence.

"If I advised the young man not to enter the law, it would be because the profession, more than any other, is, and will be for many years to come, an overcrowded one.

"The formation of trusts, whatever may be their beneficial attributes, — and they are many, — has, by reason of consolidation and concentration, limited the clientele which existed while the constituent companies or firms were independent and competitive.

"The formation of real estate, mortgage, and title-guarantee companies has rendered the branch of the profession known generally as conveyancing of little importance.

"The existence of arbitration committees, in the great exchanges, has diminished litigation greatly.

"A uniform bankruptcy law, containing features which render the issue of mesne process valueless, and which gives no advantage to the diligent over the dilatory creditor, has greatly diminished the volume of debtor and creditor litigation.

"It is true that the calendars are crowded, but with a large preponderance of cases arising from negligence in the operation of public service companies, the elements of which are generally understood and require no high order of attainment in their conduct.

"Other reasons might be adduced, but these of themselves, it seems to me, are sufficient to justify the belief that, with the limitation of proper opportunity, only those exceptionally qualified should enter upon the profession of the law."

The Hon. Charles S. Hamlin, A.M., LL.D., of Boston, late Acting Secretary of the United States Treasury, in a letter to the author, says:

" Whether or not I would advise a young man to take up the practice of the legal profession would depend somewhat upon the man himself. It is a profession that is exacting, yet it offers very great rewards to those willing to devote themselves to it. In addition to that, a legal education equips a man well for many positions not directly connected with law.

" A legal education presupposes a well-trained mind, and this may open a wide avenue to other fields of usefulness. I think that a legal education could never be a handicap, but probably would be of the greatest assistance in almost any business. To one who takes it up as his profession, it certainly, as I have said, offers the highest prizes for ability and capacity for hard work."

THE STENOGRAPHER

UTSIDE of the courts and newspaper offices more than eighty per cent of the stenographers and typewriter operators are women; and even in the courts to-day women are vying with men for the occupancy of these clerical positions.

The reason for this is obvious. The work is not particularly difficult after the necessary speed has been acquired; and women, rightly or wrongly, are willing to work for less pay than would be accepted by men occupying parallel positions.

Business is cruel, and there is no philanthropy about it. It buys what it wants at the lowest possible price consistent with reasonable efficiency. So long as the woman continues to work at a lower price than is paid to the man for a similar service, the man cannot compete with the woman on what may be assumed to be the woman's ground.

The woman stenographer has become an office fixture and necessity.

However, as this book is for boys and young men, I cannot here discuss in detail the advantages and disadvantages of stenography as applied to girls and women.

There is little demand in the country for stenographers because the majority of country business and professional men attend personally to their correspondence, and a large porportion of the stenographers employed in the country are engaged by lawyers or are in factory offices. But in the city they are as common as book-keepers, and the demand for them is rapidly increasing.

The principal work of the stenographer consists of taking down in shorthand what is dictated, and of transcribing the notes upon the typewriter.

Comparatively few stenographers perform any other service than that of shorthand or typewriting, although there should be no reason why they could not attend to other duties, and thereby enhance their commercial value. In many cases there is not enough stenographic work to keep one busy, and this condition gives the stenographer opportunity to learn something of the business, and to perform other duties; but for some reason, which need not be discussed here, the average stenographer, whether man or woman, is seldom more than a stenographer, and seems to have no thought, or no desire, beyond the note-book and the typewriting-machine.

The higher grade of stenographer, however, is often more than a machine. If he did not have the ability to be more than a routine stenographer, he would probably not be an expert in that art. In connection with his stenographic work, unless he occupies some government position, he frequently has more or less to do with the confidential duties of the office, and sometimes occupies the position of private secretary.

Some of our most eminent business men were once stenographers, and rose from the ranks to commanding positions in business. But it must be admitted that comparatively few male stenographers of not more than ordinary ability obtain advancement other than a moderate increase in salary from time to time; and when they become too old for office work, they usually drift into some subordinate clerical position, where they indefinitely remain. This sad condition, however, is not limited to the stenographic profession.

The court stenographer, so far as stenography goes, is next to the top of his profession, and is second only to the official government stenographer, who is capable of reporting legislative sessions, and receives a salary of several thousand dollars a year. Few court stenographers earn less than a thousand dollars per annum, and often their salary, or income from all sources, is in excess of three thousand dollars a year. They frequently receive as much from their outside work as from their salaries. The attorneys on both sides often desire extra copies of testimony, or minutes, and sometimes several extra copies, which the stenographer furnishes at a profitable price.

Although there are comparatively few high-salaried stenographic positions, yet there are more of these positions than there are men competent to fill them.

The top of stenography is by no means crowded, and the high-class, verbatim stenographer is seldom out of a position. His income, as a rule, is considerably in excess of the ordinary clerical salary, and sometimes equal to that enjoyed by the manager of the department in a business house. Still, even with his comparatively high salary, he has little or no opportunity for advancement beyond certain limits, unless he goes outside of his duties as stenographer.

It is quite easy to acquire a stenographic speed of

from eighty to one hundred words a minute, and to read notes taken at this rate with a reasonable accuracy, but every word over the hundred mark comes harder, and the majority of stenographers cannot, for any length of time, maintain a speed much in excess of one hundred words a minute.

The stenographer who can easily, and with accuracy, write one hundred and fifty words a minute, for a period of an hour or more, is an expert, who ought to enjoy an income of from a thousand to twenty-five hundred dollars a year, and occasionally in excess of this latter figure.   But positions of this kind are not frequent, and the number of stenographers competent to fill them is small.

The ordinary commercial counting-room stenographer, usually a woman who seldom writes more than one hundred words a minute and is not always sure of her notes, receives, on the average, not over eight dollars a week at the start, with a prospect of finally earning ten or twelve dollars.

Comparatively few business concerns pay over eight dollars a week to a green stenographer, man or woman ; and many stenographers, just out of school, cannot hope to begin on more than six dollars a week.

It may be said that almost any one of ordinary capacity, with a good common-school education, who is willing to apply himself to faithful study and practice, can become a fair stenographer, and is reasonably sure of a salary of from eight to twelve dollars a week.   If he can increase his guaranteed speed from one hundred to one hundred and twenty-five or more words a minute, and combine with stenographic speed some skill in correspondence, the prospect of fifteen dollars a week will be good, and he may rise to an annual salary of from a thousand to fifteen hundred dollars, or even to two thousand dollars.

The stenographer needs a first-class common school education, and should be preferably a graduate of a high school. Unless he is a good speller and grammarian, he has little hope of stenographic success. The average business man has forgotten or disregards much of his grammar, and often does not know much about rhetoric or construction. He therefore depends, in these respects, upon his stenographer, who must take down in shorthand what he says as he says it; but unless the stenographer is able to reconstruct the dictated matter, without material change, his services are not likely to be advantageous to his employer.

The stenographer can, of course, learn mechanically to do what he is told to do; that is, he can, by practice, learn to take down in shorthand what is dictated; but it is more of an achievement to properly and grammatically write out his notes, correcting them as he writes, so that the completed letter, while it does not differ in substance from the dictation, will be a finished production. The stenographer who can do this is reasonably sure of an ultimate rise in salary of from twenty-five to fifty per cent, provided the house for which he works can afford to pay it.

After one has finished the high school, the school of stenography is the next in order, if that line of work is selected. It is possible to learn stenography without an instructor, but it is difficult to do so, and considerably more time will be required than under the guidance of a good teacher.

Beware of unreliable and unknown schools of stenography. Before choosing one, consult with the principal of your public school, or with a reputable stenographer,

and follow his advice. Be sure to learn some standard
system of stenography. Keep away from short-cuts.
Remember the Three P's, — patience, perseverance, and
practice.

The stenographer's school course takes usually about
nine months, in which time any boy of ordinary capacity
ought to learn to write and read shorthand, but of
course at a slow rate of speed. Speed depends upon
practice, and no stenographer can hope to be more
than moderately proficient in less than a year.

The superabundance of stenographic schools turns out
stenographers with almost incubator speed, and actually
gluts the market. The reliable stenographic institution
never misrepresents, and fulfils its promises, but there
are, in every large city, irresponsible schools of stenography, which literally prey upon every scholar. Their
advertisements and announcements are flagrant misrep-
resentations. They give the scholar and the parent to
understand that not only is stenography very easy, but
that numerous vacancies exist at all times for their
graduates. Without legally doing so, they apparently
guarantee to place their graduates in business. The
parent, with a worthless or idle boy on his hands, and
not knowing exactly what to do with him, places him in
a school of stenography, where, in an indifferent, slip-
shod way, the scholar masters the rudiments of shorthand, and sooner or later possibly obtains a position at
from five to eight dollars a week. Of course he does
not remain long in this position, but is soon out of work
for an indefinite period ; then he gets another position,
and so on, never succeeding in obtaining a permanent
situation.

Stenography is a possible stepping-stone to better
things, and from that view-point is worthy of considera-

tion on the part of the ambitious young man; but it must be admitted that stenography is not one of the best preliminary steps for those who have more than ordinary ability, and who are capable of planning and executing the active work of business.

There is little demand for the man office-stenographer. The merchant knows full well that he can obtain for such work a woman of equal or greater efficiency at a smaller salary than the man would require. Because a few male stenographers have gained commanding positions, it does not follow that stenography, in itself, offers unusual opportunities. These successful men would probably have succeeded whether they had become stenographers or not.

Typewriting is an essential part of the stenographer's work, and all stenographers use the typewriter. The average typewriter operator has a speed of from thirty to fifty words a minute. Comparatively few can exceed sixty words a minute, still fewer can attain seventy-five, and only a very small number can approximate one hundred words a minute. There are, however, a few typewriter operators who can maintain a speed equal to that of ordinary dictation, and are able to follow dictation directly upon the machine. Nevertheless, stenography should be learned, even by expert typewriters, as few men are willing and able to dictate directly to the operator at the machine.

Shorthand is not especially difficult of acquirement for one of ordinary ability, but its thorough mastery requires close application and long-continued practice.

Accuracy is all-essential; speed without accuracy is worth next to nothing; and accuracy without speed has little commercial value.

I would advise the boy who thinks seriously of becoming a stenographer to pause and reflect, and then to pause again, and to continue to reflect, for several days or weeks, before entering a profession which has comparatively few prizes to offer, and has very little substantial reward even for those who draw a prize.

Mr. W. S. Townsend, of New York City, private secretary to the president of the Southern Railway, in a letter to the author, says:

" My views are:
" That the principal advantage of stenography to young men lies in the mental training which tends to concentration of thought and purpose, and thus establishes mental habits, which are valuable in any business or profession. No young man can be a good stenographer unless he is temperate, alert, accurate, and thorough; and these qualities cannot fail to prove of material value, whether or not he remains a stenographer.

" That the principal disadvantage of stenography lies in the absence of responsibility and the consequent neglect of some of the most important qualities necessary in the conduct of business affairs. The average stenographer is not called upon to assume responsibility, other than the proper transcription of his notes, and therefore does not mentally grow after finding his level, but gradually deteriorates, and falls into a rut from failure to cultivate his powers."

Mr. W. B. Kirkpatrick, of the Navy Department, at Washington, D. C., in a letter to the author, says:

" At no time in the history of shorthand has it been necessary, in a town of five thousand or more inhabitants, where the English language is spoken, for a stenographer of even ordinary intelligence to go hungry or remain out of work for any length of time; and as business develops competition becomes keener, and the necessity for quick, sensible action increases, average salaries are higher, and the demand for competent stenographers grows more urgent.

" To be a successful stenographer a boy must first obtain a basic education in the common English branches. Having secured such a basic education, every boy should learn to write shorthand. It requires less time than to learn any of the trades or professions, and the returns are quicker and surer. As ' job insurance,' in times of trouble, it has no equal. If a competent stenographer should at any time fail in other business, he can at once return to his old work, and pay rent and living expenses until he can again get on his feet. As long as he is able to do any work, it is not necessary for him to ask for aid from others. He is independent, and it gives him a feeling of security, which prolongs his life and helps him to succeed in other lines of work on his own account.

" Every man should be a stenographer.

" While a stenographer usually starts at a higher salary than other employees, he will sooner or later find that there exists a kind of prejudice against promoting a stenographer to the highest places in private concerns, industrial and railroad companies, and government and state offices. A few stenographers of unusual strength win out and go clear to the top in any business; but, as a rule, it is easier to overcome this handicap by working with another aim in view; that is, in the first place, always accept a position where a business can be learned and put to other use. For instance, if a man desires to succeed in his own commercial business some time during his life, let him take a stenographic position under a good man in a commercial house; if in law, with a judge or lawyer of the highest standing; and if in railroad or government service in the best office, where he can learn the whole business, and afterwards open an agency for handling some special line of work where such knowledge as he has acquired through his stenographic position will be of value to his patrons. He can in this way honorably overcome this unjust prejudice, and without friction with his employer or co-employees.

" When employers see stenographers successfully handling their own business, they will allow them to work up to their proper level. I say this from general observation, and this statement has no reference to my personal experience."

THE STAGE

ALL the stage is a big trap-door through which most of those who tread its boards fall into the cellar of obscurity.

There is no vocation of more uncertain results, either in fame or in moneyed remuneration.

The glitter of the footlights, and the charm and mystery of stage-land, have been the blazing flame which has attracted the million moths of failure.

As we, the outsiders, view the actor and dramatic conditions from the auditorium, we see only the painted and finished side, and naturally obtain little correct idea of the inside life of the profession, which is acknowledged by those in it, and by those who are familiar with it, to be the most difficult to master and traversed with frequent and deep pitfalls.

The desire to become an actor will not make an actor of anybody. The greatest amount of study and most severe and continuous training never transformed into an actor a person who did not possess natural dramatic ability; nor has any one ever become a finished tragedian, a fairly good comedian, or ever successfully filled any stage part, unless of the lowest grade, who did not develop his natural talent by the hardest and most painstaking study.

The actor must be born, for natural ability, no matter how marked it may be, in itself will not finish and polish him for a successful stage career, except in the most exceptional exceptions, which are altogether too infrequent to be worthy of consideration. Even these so-called spontaneous actors, who seem to leap at a bound into the centre of the stage, would have been much better off had they passed through years of preliminary training.

The actor himself, and his teacher, without exception, will tell you that there is no study or training more difficult, more wearing, and more discouraging than that necessary to place an actor in the line of promotion. The ordinary boy may become a fair lawyer if he studies hard enough. He may not be a good pleader, but conscientious and long application will probably give him some foothold in the law and present him with an opportunity for earning a livelihood, and all this without any special adaptation to the legal profession. The ordinary boy, by continuous study and application, may become a fair success in some of the professions, and in many lines of trade or business, without pronounced aptitude; but unless Nature struck the first spark of histrionic fire he will never become, try though he may, more than a flickering candle of dramatic light. He will not blaze; he will just burn, and burn out.

I am not advising the boy who has no talent for the law to enter the law, or to go into any other profession, unless he feels a reasonable certainty that his inclination and abilities tend that way. I am simply bringing out the point that, while he may make a fair success along certain lines, often against the grain of his incli-

nation and his ability, it is well-nigh impossible for him
to even fairly well succeed upon the stage unless Nature
has given him, not only a love for it, but a well-defined,
sharply cut ability in that direction.

Unless he has an intense love for the drama and positive dramatic ability, he cannot hope to be more than an
insignificant seventh or eighth grade actor, with substantially no prospects and a cloud for his future. It is
absolutely essential that Nature give the start, and it
is as necessary that study and training follow.

Like all other professions, and like almost all other
callings, whether of trade or business, the stage is overcrowded, not only with actors, but with really good
actors. It is true, however, that the dramatic top is not
fully occupied; but the road to superlative fame is a
virtual hurdle race of difficulties, and most of those who
attempt to run it perish within sight of the half-way
post; and from that point the road is strewn with the
emaciated bodies of beaten, yet struggling, aspirants for
never-to-be-gotten fame.

It is a popular notion that the stage offers unusual
temptations, and that actors, as a rule, are of loose
morals. It is useless to attempt to deny that the stage
gives opportunity for about every kind of immorality,
for it does. But so do many other callings. There is
temptation everywhere, more on the stage than in some
other walks of life; but there is nothing about the stage,
or stage life, which will drive a boy of character to
the bad. If the boy has not character in the first place,
he will fail morally, whether he goes on the stage
or not; perhaps he will fail more quickly on the stage
than he would in some other profession. The character
of the average actor is as high as is that of the majority
of other professional men. He is no worse, and proba-

bly no better, than are the rank and file of the people whom we see on the streets or in the stores. His vocation, which sends him from place to place, and which pushes him to the front, gives the public an opportunity to judge him more accurately than it can those in the ordinary walks of life. Consequently, the evil in him is more readily seen. I do not think that the temptations of the stage or the morality of the actor should prevent any one from entering the dramatic profession. Other considerations and conditions are of more consequence.

The dramatic profession appeals to the higher sensibilities and to the artistic temperament. The great actor is a great man, and deserves the honors bestowed upon him. The competent actor is one of the gems of civilization and one of the brightest stars in the public-seeing firmament. The profession of the stage, no matter what it may have been in the past, is to-day an honorable and thoroughly legitimate vocation.

The good actor is an artist, and one of our most prominent citizens ; but the poor actor is without honor upon the stage, an outcast behind it, — unknown, uncared for, and poorly sustained. His salary is small, often below the living-point. His prospects — really he has none. The poor actor never rises from the ranks, and he will probably not even remain stationary, but is likely to drop lower as the years go by.

The world cares nothing about the poor or ordinary actor. He has no standing on the stage or off it. The small storekeeper, or ordinary representative of almost any other calling, if he be a decent fellow, has some sort of a position in the community; but the poor actor — never.

From the ranks of good actors spring most of our

great ones. While training and experience do not make an actor, very few actors reach any kind of dramatic success at the start. The great actor in embryo never began as a poor actor. He was merely an inexperienced actor. No matter how crude and unfinished his attempts, he invariably showed, at the very beginning, some indication of the growth of success.

It is necessary for the embryo actor to wait for fame, perhaps a dozen years, unceasingly acting and studying himself and his characters, that his acting may not be that of the mimic sort, but the outward manifestations of his innermost self.

No actor ever made a continuous success who was not an actor at heart as well as in name, his visible work being the reflection of the true artistic quality of the actor's real and complete inner-self.

Nearly all of our great actors have passed through years of hardship and privation; and some of them, for extended periods, have really suffered for want of proper food.

The actor must anticipate, and be willing to experience, disheartenment and discouragement. He will be snubbed and abused, and probably kept in minor rôles long after he is competent to assume important ones. His life, even when he has become a star, is devoid of many of the pleasures which seem essential to a comfortable amount of human happiness.

Nearly all actors, whether they be stars, leading men, or ordinaries, are obliged to spend from seven to nine months of the year upon the road. Although the home stock company is being revived, probably ninety per cent of the legitimate actors play what is known as one-night stands; that is, with the exception of a few weeks, they visit six different towns or cities a week, and thus are travelling continually, with little opportunity for rest. They are away from home the greater portion of the year, and a part of the time they are on sleeping-cars and eating their meals anywhere and everywhere.

The vaudeville artist's life is not so hard as that of the legitimate actor, because he is generally allowed to play a week in one place, but even he enjoys the comforts of home for only a small part of the year.

He who would be an actor needs to deeply impress upon himself the solemn, and by no means agreeable, truth, that the stage demands a sacrifice, the like of which does not accompany many other callings.

The actor seldom has a home. He is without a home, and at times without a country. He cannot often exercise the prerogative of citizenship. In the years of his struggling, the only home life that he can hope to experience is, at best, a summer vacation, and this vacation he may not fully enjoy, because he cannot often afford it, and accepts it because there is no help for it. When he becomes a great actor, or an actor of moderate success, he still has no home save in the summer, and that cannot be considered a genuine place of residence.

True, an actor is not much more unfortunate than is a commercial salesman on the road; but the salesman has this one advantage, — there is a fair chance of his eventually being permanently located somewhere. This opportunity is seldom presented to the actor. Success on the part of the commercial traveller means a permanent home, if he wants it. Success on the part of the actor keeps him still on the road.

The boy, enjoying the comforts of home, with playmates and friends about him, does not, and cannot, realize what it is to sleep in a different bed every night, or a different bed every week; what it is to travel from point to point, continually on the move, with a comfortable room one day and an uncomfortable one the next, with good food to-day and poor food to-morrow, with midnight transfers, cold cars, and chilly hotels, with no opportunity to make friendships, save among those of his own company and of the few companies he meets. The fascination of continuous travelling remains with those who do not continuously travel.

True, an actor may marry some actress, and they may travel together, but this does not mean a home, nor is it certain that they can stay together for any length of time.

The resident stock company actor, located near his theatre, may have a permanent home of his own, provided, of course, that he remains with his company. Comparatively few do that for any length of time. In the first place, the actor is likely to become dissatisfied, and frequently the home audience demands a change, so that few stock company actors remain more than four years in any one place. During the season, the stock actor has little time to himself, and if it were not for the long summer vacation, he would probably break down after a third season.

Most of the home stock company actors play in what are known as popular-priced houses, with two performances a day, — afternoon and evening. These theatres, as a rule, run a different play each week, although they occasionally hold the same play for two or more weeks ; consequently, the actor gives substantially his whole time to acting and rehearsing. He has no afternoons or evenings off, except when he is temporarily dropped from the cast, which does not occur often. From the opening to the close of the season he is probably cast in thirty different plays, in some of which he has never appeared before, and he must rehearse these plays whether he has ever played them or not. The rehearsals are held in the morning and on Sunday, and the stock actor, therefore, spends most of his time in the theatre, which amounts to about the same as appearing three times a day.

If he is a competent actor, he is given prominent parts; but even with a good memory it is no small task to become letter-perfect in thirty or more plays a year. Exercise of memory is only a part of his work. He must enter into the spirit of the character and train himself at rehearsal to the proper portrayal of it. The home stock actor actually has to be thirty different types of men in about forty weeks, and these different kinds of men he must portray twice a day; and to do it properly he must feel the rôle which he assumes. To do this, strains the mind and often makes a man altogether too versatile, so much so that he is not likely to become a great success in any one rôle.

The travelling actor plays fewer parts, and consequently is not obliged to appear continuously at rehearsals. Many of these actors do not assume more than one rôle a year. This limits their labors to about eight performances a week, assuming that they play two matinées, and to comparatively few rehearsals, since a rehearsal is not held except when a new play is put on, or when there is a change made in the cast, or a poor performance is given.

As a rule, the star and the star's company do not play more than two rôles in a season, although some stars have a long repertoire; but unless of the brightest magnitude, they cannot expect to remain in one city longer than a few weeks at a time, and substantially all of them, for a portion of the season, play one-night stands.

The fabulous salaries popularly supposed to be enjoyed by actors do not often materialize. It has been said that the greatest star, with an acceptable play or opera, has been known to net as much as ten thousand dollars in a single week, — this week, of course, occurring in the height of the season; but no star ever received this figure for an extended period. Many a star of respectable quality does not receive, on an average, more than two hundred dollars a week in a season of from thirty to forty weeks.

Although some stars net from five hundred to a thousand dollars a week during the season, few receive the latter figure, and very few exceed the thousand-dollar mark. The "top-notch" stars usually play for a percentage on the receipts, and sometimes own the play, with or without a partner. Even the most successful, who receive from five hundred to a thousand or more dollars a week during a profitable season, may earn in reality very much less, on account of the losses through an unfortunate play, which may in a single season wipe out the profits of several successful years.

There is no business more problematical than that of the stage. It seems to be well-nigh impossible for any one to anticipate the success of a new play. Many a play which has successfully passed the critics, and has been dubbed a winner at rehearsals, has fallen flat when presented to the public; and many a play which owes its presentation more to luck than to discovered merit becomes an instantaneous success, sometimes running into several seasons. Continuous profit or income is almost unknown in the dramatic business; therefore, in calculating incomes one must deduct the losses, which would bring the aggregate profit far below its apparent magnitude.

Second-rate stars earn anywhere from one hundred to five hundred dollars a week. By "second-rate stars" I am not referring to those who are thoroughly first-class and highly popular with the public, but to stars who play at ordinary prices; that is to say, if the usual price of the theatre is one dollar a seat, this price is not raised when the actor appears. The majority of stars belong to this class.

In reckoning an actor's income, it must be understood that the majority of them do not play more than thirty or forty weeks, and that few of them appear the year around, except those in the variety business. Probably the first-class leading man, — that is, the principal male support under the star of the first or second magnitude, — earns from a hundred and fifty to two hundred dollars a week, the average drawing a salary of slightly over a hundred dollars a week. Out of this salary he must pay his hotel bills, and all expenses other than for transportation; that is to say, he must pay for lodging, for meals, for sleeping-cars, for staterooms, for everything except the actual cost of his transportation ticket. This condition applies to all actors of every grade from the star to the chorus. Some managers, however, make a slight increase in salaries while on the road; or, to put it conversely, decrease the salaries while on long stands.

A plain, ordinary, every-day actor, even if he possesses some ability, does not receive, on the average, more than twenty-five dollars a week, and comparatively few get above the fifty-dollar mark.

Many a good actor, playing rôles below the fourth position in the cast, does not receive exceeding thirty or forty dollars a week; and all-around actors, capable of acceptably filling almost any part except leading rôles, can often be obtained for considerably less than sixty dollars a week.

Again let me impress upon the reader that these salaries are paid only when one is actually on the stage, and that substantially all actors, barring the vaudeville artists, have nothing to do during at least three months of the year.

All actors are engaged by contract; that is, they receive from the manager a written agreement specifying what they shall do and what they shall receive for it. Most of these contracts cover the season of from thirty to forty weeks, but in every contract there is a clause which gives the manager an opportunity to cancel the engagement on a week's notice. On account of this condition, which invariably appears and is accepted by both parties, there are many cancellations and changes. Consequently, the average actor does not act and draw a salary for more than thirty weeks a year. During these weeks he must earn substantially all of his yearly income, and pay all of his expenses, whether at home or on the road, except the one item of car fare.

Assuming that an actor receives fifty dollars a week for thirty weeks, his yearly income is only fifteen hundred dollars. Out of this he must pay all expenses, save car fare, while on the road. If he has a family, this means that his salary is equivalent to the thousand dollars received by the clerk who has a permanent position and does business near his home.

In most cases the actor pays for his ordinary stage costume, like a dress suit, business suit, and Prince Albert suit, the manager generally contributing the fancy costumes.

The modern stage is said to be divided into three distinct branches: opera, grand and light; drama, including both comedy and tragedy; and the vaudeville or variety, including the so-called continuous performance.

Success in the opera depends more upon the voice than upon the stage presence; but a handsome man, with a prepossessing figure, who is a good actor, with a fair voice, may be a greater success than an unprepossessing man with a much better and stronger voice.

The average income of a male opera singer is about the same as that of an actor of the same grade.

The enormous salaries paid to operatic artists are usually confined to prima donnas. No male opera singer has ever received anywhere near the price earned by the greatest prima donna.

The male chorus does not earn, on an average, more than fifteen dollars a week, with a few additional dollars while on the road.

The vaudeville or variety actors, as a rule, are better paid than the regular actors, and many legitimate actors have permanently or temporarily taken up the variety stage.

Some years ago the continuous performance sprang into life. It was a new idea, and readily found public favor. It gave respectability to a class of performances which had hitherto never been patronized by the better class of people.

While the vaudeville craze or fad has somewhat subsided, the vaudeville remains a permanent institution, and will probably continue to exist.

A very few vaudeville artists receive as high as a thousand dollars a week. Undoubtedly a number of them earn as much as from one hundred to three hundred dollars a week, but the great majority are below, and some of them much below, the hundred-dollar mark. Many a vaudeville artist does not receive more than thirty dollars a week, which does not net him more than twelve dollars, for these artists are obliged to pay all of their expenses, including their transportation.

Generally speaking, it may be said that the vaudeville artist receives from ten to twenty-five per cent more net profit than does the same grade of legitimate actor.

The vaudeville presents substantially every kind of entertainment, from the tragedian in a short tragedy to the trainer of dogs and monkeys. Many of them play in what is known as teams, two usually, and sometimes more, being in partnership. Nearly all of the singing and dancing artists do team work.

The program of the average vaudeville performance is about as follows : a singing and dancing team of two persons, either two men or two women, or a man and a woman; a juggler; one or more gymnasts or acrobats, usually in teams of two, — two men, two women, or a man and a woman, — and sometimes in teams of from four to eight; trained animals, generally dogs, monkeys, or horses; one or two short plays, usually comedies, with two actors, — a man and a woman, — although sometimes there are three or more; a so-called conversational team, which may be in the form of Jew imitators, Irish talkers, or Dutch comedians, usually confined to two men ; a vocalist, generally alone ; stereopticon views; and moving pictures.

Vaudeville actors, playing short plays, earn about twenty-five per cent more than they would be likely to receive on the regular stage.

The vaudeville artist has an easier life than does the legitimate actor. He has substantially no rehearsing to do. He is his own manager, and usually has but two performances a day, each performance lasting about twenty minutes. Reckoning the time required for two

appearances, including dressing, the average vaudeville
actor is not employed at actual work more than three
hours a day. This gives him considerable time for diversion and rest; altogether too much time, in fact, because
he is not likely to employ it to advantage, the average
actor, like the average man of the other lines, not caring
for reading or study; consequently, this extra time is
used for loafing and resting purposes.

The vaudeville performer has another advantage over
the legitimate actor in that his engagements are likely
to be for a week or longer, as he plays to few one-night
stands. He has much open time, however, and suffers
greatly by cancellation of engagements. He probably
does not play more than nine months in a year, even
including summer dates at picnic groves, at beaches,
and at semi-outdoor theatres.

Not one boy in two thousand who wants to be an
actor, and not one boy in a thousand who thinks he
has dramatic ability, is likely to make much success upon
the stage. The fact that he wants to be an actor is of
little significance. Almost every boy, at some time in
his career, wanted to be an actor; and, for that matter,
wanted to run a street-car or to be a soldier or sailor.

The boy with the dramatic fire in him will be an actor
against all opposition. The histrionic flame is in him.
It demands the stage for its burning. This boy should
show such marked dramatic characteristics, such intense
desire to perfect himself for the stage, that the parent,
and every one else connected with him, cannot help seeing the dramatic flash of his eye. Such a boy can be
successfully trained for the stage.

The funny boy, the boy who can recite comic pieces
and make people laugh at a home party, may not possess one spark of dramatic fire. As an amateur, he may

be a success in a small way, but mere appearance of dramatic talent is not sufficient.

The precocious child, who recites at every opportunity, will probably outgrow what seems to be dramatic quality.

A mimic, even if the mimicry is humorous, may possess only flashing talent, and none of the intensity necessary for more than transient success.

Because many a great actor began as an amateur, the amateur actor, achieving local success, may honestly believe that the stage should be his goal, and this opinion may be possessed by some of his friends and relatives.

As a matter of fact, not one good amateur actor in a thousand is fitted for the stage. The amateur almost always acts for the fun of it, without giving it much serious thought. The real actor is serious, serious as an amateur actor, and serious all along the line from the bottom to the top. The born actor not only shows ability at an early age, but his whole interests are centred upon stage-craft. To him the stage is all the world, and real — very real. No matter how careless he is, no matter how dreamy he is, he devotes all of his available energy to perfecting himself and to studying along dramatic lines. He realizes the necessity of training, and that it must be long and tedious, and he accepts this condition.

The boy fitted to be an actor goes into it as the boy adapted to medicine takes up the study of medicine, or the boy predisposed to be a lawyer naturally gravitates toward the law.

No boy should choose the stage for a living unless he has decided dramatic ability, and sufficient ability to show at an early age, — not the ability of the mimic, but the ability which flames and burns. This boy will not smother his fire under a bushel. It will be bright enough and free enough to impress his relatives and friends. It will not be a fad with him, but a lasting desire.

The boy who cannot make any one besides himself feel that he is naturally stage-bound is fooling himself, and has no business in dramatics.

The boy who seriously wants to be an actor should be taken to the stage and shown what it is. He should see it in its reality, and particularly should he be shown every disadvantage. He should be allowed to talk with actors who have failed, and with actors who have succeeded, and especially with actors who have not reached the top nor sunk to the bottom. As he progresses, great will be the discouragement before him, and unless he has the real "stuff" in him, not one boy in a thousand will go beyond the second and third degree, although occasionally the stage-struck boy will doggedly stick to it against every obstacle and without a particle of ability.

Generally, if a boy persists against all obstacles, and continues to study and to train himself for his life work, it is evident that he was born for the stage, and the stage then offers to him the realization of an honest ambition.

When in doubt about going on the stage, don't go.

Now, how best to go on the stage. The best way to go on the stage is to go on the stage, to begin at the bottom and work up. Theatrical managers do not often play favorites. Ability, and the ability to use ability, may be considered the only steps to histrionic fame.

Education is necessary, perhaps the more of it the better. A common school education is essential. A

EDWARD H. SOTHERN

America's foremost actor; born in New Orleans, La., 1859, son of Edward
A. Sothern, the famous comedian; educated in the United States and
England; first appeared on the stage in New York in 1879 in a small part
with his father; later toured the United States with John McCullough;
toured England, 1882; first took leading role, Lyceum Theatre, New
York, 1887, and has since starred with his own company

high school education is next to necessary. Graduation from a college, if one does not have to make too great a sacrifice to accomplish it, is to be advised; but I do not consider it necessary.

There is no denying, however, that a broad and liberal education, and college association, will add materially to one's chances of success upon the stage. A college teaches, above all things, how to use what one has; and actual dramatic ability, unless one understands how to use it, is worth little upon any stage.

The dramatic school is to be recommended, generally; but the claims of dramatic schools should be investigated in advance, as there are undoubtedly many institutions which are dramatic in name only, and which are presided over by actors who cannot teach one to act, partly because they do not know how to act themselves.

The good dramatic school, and there are several, naturally and logically, comes between the school education and the stage itself; and I would advise any aspirant to spend a year or more at such a school, provided he can afford to do so.

But the dramatic school graduate should realize that, even after graduation, he is in no sense a full-fledged actor. He must begin at the bottom, or close to the bottom. His dramatic school education, while it may not help him materially at the start, will most likely assist him to rise more rapidly.

Mr. James S. Metcalfe, dramatic editor of *Life*, in a letter to the author, says:

" I am asked whether or not I would advise a young man to take up the profession of acting for a livelihood and to state the reasons for my advice either for or against this calling.

"In the first place, it would be absolutely impossible, in so important a matter, to lay down a general rule which would apply to each individual case. Some young men obviously have not the natural equipment necessary to success as an actor, and advice in such cases would be emphatically against the adoption of the stage as a profession. Even of those who seem naturally adapted in a physical way for the calling, there are many to whom, on less material and more subtle grounds, it would seem advisable to say, ' Adopt some other way of gaining a livelihood.'

"Physical qualifications enter so largely into the attraction of the actor that they are the first essential, because without them there exists a handicap almost impossible to overcome, no matter how well adapted the aspirant for Thespian honors may be in other ways.

"Next must come the temperamental qualification, which it is, however, practically impossible to describe. It includes a receptiveness of ideas and thoughts and impressions, and the power of giving them outward and physical expression. This is not so much a matter of intellect or brain power as it is a matter of feeling. Those who possess it seem to have an instinctive knowledge of the mimic art; and I know of no test which will demonstrate its possession except that of actual experience. It is a quality which in one of its aspects is known as ' personal magnetism.' No amount of education or practice or study seems able to create it, although these may bring it into evidence when it lies dormant, and certainly lend effectiveness in its use to those who are born with the gift.

"Granted the possession of the physical and temperamental qualities, I think that a love of the stage and its accessories is also largely important in an art where personality counts for so much. Personal enthusiasm, ambition, and interest in the work itself are all essential to success.

"In no other career does it seem that these sterling qualities, which mean the power to resist temptation, are so strongly needed, because stage life is one which is surrounded with temptations due to the fact that it is a world by itself, and the social life possible to those with a fixed abode and stable acquaintance is here largely impossible.

"The depressing influences which are encountered in the early stages of work in the theatre are many, and the refuge from them is too often found in things destructive to character and continued effort. The young man who engages in this work must be thrice armored to resist a host of enemies from without and within.

"The rewards of success are tempting, but they are not secured so easily as might at first appear.

"As in other walks of life, accident occasionally brings success; but, as a rule, eminence in this career is the reward only of long and persistent effort and at the end of a very rugged path.

"This is especially true in the condition of the theatre at the present writing. The artificial conditions which exist in the business control of the theatre in America make favoritism, more than formerly was the case, the basis of a certain kind of success. Proper training is difficult to acquire, because proficiency in legitimate acting has less influence, and is less a factor on the stage to-day than ever before, and the meretricious aid of advertising and the capricious support of managerial influence are powerful where art alone should be supreme.

"Finally, to the young man who has any idea of undertaking this kind of work, I would strongly urge that he cast aside all personal vanity as an influence in reaching his conclusion, that he prepare himself for a life of self-denial, study, and hard work, and that he be very sure that he has the natural physical and temperamental qualifications.

"With all the questions in this self-examination answered in the affirmative, he must still be prepared to find the laurel wreath long withheld from him."

Mr. Harrison Grey Fiske, editor and proprietor of the *New York Dramatic Mirror*, and manager of the

Manhattan Theatre, New York City, in a letter to the author, says:

"I should not advise any boy to become an actor.

" A stage career generally should not be begun before a youth has attained his majority, or until he has reached the age when he would enter upon the practice of any serious art or profession.

" Precocious talent for the stage rarely results in mature achievement. It is scarcely safe for a boy to select any career before he is old enough to realize its demands and responsibilities, its advantages and disadvantages; and decidedly no youth is qualified to adopt acting as a profession until he has passed the period when impressionable natures are apt to be 'stage-struck.' In many cases men have passed thirty before they have learned that in choosing the stage they have committed an irretrievable blunder. Rarely does any actor reach the fulfilment of his ambition, or the complete development of his powers, until he has passed into middle age.

" The dramatic profession, under the conditions that rule at present, is a precarious means of livelihood, except in the cases of a chosen few. With the majority, engagements are difficult to obtain; the supply of actors is treble the demand; there is very little permanence of employment; and, as a rule, employment, even among those fortunate enough to obtain consecutive engagements, rarely covers more than thirty-five weeks out of the fifty-two in each year.

" While a few actors, with special gifts, accomplishments, or popularity, command, on account of their rarity, large salaries, the majority of the workers of the stage are underpaid.

" Considered merely as a means of livelihood — except where young men possess undoubted talent or the spark of genius — the stage should be avoided. The man of small capacity for dramatic work can better bend his energies to almost any other occupation with greater expectation of substantial returns.

"It is only the young man who unmistakably reveals the possession of those qualities that make for success on the stage who should for an instant seriously consider it. And such a man, to obtain eventual recognition, must serve an arduous apprenticeship, confront constant difficulties and disappointments, possess personal and artistic ideals of a high order, and be prepared to maintain them despite every insidious inducement to destroy or cast them away. And even then, it is more likely than not that at the close of his career, however brilliant its achievements may seem to have been in the eyes of the world, he will ask himself the question, 'Was it worth while?'"

THE STEAM RAILROAD

THE railroad business is divided into two distinct and widely separated branches, — the operating department and the business department.

The operating department is responsible for the running of trains and for all that directly pertains to the mechanical action of the road.

The business department does the financiering, fixes the rates, is in charge of the clerical forces, and attends to the business part of railroading; and, further, exercises a general supervision over the operating department.

A railroad is a corporation, operated under the official direction of a board of directors, which is elected annually by the stockholders. This board is in control of every department, and delegates its power to its active and appointed officials.

For the sake of convenience and expediency, the board of directors elects, as its representatives, what are known as railroad officials: a president; one or more vice-presidents; a treasurer, with his assistants; a secretary; a general superintendent, with any number of assistant superintendents;

a chief-engineer and assistants; a master mechanic, with his assistants; a general freight agent and assistants; a general passenger agent, with one or more assistants; in some cases, a general manager and a traffic manager; and the department heads, with their assistants. By assistants I am referring to assistant officers, not to clerks.

All of these officials may or may not be elected directly by the board of directors, as it is usual for the chiefs to appoint some of their assistants.

The president is not always the working head of the railroad. He may not be a practical railroad man, and may hold his office on account of his business capacity, which enables him to finance any commercial enterprise. But most railroad presidents are practical men, understanding railroading in general, and often its management, even to the smallest detail.

The vice-president, if active, usually has some distinct duties, and is in charge of certain important matters.

The treasurer, as his name implies, is the custodian of the railroad's money.

The secretary may or may not occupy a position of responsibility. It is his official duty to keep the records of the meetings and to perform such other functions as may be designated by the board of directors. His position is, to an extent, clerical.

The general superintendent is the executive officer of the operating side of the road, and is responsible for everything outside of the clerical and financial departments, except that he does not, as a rule, interfere with the duties of the general freight, passenger, and ticket agents. He is almost invariably a mechanical expert, and always a disciplinarian, who understands the handling of large bodies of men.

The chief engineer occupies a position equal to that of the general superintendent, and in some cases he outranks him in salary and in importance. He has charge of the civil engineering and of other matters. A railroad must be surveyed and constructed, with its bridges, tunnels, and track-work, before the trains can be run; and the chief engineer is responsible for this work, and for the constant re-building and enlargement of the road.

The master mechanic is at the head of the mechanical work of the road, and is responsible for the condition of the locomotives and cars.

Large railroads are divided into divisions, each of which is under the direction of a district or division superintendent, who, in turn, is responsible to the general superintendent.

The general freight agent has charge of the freight department, a position of much responsibility.

The offices of general passenger and ticket agent are usually combined under one man, as the duties of each are frequently too similar to warrant separation. This official has charge of the railroad's passenger business, including the ticket offices.

Comparatively few roads have traffic managers. These officials are in control of the traffic, and outrank the freight, ticket, and passenger agents.

With the exception of a few railroad presidents, who are chosen solely for their financial ability, substantially all railroad men began at the bottom, or close to the bottom, and worked up. This is as it should be, in other lines of business as well as in railroading; but railroading, perhaps more than any other calling, requires a specific knowledge and experience obtained on the premises. It is a special business, and the ordinary business man, successful along general lines, cannot immediately adapt himself to railroad conditions. For this reason, the greater part of successful railroad men, including the presidents, began in subordinate positions, and rose from them to those which they now occupy.

Railroad presidents are not usually heavy stockholders, but they invariably represent the pleasure of the majority of stockholders; otherwise their election would be impossible. A few presidents, however, own controlling interests, and therefore may be said to be in business for themselves; but the majority of them, and practically all of the other officers, are employees in every sense of the word, — men who depend upon their salaries for their livelihood.

The principal officials are well paid, their salaries ranging from a few thousand dollars to as much as a hundred thousand dollars a year. This higher figure, however, has never been paid to more than a few railroad presidents. Comparatively few presidents receive less than five thousand dollars a year, and ten thousand dollars is by no means an unusual figure; in fact, there are quite a number drawing salaries in excess of twenty-five thousand dollars a year.

The average salary enjoyed by the official whose position is not relatively lower than that of the general passenger and ticket agent is not far from five thousand dollars a year, and it is doubtful if any competent head of a responsible department ever receives less than fifteen hundred dollars.

Railroad clerks and other employees receive salaries equal to those paid by the regular mercantile houses. They have, up to a certain point, the same opportunity for advancement as is enjoyed by those occupying similar positions in general business. But it must be borne in mind that the clerical railroad employee has little chance of becoming a factor in the controlling ownership, as this is likely to be held by capitalists, who may not have anything to do with the active management, and who may confine their action to the dictation of the road's policy. The railroad clerical employee has little opportunity to rise beyond a head-clerkship or to the head of an under-department.

Success in railroading depends either upon great mechanical or disciplinary ability or upon extraordinary business capacity.

The heads and subheads of the operating department are men of unusual ability. They are specialists, possessors of mechanical skilfulness, and if in charge of many workers, are natural controllers of men. They know how to work themselves and how to direct the labors of others. They are also equipped with minds capable of instantaneous action.

The operating department is divided and subdivided into many divisions, all under the direction of the general superintendent. There are division superintendents, mechanical engineers, and a large number of foremen and assistants, each man below the general superintendent being responsible for one thing or series of similar things, in which line or lines he must be an expert.

Comparatively few railroad boys or men are promoted unless they deserve advancement. While favoritism may be in evidence occasionally, it is seldom indeed that a " favorite " without ability gets ahead of a person of real ability.

Every operating railroad man is a specialist, and differs from the rank and file of ordinary business men. His success depends upon his ability and training along certain lines. Without this special ability and hard training, he will never make a success of the railroad business.

The boy who intends to enter the clerical side of railroading needs the same preparation as he does to take up any regular business, although some mechanical knowledge, even in the clerical department, will not come amiss. But the boy who intends to go into one of the operating departments, and this is the side which offers the greatest opportunity, needs to be equipped with a liberal and broad technical education. From the common or high school he should pass into some institute of technology, and graduate. The college is hardly to be advised, because the first-class institute of technology, or other high technical school, gives all the general education essential to successful railroading.

There are few callings which need more training and discipline than this. Promotion in the operating department is impossible without experience, and a strong, broad, general technical education exhilarates experience and widens one's capacity.

A well-educated boy stands a many times better chance of advancement than does the boy who enters the operating department from the common school without any definite knowledge of mechanics. The successful railroad official is an educated man. If his early or scholastic education has been insufficient, he must acquire the training later in life, and his progress is therefore naturally retarded. It takes less time, and costs less, to receive education when one is in the receptive educational state than to properly acquire it after one has started his career.

I would not advise any boy to enter the operating side of railroading who is not naturally of a mechanical turn of mind. If he has no mechanical ability he will not rise much above the lower levels.

True, there are many railroad engineers, and others, who are successful, and who have enjoyed little school-education. It is also true that one may learn to run an engine, or to do other mechanical work, without a technical school-training; but this school-training is far more effective, and far more economical, than is the training of experience, although it does not take the place of actual experience. The boy, properly school-trained, can much more quickly absorb experience, and utilize it, than one who never had a school-training.

But the boy with only a school-training has little in the way of assets. He is simply in a position to advance more rapidly than would be possible without this school-experience. A general, broad mechanical education is valuable, even though only a part of it may be actually utilized in real life, for the very broadness of this training allows its possessor to be more successful in a specialty than he would be if he had given his scholastic life exclusively to the practice of that specialty.

Railroad locomotive engineers are paid as high as two thousand dollars a year, and from that the salaries grade down to seven hundred and eight hundred dollars for drivers of freight and switch engines. Passenger conductors receive from a thousand to twelve hundred dollars a year, and brakemen from seven hundred to eight hundred dollars. Freight conductors are paid about eight hundred and fifty dollars a year. Conductors, as a rule, begin as brakemen, this experience being extremely valuable to them. The engineer usually develops from the fireman, and most firemen start in as wipers or as roundhouse helpers.

Superintendents have almost invariably occupied some subordinate position, often the lowest. There are men of commanding position and of enormous capacity who may have begun as firemen, as workers in the round-house, or as mechanics in the repair shop.

Ordinary mechanical ability, in the railroad business is subject to reasonable promotion, but it is not likely to lift its possessor much above the head of a subordinate department, while extraordinary ability is pretty sure of reaping an adequate reward.

The railroad man, barring the clerical clerk, is a man of action, and a man of quick action, a man able to do in a minute, in safety, what men in other lines of work may require hours for execution.

It has been said that the railroad man never sleeps, that if he does sleep he has the sleeping mind of a dog, the kind which a whisper will awake. At any rate, the railroad man, like the active steamship officer, is necessarily the most alert of all men of business action.

The lazy boy, even though he may be a mechanical genius, would better keep away from railroading.

To sum up, let me say that the clerical side of the railroad business offers good opportunity, but probably not so much as does the clerical side of the mercantile business. The operating department usually presents good opportunities to the boys of mechanical capacity, who are able to master their ability, and to practically utilize it, and who, moreover, are natural workers and willing to work hard, to begin at the bottom, with a full realization that promotion depends upon ability and upon the safe, yet quick, action of ability.

The slow boy has no business in the railroad business; nor has the quick boy, if his rapidity is not under the control of dependable discretion.

The boy who is considering the railroad business is advised to place himself in direct personal communication with railroad men. I would advise him to talk with men representing various departments of railroading. All of us are more or less biassed, and occasionally we unintentionally give false advice. For this reason, a consultation with several railroad men, each representing a different department, will enable the boy to obtain in advance a better idea of what the railroad really offers, — its real advantages and disadvantages. Railroad men, as a rule, are cordial, and are willing to give advice and information.

Mr. O. W. Ruggles, general passenger and ticket agent of the Michigan Central Railroad, in a letter to the author, says:

"I would not advise a boy who contemplates making railroading his life work, and who has already selected the operating or mechanical department, to enter any other. First, because his tastes and inclination should govern his choice; and, secondly, because it seems to me that there is a wider demand now, and will be in the future, not only for mechanical ability and engineering talent, but for men capable of handling freight, — which is the chief business of the railroads, — of routing and billing over an intricate system of railways from one part of the country to another; and capable, also, of dealing with the complicated question of rates, which, in itself, is said to rank as a profession. These duties are, of course, widely dissimilar, sometimes requiring clerical and executive ability, with a thorough knowledge of geography and of bookkeeping as a foundation; and in the operating department a sound training in mechanics, coupled with an ability to handle men.

"I would not advise a boy against entering other than the mechanical or operating departments of the railroad business. There are no particular disadvantages in any of the departments of railway work, except as affected by the temperament of the young man. If he feels that he is fitted for the freight department, or for the passenger department, and is determined to make his way in the path chosen, by close application and hard study of all the conditions and problems involved, he will, in all probability, make a success of his work; but he should not select the one because he wishes to 'boss' a large number of men, or the other because he would like to wear good clothes. He will find plenty of good hard work in either position; but if he is determined to learn the business from the very bottom and to overcome all obstacles, he will be almost certain to find a career which will at least give him a certain and comfortable livelihood, and may bring him both fame and fortune."

Mr. Roswell Miller, chairman of the Board of Directors of the Chicago, Milwaukee, and St. Paul Railway, in a letter to the author, says:

" The principal advantages of the railway business consist in the fact that there are not enough men in it who are capable of filling the best positions.

There is always room for those who have ability enough to fill a high position. And aside from merely clerical positions, there is something more than ordinarily interesting in the work, which makes it absorbing, and success is, therefore, more likely.

" The principal disadvantages are the absorption of the individual. If he is successful, he cannot do much else day or night, — week days or Sundays. So that, in most cases, the man who devotes himself to the railway business, and serves his company honestly, cannot at the same time acquire a large fortune, which he could do with the same amount of labor in other directions. Besides this, railroading, like many other pursuits, has many machine places, which are filled by men who come to be merely machines."

Mr. W. J. Wilgus, vice-president of the New York Central and Hudson River Railroad, in a letter to the author, says:

" To the young men of sound principles and good constitution, imbued with the intention to succeed, the railroad offers a career that contains all of the rewards for which men can strive.

"There is probably no field so attractive as that of the railroad for the display of the strenuous qualities that, in less peaceful times, won success in the profession of arms. Financial returns and the honors of position are at the command of the young man of ability, who is not afraid of hard work, and whose constant aim is the securing of the pleasure that comes from the accomplishment of work well done.

"The disadvantages in the field of railroading are long hours and the frequent subordination of social pleasures to the demands of duty."

Mr. J. W. Burdick, passenger traffic manager of the Delaware and Hudson Railroad, in a letter to the author, says:

" My advice in the premises would depend upon my estimate of the boy's ability and promise. If he is made of the right stuff, it is immaterial whether he enters the clerical or the operating department of a railroad. In either case, if his activities are sufficiently exercised in learning his business, he will either follow along the line of promotion or be extinguished, according to the estimate placed upon those activities by the management.

" I believe that the elements and probabilities of success are inherent in the boy himself, and that the ultimate outcome is not materially influenced by the kind of work he takes up in the beginning, if he is fitted by birth and education properly to perform the duties which come to his hand."

THE ARTIST

WHILE the term "artist" may refer to the expert in many lines, except those pertaining to business or commerce, the artist, commonly speaking, is one who gives the whole or part of his time to painting, drawing, and sketching in oil or water colors, or in crayon.

There is no closely drawn dividing line between the amateur and the professional artist. If there were such a line, on the professional side would be the artist whose brush or pencil is an instrument of remuneration and who spends the greater part of his time in his studio; and on the other would be the amateur, who may or may not devote most of his time to art, and who does not, as a general thing, dispose of his pictures for money, or, if he does, does not altogether depend upon the money earned by his art for a livelihood.

In America alone there are probably more than half a million men and women, and boys and girls, who dabble in art sufficiently to be called amateur artists, and who possess every degree of artistic temperament and ability. There are also in America upwards of fifty thousand professional artists, including draughtsmen and those who devote most of their time to the making of mechanical and other drawings for engraving establishments and lithographers, receiving salaries from these concerns and doing little or no outside work.

The true artist not only paints from life, but he gives life to what he paints. From the created he re-creates. He never copies.

The boy fitted to study art, and the boy able to make any kind of a success with his brush, not only possesses artistic ability, but is distinguished by an artistic temperament. At an early age he snuggles close to Nature, and his work, however crude, has life in it. The man-artist springs from the boy-artist. No boy awakes in the morning to find himself an artist. The artistic capacity and artistic temperament are gifts of Nature, and grow and develop as the artist grows and develops.

The artist cannot be made. All the education in the world cannot make an artist ; and any attempt to produce an artist out of one who does not possess artistic ability and temperament is a waste of time and money.

Artistic ability may be developed, and sometimes ordinary talent in this direction may be elevated to a stage beyond its original self ; but there must be some talent, some real natural talent, in the first place.

The boy or girl without ability and artistic temperament, and who has not displayed proficiency in drawing or sketching, can seldom be made into an artist of any rank, and can never be forced to rise higher than an ordinary sketcher or painter, a stencilled sort of a worker, absolutely worthless in the world of art, and of little use in the world outside of it.

No true artist can produce good work by working incessantly; he cannot cover a specified number of square inches of canvas in any appointed time. A certain something, by many called inspiration, is necessary to the highest artistic production. On some days the artist can do good work, and on others his hand seems to forget its cunning. He does not know why, but the fact remains; and therefore a portion, and sometimes a large portion, of his time is "off time" or "between times."

The price of any painting, or of any original picture, is unfortunately and unfairly considerably dependent upon the artist's reputation, as well as upon the intrinsic quality of the production. A poor creation by a great artist will invariably sell for more than a much better picture by an unknown painter. Many a famous artist could not dispose of half of his pictures at half of the price which he now receives for them if his name was not attached. Merit counts, and upon merit reputation is founded and sustained, but few things move more slowly than the progress of merit. Many an artist, shabby and hungry, is living close to the edge of fame and never crosses it.

The boy who is always ready with his pencil and brush and who produces pictures highly creditable to him at his age may not possess more than an imitative quality. The mere making of a picture does not guarantee the artist. The picture-maker, like the camera, may lack artistic essentials.

The creation of the real artist is not a mere picture. It is not a reflection of Nature. It is the soul of Nature; something which seems to live and grow as we look upon it. There is a quality to it, a something which speaks to you because it has much to say, a story from the artist's heart.

The ordinary picture, like the photograph, is a mechanical production, correct, but lifeless and soulless.

It has been said, and I am not prepared to dispute the truth of the statement, that no one ever earned his living by the production of true art; or, to put it differently, that I may be more perfectly understood, there is a prevalent opinion, perhaps largely confined to the upper grade of artists, that the best results of the brush, in their aggregate, do not more than pay the meagre living expenses of the artist.

Every artist has what may be considered an inside as well as an outside proficiency. This inside talent springs from the very centre of his true artistic soul, and is responsible for the real depth, the real feeling, and the real character of his best work; and this best work, this work which is a part of the artist himself, may have little or no commercial value, — at least, during the life of the artist. In the majority of the cases, the artist's second grade of work, or rather the work which does not represent his truest feelings, is the principal support of him and his family. For instance, a great landscape painter, who wants to act as Nature's agent when he paints, may find it necessary to do sketch-work, that he may earn a comfortable living.

I do not mean to give the impression that it is not possible to earn a living from the product of one's highest work, but I do not think that any true artist ever earned a livelihood with his brush until he had reached the very pinnacle of fame, unless he allowed himself to produce paintings or sketches of minor quality, and which did not represent the true inwardness of his possibilities.

Designers of wall-paper, of carpets, of tapestries, of fabrics, or of the various kinds of dress-goods, may be considered artists, for none of them succeed unless they possess the true artistic temperament. The demand for this class of competent designers is far below the supply. However, the man who can not only design a piece of furniture, but can fit the furniture to the room it is to occupy, is in every sense an artist, and fortunately his services are beginning to receive commercial recognition.

There are probably not over two or three American artists receiving an annual income exceeding twenty-five thousand dollars. The minimum earnings of a professional artist, with a studio, are not much more than three hundred dollars a year, and the average receipts of a good artist are in the vicinity of fifteen hundred dollars per annum. A very few salaried artists receive between five thousand and ten thousand dollars a year, the average, however, being not over thirty-five dollars a week.

Comparatively few artists, capable of earning a salary, are paid less than seven hundred dollars a year. There are, however, several hundred first-class artists, maintaining studios, who annually receive from two thousand to five or six thousand dollars a year, but these artists are in no sense ordinary, nor are they extraordinary, and they are first-class in that they never do poor work, and occasionally do remarkable work. They are generally what is known as all-around artists, able to paint almost any subject from a landscape to an interior. Probably half of their work is ordered; that is, they know in advance what they will receive for it, these orders coming from book or magazine publishers and advertisers.

The field of advertising, which is growing broader every day, has opened new opportunities to the artist, and in many cases has added from twenty-five to fifty per cent to his income.

Many of our leading artists, barring those at the very pinnacle of fame, offer their services to advertisers. A goodly number of our highly artistic designs, and those that show great skilfulness, appear in the advertising columns of magazines and newspapers, and are the work of artists who, a few years ago, could not have been induced to execute a commission from an advertiser.

All lithographers and engraving establishments employ from one to twenty artists, the most of whom are young men and women, many of them of no particular ability, except for mechanical work.

A great lithographic establishment occasionally pays as much as five thousand dollars a year to an artist, the artist giving his whole time to the work of the establishment, but these prices are exceptional, comparatively few artists on salaries receiving more than fifteen hundred dollars a year, and many of them not much more than one-half of that sum.

Few illustrated newspapers or magazines employ artists by the year, but pay them for each picture or sketch produced. This is better for the publisher, and also better for the artist, because it enables the publisher to get finer work and a greater variety of work, and the artist to receive a higher price per picture.

It is said that a well-known sketch artist, whose work has attracted international attention, was recently engaged by one of the great illustrated weeklies, at a salary of twenty-five thousand dollars a year, it being understood that he produce at least one sketch a week; and a further condition was imposed upon him, namely, that he must not have but one other customer; that is to say, his work must be limited to two customers during the term of his engagement. This, however, is too exceptional to be considered.

Cartoonists, connected with the great daily newspapers, are well-paid, some of them receiving as much as ten thousand dollars a year, although probably the average salary does not exceed three thousand dollars.

Anything below ordinary ability has little earning capacity in art, and ordinary ability is not likely to obtain more than a livelihood; while exceptional ability will live comfortably, and extraordinary ability can obtain a competency.

The high-grade artist works at will, disposing of his productions from time to time; while others work under contract, and are paid a stipulated price for a certain amount of work, or by the year, their income coming from the publishers of magazines and illustrated papers, book publishers, and lithographers. Many artists derive their income from all of these sources.

The medium and lower grade artists are employed by engravers and lithographers, and their work is largely what might be called semi-mechanical.

Portrait painters are extremely well paid, the income of a good portrait painter running into thousands of dollars a year, but comparatively few artists can paint portraits. The painting of portraits seems to be an art in itself, requiring a different skill and temperament from that necessary to the painting of almost any other subject.

The boy fitted to be an artist brings to the parent

illustrative evidence of his right to study art; but, unfortunately, the parent, unless an artist himself, too often mistakes the imitation for the real. Naturally proud of his boy, he magnifies his boy's ability, and imagines he sees in the boy's cold work the warmth and glory of genius.

No parent should advise his boy to enter art as a profession until the boy's work has been critically examined by several competent art critics. Do not trust to one critic's opinion. He may be biassed; trust only to the composite opinion of several artists and critics.

If the boy has art in him he will show it, and he will manifest it so plainly that no competent artist is likely to diagnose his case incorrectly.

Unless the boy can show marked proficiency, and show it beyond peradventure of reasonable doubt, his sphere is not within the realm of art.

Love of art, love of Nature, and an artistic temperament, will not, of themselves, make an artist. The true artist has the love of art, the love of Nature, and the artistic temperament; but he has something else, — he has the power to express himself, his inmost soul, upon canvas.

How should the would-be artist begin to become an artist? How should he prepare himself for his life work? If he is of true artistic temperament, and has been Nature-endowed for his work, he involuntarily began to prepare himself long before he was out of his boyhood.

Rather let me differently frame the question. What method should the embryo artist pursue? What education is necessary or advisable?

Let me say at the outset, that one cannot learn to be an artist. It is impossible to teach art. At best, education can but develop, and development is impossible without a basis.

The art school? Yes, if the art school is a good one. A European trip? Advisable, most certainly. The centre of the world's art is not located in America. Abroad there are art centres, reeking with art atmosphere, where one breathes art, lives with it, and sees little else.

A year, or several years, abroad, studying art where art began, will permit of the very acme of development, and will enable the artist to reach the extreme of his capacity.

But an art trip abroad should not be considered essential. Development is possible with the assistance of American art schools and by keeping in close touch with the Great Artist — Nature.

If you feel that there is art in you, and impress your friends with your artistic ability, better visit several artists of note — real artists — and follow their advice; not the advice of any one, but the composite advice of all.

Mr. John J. Enneking, of Boston, in a letter to the author, says:

" I would advise a boy to take up art as a profession if he is convinced that he has not only ability, but capacity for hard work and plenty of pluck sufficient to overcome the many obstacles in the way of gaining a permanent foothold.

"Sir Joshua Reynolds, in one of his lectures before the Royal Academy, said that the older he grew the more he was inclined to believe that it was not genius, but a great capacity for hard work, that succeeded in art.

" The older I grow the more inclined I am to believe that he was right.

"Very few artists in this country can make a living creating works of art in which they are trying to realize their highest ideal. Almost all those who try seriously to represent only the best there is in them have to rely for a living on side occupations, like teaching, illustrating, etc.

"The mere 'making a living' in art does not always depend on the artist's reputation or the qualities of his pictures, but quite often it depends on whether the artist can furnish such art as the times and buyers demand. Millet's pictures were not in demand during his lifetime; people did not understand his pictures, therefore he was poor while he lived, and very poor when he died.

"A boy with a will to work, who is born with art ability and love for the profession, ready to turn his hand to anything to further his chances to get nearer his ideals, has every chance of success.

"If a boy has ability and a love for art, but not much courage and pluck to struggle with the many and almost unsurmountable difficulties and deprivations, I would advise him to choose a more ordinary calling where his artistic feeling can also be a factor.

"The years of training in an art school, spent in acquiring the grammar of art, the ability to express through drawing, painting, etc., breaks down over half of those who commenced with every hope of winning. Half of those left, after they have learned to express themselves, have very little to express, and that little 'not worth the powder.'

"'Many are called, but few are chosen.'"

Mr. Gustavus H. Buek, the vice-president and head of the art department of the American Lithographic Company, of New York City, in a letter to the author, says:

"My principal reason for advising a young man to become a professional artist would, of course, be because I detected the art microbe in him, and because I thought this indestructible art microbe had him more firmly in its clutches than any other microbe had. Then in the world of art, as in the world of music, literature, finance, or mechanics, there is always plenty of room at the top, which, if reached, bestows honor and pecuniary benefit upon him that reaches it, whether it be in the direction of the painters' or illustrators' art, or only as a so-called commercial artist. This latter field, however, oftentimes gives as great distinction and opportunity as that of the successful painter, and not infrequently gives greater pecuniary reward.

" My principal reason for advising a young man not to become a professional artist would, of course, be because I did not detect the art microbe in him; and without this necessary microbe no success in the art world could reasonably be expected.

" While I believe that honest, hard work may make a more or less successful mechanic in any field or occupation, it never can, and never will, make a great musician, littérateur, and, least of all, a great artist; and I would rather start a young man in a direction which I believed he might reach by industry, at least the snow-line, than know at the start that there would never, by any possibility, be a dividend paid on the investment."

THE BANKER

THE banker, specifically or commercially defined, is an officer, or part owner, in some banking institution.

There are five classes, or kinds, of banks:

The national bank, the state bank, the loan and trust company, the institution for savings, and the private banking house.

As its name implies, the national bank is a national institution, under the jurisdiction of the federal government and amenable to special national banking laws. It is a corporation, but is unlike the ordinary commercial corporation in that it is incorporated under special national law and subject to national jurisdiction. Its officers consist of a board of directors, a president, one or more vice-presidents, a cashier, sometimes one or more assistant cashiers, a discount-clerk, one or more paying-tellers, one or more receiving-tellers, — although comparatively few banks employ more than two tellers, one a paying-teller and the other a receiving-teller, — a bookkeeper, with any number of assistants, one or more messengers, and such other officers or employees as the extent and requirements of the business demand.

The national bank receives money on deposit, subject to withdrawal by check; that is, the depositor may, at any time during banking hours, draw out the whole or any part of his money.

The depositor pays nothing for the privilege of keeping his money in the bank, the bank receiving its remuneration from the use of the money deposited, which it loans to its depositors, and to other borrowers, at varying rates of interest, not exceeding the rate fixed by law.

The success of the bank depends primarily upon how profitably it can loan its money, and upon the volume of its deposits. Some banks materially increase their profits by doing a foreign business; that is, they issue bills of exchange, which are good in foreign countries, and charge a fee for this service.

A national bank cannot exist without a paid-in capital of as much as twenty-five thousand dollars. A few national banks have capitals of several millions of dollars, but probably the average city bank is capitalized at about two hundred thousand dollars; and the average country town bank has a capital of from twenty-five thousand to fifty thousand dollars.

The national bank is the only institution which issues what is known as bank-notes; that is, paper money bearing the name of the bank and signed by its president and cashier.

The government allows this privilege to other banks complying with certain conditions, but levies upon them a ten per cent tax, which operates as prohibitive.

Before proceeding further, a little explanation is

necessary. The United States issues five kinds of money:

First, gold coin. Gold is considered by this country as the National Standard. Gold money is in the form of coins, and is little used in commercial circulation.

Secondly, silver coin of the denominations of one dollar, fifty cents, twenty-five cents, and ten cents. Formerly there were issued silver twenty-cent pieces, five-cent pieces, and three-cent pieces, but the government has discontinued their coinage.

Thirdly, government currency or bills, printed upon paper especially made for the purpose. These bills are really promissory notes, the government promising to pay the bearer, on demand, their face value in gold or silver. They have no intrinsic value beyond what they represent. Of course, the government is seldom called upon to redeem these notes, the credit of the national government being sufficient to make the notes good for all purposes of exchange.

Fourthly, national bank-notes. The national bank-note is virtually double paper; that is to say, it is a note issued by the bank and endorsed by the government. Both the national bank and the national government are responsible for its payment. Theoretically, the national bank-note is worth more than the government note, because it is double instead of single paper; but practically there is no difference, because when the government credit is gone, making valueless the government bill, the national bank will, in all probability, go out of existence, and its responsibility for the bill will cease, and there will be no redemption value. As security for these bills, the national bank deposits United States Government bonds with the United

States Treasurer at Washington, which bonds are held by the national government as collateral.

Bank-bills are issued in order to secure a convenient and economical medium of distribution. They are not national bank bills in any practical sense, the failure of the bank having no effect upon the value of its currency.

Fifthly, coins made of a composition of metal, and known as five-cent pieces and cents or pennies. The government, some time ago, did away with the coinage of the two-cent and three-cent pieces, and now one-cent and five-cent pieces are the only metallic money in circulation, which are not either silver or gold coin.

National banks are not only under the control of the national government, but they are examined at stated intervals by government inspectors, known as bank examiners.

The state bank is practically the same as the national bank, so far as its management is concerned; but it is not under the control of the national government, and is not inspected by the United States bank examiners. Many state banks are fully as strong as are the national banks and merit the confidence of the community. They do not issue bank bills.

The loan and trust company is a corporation organized under a state charter, and doing a general banking business. Its management closely resembles that of the national and state banks, differing from them chiefly in the broadness of its methods of loaning money and of holding property. It may or may not take money on deposit, subject to check; but in most cases it does a regular banking business, similar to that done by the national or state bank, in connection with its other financial work.

The savings bank, as its name implies, is an institution for savings. It receives money and pays interest upon deposits. It is of especial benefit to those who are able to save a monthly proportion of their salary or wages, giving them a safe investment, where their money is as easily accessible as it was in the stocking of the old days, and where it earns the highest rate of interest consistent with almost complete safety.

The savings bank increases the money, from which it pays interest, by loaning money, and by other investments; but its methods of loaning are different from those of so-called business banks. It is amenable to state laws, and in most cases is subject to very rigid state regulations, the majority of states requiring their savings banks to invest only along lines of the greatest security, and forbidding them to take speculative chances.

Comparatively few of these banks pay more than three and a half per cent, although a few pay four per cent. They cannot consistently pay more than four per cent unless they take speculative chances, which would not be expedient for them to do, even if they were not restrained by the law, which in most cases prohibits it.

The savings bank officers consist of a president, one or more vice-presidents, a treasurer, a teller, bookkeepers, and other officials. The savings bank is, to a great extent, a philanthropic institution. It seldom pays large salaries to its officers, and there is little opportunity for one to rise above a clerical position, except in states where savings banks are allowed by law to do a general banking business, and are, therefore, at least in part, business banks.

Private banking houses are private institutions, doing

business in the form of a mercantile partnership or corporation. In most cases they deal directly in stocks, and bonds. Private banking houses, if owned by men of solid, well-invested wealth, offer substantially the same opportunities as do the national and state banks, and in many cases much better business futures. The private banking house, as a rule, accepts money on deposit, subject to withdrawal by check, and generally pays interest on deposits, usually at the rate of two per cent. This paying of interest on deposits is also universal on the part of loan or trust companies, and some national and state banks pay this interest to favored depositors, but national and state banks generally do not pay interest on deposits.

Banking is a good business. It is essential to the movement of trade. Without the bank, business could not be done economically or easily.

Bankers, generally, are a high-grade class of men; they are usually well-educated, financially broad-minded, and good and patriotic citizens. They rank as high as any other class of business men, and by some they are considered as occupying the highest place in the business world.

The salaries paid by business banks are substantially the same, whether the bank be a national bank, a state bank, a loan and trust company, or a private banking house, the size of the salary depending upon the amount of business done and the responsibility of the position.

City bank presidents seldom receive a salary exceeding twenty-five thousand dollars a year, and this figure may be considered the maximum. Comparatively few draw salaries of less than four thousand dollars a year, the average being somewhere between eight and ten thousand. In some banks, the president occupies a

J. PIERPONT MORGAN

Banker, financier; born in Hartford, Conn., 1837; educated in Boston and Germany; entered banking business, 1857; became agent for George Peabody & Co., London bankers, 1860; became member firm Drexel, Morgan, & Co., now J. P. Morgan & Co., leading private bankers of the United States, 1871; organized many big corporations, including United States Steel Corporation, capital $1,100,000,000. Famous as collector and patron of art.

nominal position, and may receive only a nominal salary. In others, the president is the actual working-head, and the man of responsibility, and is paid accordingly.

Presidents of country banks are non-working heads much more frequently than are presidents of city banks. Where the president is an active officer, he receives up to five thousand dollars a year, although comparatively few are paid annual salaries of over three thousand dollars. A nominal president may be paid as little as five hundred dollars a year, but the average salary for an inactive president is about eighteen hundred dollars a year.

City bank vice-presidents, if active, are sometimes paid as much as ten thousand dollars a year, and occasionally considerably more, if, while holding the office of vice-president, they are doing the work of the president. But the maximum, as a rule, is not much over five thousand dollars a year, and the minimum about one thousand dollars; while the average, unless the work is merely nominal, is about four thousand dollars a year.

Comparatively few country banks have active vice-presidents, and in many of the country banks the vice-president receives no salary. The maximum salary is about three thousand dollars a year.

The second and third vice-presidents generally do not take any active part in the work of the bank, and in many places such officers do not exist.

The cashier is usually the executive officer. The duties of a cashier in a bank are different from those in a mercantile house. The cashier in a mercantile house is the one who takes in the money. The cashier of a bank seldom, if ever, handles money. He is not a cashier in any sense, except that he is the custodian of the cash. The name is really a misnomer, because the cashier should be called the superintendent. In the savings bank and in many trust companies the cashier's position is held by the treasurer, there being no distinct office of cashier. In some banks the cashier is not only the executive officer, but the virtual manager of the bank. Where there is an active president or vice-president, the cashier occupies the position of a head-clerk; consequently, the cashier may or may not hold a place of great responsibility. Probably no cashier of a city bank has ever received an annual salary of more than fifteen thousand dollars, while the minimum salary is about three thousand dollars a year, and the average not over four thousand dollars.

Cashiers of country banks are more likely to be the working-heads of the banks than are their city brethren, and their salaries run anywhere from three thousand dollars a year down to one thousand dollars, the average being not far from two thousand dollars. Some country bank cashiers receive as much as five thousand dollars a year, but this figure is very exceptional.

Assistant cashiers are, as their name suggests, assistants to the cashier. The maximum salary in the city is four thousand dollars, the minimum two thousand dollars, with an average of about twenty-five hundred dollars. Country banks, as a rule, do not carry assistant cashiers. When they do, these are seldom paid more than two thousand dollars per year, with a minimum salary not far from one thousand dollars, and the average about twelve hundred dollars.

Discount-clerks usually rank next to cashiers, or to assistant cashiers where they are employed; but in some cases the discount-clerk is ranked below the teller and even below the bookkeeper. Quite often the discount-clerk holds the dual office of assistant cashier and discount-clerk. When rated next to the cashier or to the assistant cashier, his maximum salary in the city is about twenty-five hundred dollars, the minimum being about eighteen hundred, and the average about two thousand dollars. In the country they receive from twenty-five to forty per cent less.

Discount-clerks have charge of the notes. It is their business to see that they are paid at maturity. As a rule, they have no voice in making discounts; that is to say, they have no authority to discount a note, this power not being given to one below the position of cashier, and seldom even to the cashier.

The teller either pays out money, or receives money, or does both. Some banks combine the offices in one teller, while large banks have two or more tellers, one or more paying-tellers, and one or more receiving-tellers.

The paying-teller outranks the receiving-teller, as his duties are of greater responsibility. If he makes a mistake, the bank is likely to suffer an irrevocable loss, while the mistake of the receiving-teller can usually be rectified without material cost.

Paying-tellers in large city banks seldom receive more than four thousand dollars a year, while the minimum salary is not far from sixteen hundred, and the average is about twenty-two hundred dollars a year. These positions in the country pay about fifteen hundred dollars a year for the maximum, six or seven hundred dollars for the minimum, with an average not far from one thousand dollars a year. The receiving-teller's salary is from ten to twenty-five per cent less than that paid to the paying-teller.

The bookkeeper, or head-bookkeeper where there is

more than one, may or may not outrank the tellers. He has charge of the books and keeps the accounts, but he is generally a man of a much greater ability than one occupying a similar position in a mercantile house.

Bank clerks seldom make mistakes; in fact, a bank is supposed to be exempt from error; consequently the bookkeeper must be as exact as possibility admits.

Bookkeepers in city banks seldom receive more than two thousand dollars a year, although a favored few, in great institutions, draw salaries of not far from five thousand dollars. The average salary is about fifteen hundred dollars. Bookkeepers in country banks are not often paid more than one thousand dollars a year, the minimum being about four hundred dollars, and the average about seven hundred dollars. Assistant book-keepers usually receive from ten to twenty per cent more than is paid for about the same service in mercan-tile houses.

Messengers are virtually collectors or errand men. They present and collect drafts, and carry checks, notes, and money from bank to bank, and sometimes to the clearing-house. Because they carry money, often large sums, they are paid higher salaries than are enjoyed by any one else doing similar work. Some city banks pay their messengers as much as two thousand dollars a year, but comparatively few messengers receive over fifteen hundred dollars, the minimum being as little as six hundred dollars, and the average about eight hun-dred dollars a year. Country bank messengers are paid salaries anywhere from twenty to fifty per cent less than those paid in the city.

The banker, other than the president of the bank, generally begins as a boy, doing an office-boy's work as he would in any mercantile house; although sometimes he starts as a messenger. He is in the line of promotion, and if he is faithful and of good capacity, he will, sooner or later, become an officer; but he is not likely to rise higher than cashier, and it may take twenty years before he can reach that position.

Bank promotion is reasonably sure, but is very slow. When an officer or clerk dies, or his position becomes vacant for any other reason, the one next in line is reasonably sure to obtain his position, provided he is competent to hold it; and this evolution continues up to, and including, the office of cashier.

I do not mean to say that every faithful boy entering a bank as a boy, even if he has the necessary capacity, stands a chance of becoming a cashier in time, because unforeseen conditions may interfere; but he certainly has a fair prospect of reaching that position if he has the capacity.

The reason that there is little opportunity for rising higher than cashier is because the presidents of banks are generally leading men of financial or other prominence, who may not have started in a bank, and whose first experience in banking may have begun with their presidency. They are elected, partly because of their great financial ability, but largely because of the business they can bring to the bank. They are not likely to be clerical men in any sense, and many of them have not had any actual banking training. They may be simply financiers, men of property, men of influence, and men who know how to properly finance a banking institution.

The banker, more than any other class of business men, is a custodian of money, and his success is not independent of public confidence. If he is not a man of character, of recognized honesty, of caution, and of strong stability, he cannot become more than a temporary banking success. People will not willingly deposit money in any bank owned by speculators or men of careless financiering. They demand that their banker be a safe man, and unless he is a cautious man, he will sooner or later cease to be a banker.

The embryo banker needs a common school education; without it he is materially handicapped. He should not stop below the high school, and a liberal college training may be of considerable benefit to him. Of course the technical school can be of no use to him, for his work is in no sense mechanical.

The question is asked, What kind of boy will make the best banker? This question is exceedingly difficult to answer. The boy fitted to be a lawyer shows distinct characteristics, which may guide the parent; the boy adaptable to the ministry presents unmistakable tendencies; but the to-be-banker boy may not have any characteristics by which one can determine, with any degree of accuracy, whether or not he is well suited to banking.

There are hundreds of boys who will not make good bankers; the careless boy, the boy who takes no thought for himself or for others, who cannot be depended upon, who knows little of figures, and wants to know even less than he does know, who is always behindhand, and who is unreliable, will not make a good banker. Then there is another kind of boy who may not be adapted to banking, and that is the boy who has an unmistakable tendency in another direction.

The boy more fitted by Nature to be a lawyer, doctor, minister, or journalist may make a good banker, but he will make a much better lawyer, doctor, minister, or journalist than he will banker.

The bank, from a clerical point of view, may be considered as between the mercantile and the professional, requiring a somewhat different class of ability than the purely business or the wholly professional occupation. For instance, the boy adapted for a profession is usually not adapted for business; the boy adapted for business is not likely to be fitted for a profession; and the boy adapted for the bank may not be as tradesman-like as a boy inclined to the purely mercantile life. He may even be inclined toward a profession. The banking business outside of the office of president and of vice-president is largely a clerical proposition, not to the extent that pure and simple bookkeeping is, but to a greater extent than is found in much of the work of mercantile houses. It is extremely difficult to point out this banker boy.

Perhaps the best advice that I can give to the boy who is considering banking is to tell him to enter banking if he is positive that he has no pronounced tendency in some other direction, and is sufficiently careful and methodical, is one who seldom makes a mistake with his pencil or with his pen, and who is reliable in every sense. This boy, if he chooses banking, will make his living out of it; and if he has business sagacity, will rise from the ranks. But I must admit that the boy of much business capacity, the boy with a natural trading tendency, will stand a better chance in regular mercantile work as a salesman than he will in the banking institution.

And yet I do not wish to give the impression that I do not think banking offers good opportunities, for it does.

The boy adapted to banking, who is careful, exact, and with fair education, is pretty sure of a good living, perhaps of the comforts of life; and I may say that he is even surer of a living than is the salesman and other mercantile worker, because there is a permanency about the bank which exists in few other classes of business. Yet the opportunities offered by the bank to the bright, aggressive boy are not so great as those presented by a mercantile house. In other words, the bank draws a line, beyond which there is little possibility of going. Inside of that line there is a reasonable certainty of a living success. The mercantile business does not draw any line of limitation, but the work has more of the elements of risk and of speculation.

Perhaps the most serious objection to entering the banking business is, that after one has become imbued with the work of the bank he is of little use in anything else; and if after his prime the bank fails, or he leaves it for any other cause, he is, to a very large extent, unfitted to enter any other calling. But this objection is not necessarily confined to banking. Comparatively few men, who are thrown out of work after they reach the aged side of their primes, can easily adapt themselves to other things; and therefore business failures can earn comparatively little and are objects of pity, unless they have in the meantime saved a competency.

The banking business, as a rule, does not broaden one's ideas. It confines one largely to finance, or rather to dealing with the mass of detail having reference to the handling of the money of finance. It does not generally carry one out into the Great Open, where he can see men and things from the broadest viewpoint. The bank clerk, or bank officer, is, to a large extent, confined to his banking-room. True, he meets all kinds of men, and gets an insight into all kinds of business;

but he only comes into direct contact with the financial side of those men. He sees them when they have money to deposit, and when they want to borrow money. He sees them when they are flush, and when they are in need. He may not see them in the action of their business.

But again, let me say that this condition is not confined to banking. I simply want to prevent the boy from rushing into banking, as I want to prevent him from rushing into any other calling. I must repeat that, while banking is a good business, I would not advise any boy to enter a bank unless he finds that he has not, and shows that he has not, unmistakable or marked ability, or well-defined inclination, in some other and broader direction.

Mr. Frank H. Barbour, cashier of the National Shawmut Bank, of Boston, in a letter to the author, says:

"In response to your request, I will give you some reasons why I would advise a boy to enter the banking business.

"Of course, I assume that he enters business life with the determination to succeed, otherwise this business has no place for him. Assuming, therefore, that he is in earnest, I would advise him to enter banking, because it is a clean, honorable business, commanding the respect of the community ; and deservedly so, for, though it has its defaulters, whose betrayals of trust are always spread before the public under heavy headlines, their percentage to the number in the business is creditably small, a tribute to the integrity of the members of a profession in which temptations to dishonesty are great.

"Banking is among the oldest lines of occupation, and so long as the business world exists it must have facilities for the safe keeping of its funds and the handling of its credits.

"The boy, therefore, who enters banking determined to make himself valuable to his institution may feel more assured of a permanent situation than one who enters business life as clerk in a mercantile establishment. The chances of the failure or withdrawal of his institution from business are less. His income may be smaller than that of the average business man, but it is assured and regular; and, knowing this, he can adjust his expenses accordingly, laying by monthly the little sums which will in the end provide for his comfort, when he is retired, and, let us hope, reasonably pensioned.

"Availing himself of the somewhat shorter hours of office work than the average clerk, or even business man, enjoys, the bank clerk may improve his opportunity to indulge in some healthful form of out-of-door amusement, or the study of some natural science, perhaps irreverently called a "fad," which will clear the cobwebs from his brain and make him a broader, better man.

"The tendency of the times is to more intense application during business hours, making necessary more frequent intervals of rest and relaxation. The bank clerk is, perhaps, in a better position to avail himself of such relaxation than are others.

"Banking furnishes large opportunities for the development of the faculty of reading character, and forming rapid, accurate judgment of men. The good banker must have the ability to say " No," and if he can say it in such a way as to keep the good-will and respect of his clients, he has tact which all must acknowledge.

"This business, also, furnishes opportunities for the study of the great financial problems of the day, as well as for the development of honest impartiality. Who can better serve the interests of the business world than the fearless, conscientious banker, before whom, in the exercise of his duty as the lender of the money others have placed in trust with him for that purpose, come the financial statements of would-be borrowers to be analyzed and sifted, and on which he must pass judgment, meting out proper lines of credit to the deserving, and, with keen perception, detecting the weak points or false representations of the unworthy? The business world depends upon such men in a large measure for its safety and success. It should be the ambition of the young man to prepare himself for so honorable and important a position.

" The above are the reasons that occur to me for advising a boy to enter a bank. On the other hand, one reason for advising a boy not to enter the business is because it is a confining, sedentary occupation, and its routine of duties is narrow and tiresome, furnishing comparatively little variety.

" The boy who enters it must give up the ambition, which all have, for the accumulation of large wealth; and while he may, perhaps, see those who entered business life with him, by some fortunate speculation gain sudden wealth, he must, by virtue of his position, avoid all speculative ventures and make up his mind to be contented with a modest income in return for faithful services."

Mr. Douglas H. Thomas, president of the Merchants' National Bank, of Baltimore, in a letter to the author, says:

" I would state that the banking business is considered a most honorable profession, and a knowledge of its details will always prove of immense service to any one engaged in any of the occupations or professions of life. To any one who continues in the business, and shows ability and aptitude, a good position is always assured, with proper compensation."

THE MUSICIAN

I N using the term "musician" I am referring to those who enter the musical profession, or rather, those who undertake the performance or teaching of music as a money-making vocation, and not to the amateur musician, who neither receives, nor cares to receive, remuneration for his services.

Musicians, for the sake of convenience, may be divided into the following classes: the opera singer, the concert singer, the theatrical vocalist or vaudeville singer, the band or orchestra leader and player, the violinist, the instrumental soloist, the player of the piano or organ, other instrumentalists of various grades of proficiency, and teachers of music.

The grand opera singer may be said to occupy the highest musical position, — certainly from the financial point of view.

Prima-donnas of the first magnitude, — and there are only a few living at any one time who are allowed to occupy simultaneously the zenith of fame, — enjoy incomes of at least fifty thousand dollars a year, and some of them have received double that sum. These apparently exorbitant amounts are paid exclusively to females, — male singers, except in the rarest cases, not receiving anywhere near the first-named sum. The highest class of opera tenors, even those most conspicuously in the public eye, do not earn more than ten thousand dollars a year. The average income of leading male opera vocalists is undoubtedly less than a hundred dollars a week.

Male opera singers, one grade below the leaders, are paid, on an average, less than fifty dollars a week, with a maximum seldom exceeding seventy-five dollars a week. Male singers below this grade, that is, two grades below the "leaders," are seldom paid more than thirty-five dollars a week, with an average salary of about twenty-five dollars.

Male chorus singers seldom receive less than ten dollars a week, with a maximum salary of twenty dollars, and an average of about fifteen.

It should be borne in mind that the opera season is very short, never exceeding forty weeks, and it is often cut to thirty. The opera singer is liable to be without engagement for nearly half the year, unless he can obtain dates at outdoor theatres and summer gardens.

The opera singer should be, and generally is, a fairly good actor; in fact, dramatic ability is essential to full operatic success.

Male comic opera singers are paid about the same as non-singing actors of the same grade. Their success depends as much upon their individuality and originality as upon the quality of their voices, and in many cases eccentricity or mannerism has double the commercial value of the voice.

The theatrical vocalist or vaudeville singer, if a good actor and the possessor of extraordinary personality, may be paid as high as two hundred dollars a week, but the average weekly earnings seldom exceed forty dollars. The successful artist in this line relies upon the uniqueness and originality of his acting rather than upon his voice.

The concert singer may or may not be an opera singer. He may sing in grand opera during the season, and fill his off time with concert engagements. As a rule, his income is obtained from singing at musical entertainments and in church, and by teaching.

Concert vocalists of the highest class are paid as much as three hundred dollars a performance, the minimum being not less than fifty dollars, and the average about one hundred dollars. Those singers a grade below this may expect to receive from twenty to one hundred dollars a performance, the average amount obtained being sixty dollars.

Ordinary concert vocalists are seldom paid more than twenty dollars a performance, with an average of about five dollars. Comparatively few, even of the highest grade, receive, on an average, more than fifty profitable engagements a year; consequently their total income is very much smaller than it is popularly supposed to be.

Occasionally high-grade concert singers, who are dependent for their incomes entirely upon the quality of their voices, appear upon the vaudeville stage. These artists — for they are artists in every true sense — are seldom paid less than twenty-five dollars a week, and some receive twice, or even four times, that amount.

Instrumental musicians, and members of salaried bands or orchestras, earn anywhere from twelve to fifty dollars a week, the average player in the first-class orchestra receiving about twenty dollars a week, while the average for members of orchestras and bands of a lower grade is as low as fifteen dollars a week.

Players known as "first violin" or "first cornet," in first-class theatre orchestras, seldom receive more than thirty dollars a week, with twenty-two dollars a week as an average.

As a rule, the so-called brass or military bands are made up of those who do not depend entirely upon musical performances for their livelihood. The leader, as well as some of the members, are teachers of music.

Band players, at concerts, receive substantially the same that is paid to members of orchestras, and from three to five dollars for parade duty.

The average orchestra player in the United States, outside of the large cities, is usually an incompetent musician and in every sense an amateur, although, when he attempts to earn his whole living by music, he may be commercially considered a professional. Sometimes he works as a machinist, or a cigar worker, or a porter in a store.

The establishment of the Federation of Musicians has made prices somewhat better, but all the organization in the world will not obtain engagement. Many a theatre orchestra, in a small city or a large town, is not paid much more than a dollar and a half per player for each performance.

Dance, banquet, and reception orchestras, in the city, are paid from one to five dollars per player per appearance, and in the country from one to two dollars.

Comparatively few instrumentalists, except those regularly engaged in theatres or music halls, or by hotels and restaurants, receive more than three engagements a week; and some of them cannot hope for one a week. Therefore, the players are obliged to engage in teaching or other labor for a livelihood.

The yearly income of an orchestra or band musician

of a good grade, who is a private teacher as well, is about twelve hundred dollars.

Leaders of orchestras at regular theatres and music halls in large cities seldom receive less than fifteen hundred dollars a year, the maximum salary probably being not in excess of three thousand dollars. These leaders are usually first-class musicians themselves; but they possess something more, namely, the power of being able to get the most out of their orchestras; in fact, the quality of the orchestra is dependent as much upon the ability of the leader as it is upon the musical talent of its members. Second-grade musicians, under an expert leader, will frequently make a better showing than will first-class musicians under the baton of an inexperienced master.

Instrumental soloists may earn as much as leaders of orchestras.

Members of country bands seldom receive any actual remuneration, since the money realized from their performances generally goes for uniforms and expenses.

An organist is popularly supposed to occupy a prominent musical position, and to enjoy a large income. As a matter of fact, comparatively few receive more than three hundred dollars a year, and many a large and wealthy church does not pay its organist more than one hundred dollars a year. All over the country there are organists of great musical ability, both male and female, who preside at church organs, twice every Sunday, for not more than fifty dollars a year. A very few expert organists earn, by their playing, two or three thousand dollars a year. Usually the professional organist is a teacher.

Pianists are the most in evidence. More than one-half of our women and girls, in all grades of society, except the poorest, either play, or think they can play, the piano; but comparatively few boys and men are pianists, unless they intend to take up piano playing or teaching as a profession.

Ninety per cent of piano teachers are women, and they seem to all but monopolize this branch of the profession.

It has been said, with exaggeration, of course, that there is a woman music teacher for every scholar, and that in most districts there are even more music teachers than there are those who are willing to learn or even can be coerced into learning.

In short, teachers of the piano are a drug on the market. There are at least sixfold too many of them; not too many who have proficiency and adaptability, but there is an excess of those who can never learn to play themselves or teach others to play.

Great personal proficiency in the actual performance on an instrument is not an essential to the teacher of music, although most good teachers are good performers. The teacher, to be successful, must possess that something which allows him to impart that which he knows to others; yes, even to the extent of being able to teach others to do better than he can do himself. Unless he possesses this ability and adaptability, he can never become a truly successful teacher.

Music teachers may be divided into three classes: those who give their entire time to it, and receive a salary from some institution; those who teach music in the public schools; and those who give private lessons.

Members of the first class receive salaries ranging from five hundred to three thousand dollars a year, a favored few enjoying incomes of five thousand dollars or more a year.

The salaries of teachers of music in the public schools range between a thousand and three thousand dollars a year in the city, and a few hundred in the country.

Teachers of the last class, private instructors, are really in business for themselves, and their incomes depend upon their price per lesson and the number of pupils they obtain. Comparatively few male music teachers of this class receive, from their teaching alone, more than five thousand dollars a year, and the average private male teacher probably does not earn more than a thousand dollars from the music lessons he gives.

There are many fairly good male vocal and instrumental instructors, who, from their teaching, cannot hope to enjoy incomes of more than a few hundred dollars a year.

Seventy-five per cent of those who are known as piano teachers — and I am referring here to men and not to women — are only moderately successful, and possess little of that natural ability necessary to the efficient instructor.

Because most of the teachers of piano are women, who would rather teach music than do housework or stand behind a counter, and therefore are willing to work for nominal pay, male teachers of the piano have comparatively little opportunity of earning a livelihood, unless they are particularly proficient.

As music is not an American characteristic, a large part of our home-music is performed mechanically by players, not artists, at the instrument, people who have no conception of the true mission of music.

The average mother, with an average daughter, buys an average instrument, employs an average quality of female music teacher, and the daughter receives what the mother pays for, — a rudimentary instruction in music, which enables her to play mechanically, and, occasionally, correctly.

With this "average" training she attempts to play, not ordinary selections, but those which the true musical artist would have difficulty in performing.

Most of our home-music is music only in name, and frequently should go unnamed.

The introduction of automatic players, which, when attached to the piano, at least make it play correctly, must have driven the gods of music to feasting, — those poor old deities who, for generations, have stuffed cotton in their ears every time a home-made pianist pounded the keys of a could-not-retaliate piano.

No one can be made into a professional musician of any grade above the lowest. Unless he has natural musical talent, his case is hopeless. He can be taught to become a mechanical player of some degree of correctness; he can be made to sing in tune; but he can never truly render music, either vocally or instrumentally. He cannot even imitate music. He is, at best, an automaton, a grinder out of sound, — technically correct, but lacking in soul.

To attempt to force music into a child by a process of education is simply ridiculous. This forcing is done so often that it would seem almost as though the legislature would be justified in making it a crime for a parent to have a child taught music without a permit from the local authorities. Understand, that I am not decrying the teaching of music in the public schools. It should be taught there. Every child should understand the principles of music. He should know how to join in the chorus, and to sing in company, not by himself, but with several others. I am simply objecting to this forcing of musical training upon those who have no

musical talent, at the sacrifice of better things and at
the waste of time and money.

Great instrumentalists and vocalists gain recognition
because they have natural talent, which may have
come to them through inheritance; and when by study
and practice they develop that talent to a high degree
of proficiency, they simply take that which Nature has
given them, and make the best of it.

But natural talent, alone, will not make a great singer
or a great instrumentalist. Untrained musicians of
talent may play and sing, and do it well and with
soul, but they are not great, because they have not
developed into greatness. Musical though they may
be, they are crude and unfinished.

The musician who plays by ear, and who cannot even
read musical notation, is not a finished musician, but
simply one who is using his natural ability without
having filtered it through courses of study and training;
and, unless he develops himself, he will not climb anywhere near the musical top.

So that in the first place, the boy must have natural
talent; in the second place, he must be willing to devote
long years to study and practice, without which he will
never amount to anything.

How can the boy or his parent determine, in advance, whether or not there is musical talent in him,
such that, when developed, it will make him a real
musician?

If the boy has musical talent, it will show itself, come
what may. It cannot be restrained. He loves music.
Music is an apparent part of himself, and can be
detected by any one who stays only a few hours in his
presence. He gives you no chance to overlook it. He
loves music as he loves his life. Music to him is next

to God. Without it he would not care to live; or, at least, he would be continually unhappy.

One may sometimes doubt whether or not the boy is fitted for the law or for the ministry or for the medical profession; but there can never be any question as to whether or not a boy has musical talent. There is something about music which always proclaims its presence, and that in no uncertain manner.

The boy with music in him likes to practise. He does not run away from his music teacher, but looks forward to his coming. He is more likely to injure his health by over-practice than by under-practice. Music is a recreation worth more to him than football, or baseball, or cricket, or tennis; yet he may enjoy all of these sports; but if he has music in him, music controls him. Music with him is in the ascendant. He loves to make music, and he loves to hear music.

The best advice that I can give to the boy regarding a musical life is: Do not try to be a musician unless Nature has given you musical talent, then train Nature's gift, that you may properly use your endowment. If you have not this musical talent, develop yourself in some other direction.

From a business or professional standpoint music offers little to any one, unless he possesses great natural ability trained into proficiency.

The question is asked, Would you not advise the boy who shows musical talent to study to become a pianist, or any other instrumentalist, or vocalist?

I answer, Yes, if the boy wants to learn, and is willing to stand the hardships incident to his training; but I say, No, and decidedly no, unless talent is plainly evident, and is recognized, not only by the parent, but by the boy's associates.

From a business point of view music offers the boy substantially nothing, save the barest living, unless he has exceptional ability. The average musician, male or female, can reap far better financial results in almost any ordinary clerical position. The female music teacher, even of more than ordinary ability and adaptability, will usually make more money as a stenographer or as a telephone girl than she can hope to obtain from her music.

Do not spread yourself. Concentrate your energies. Focus them around one thing. Do that thing well or very well. To attempt to do less than that invites failure, and certainly prevents the attainment of success.

Mr. Philip Hale, musical editor of the *Boston Herald*, ex-editor of the *Musical Record* and the *Musical World*, in a letter to the author, says:

"If a young man or young woman is truly musical, it would be difficult to prevent either of them from following a musician's life. If a young musician chooses the profession simply to make money, in ninety-nine cases out of a hundred he will be disappointed. If he succeeds in making much money, unless he is a singer of phenomenal voice or a virtuoso of the first rank with personal magnetism, the genuineness of his musical sentiment may well be questioned. In other words, art is one thing and business is another. The two should not be confounded.

"The true artist may be poor, he may often be in want; but he knows a keener joy than that ever known by the successful business man, for he is an idealist. I am aware that many estimable persons do not believe in the existence of artist idealists ; but they are still to be found in music, art, literature, — perhaps, now and then, in business.

"I may add, that if a young man, whether he be musical

or not, should ask me whether music would be a lucrative calling, I should advise him at once to go into a dry-goods store or broker's office."

Mr. Frank H. Damrosch, Mus. Doc., the director of the Institute of Musical Art of the City of New York, in a letter to the author, says:

" One of the first considerations in choosing a vocation is whether it will offer a decent living, and from this point of view, given aptitude, a good personality and character, and honesty of purpose, any profession will provide a comfortable income.

" Music is no exception in this respect, and we may as well dismiss this part of the question from further discussion. While the musician rarely acquires wealth, he can usually, given the presence of the qualities enumerated above, earn a good living.

"The question then remains, if music is not likely to offer great pecuniary inducements, what would make it worth while to devote one's life to it?

" The answer lies partly in the heart of each individual. If the heart says: I must follow music because it is my life, nothing more need be said. But even when the heart does not speak so confidently, and when plain reason seeks for ground upon which to build a decision, we will find that music is an art which appeals to the intellectual faculties, and therefore tends to improve the mind; that it is an expression of the beautiful in sound, and is therefore uplifting to the spirit; that it makes for gentleness, nobility, and spirituality, and therefore brings one in contact with the best men and women in the community.

" I speak not, of course, of the trade musicians, the people who look upon music only as a plumber or a bricklayer does upon his job, which is to bring him so much in wages. That class is largely represented and has its uses;

it can often make a fairly good living, but it does not represent the true musician.

" The true musician is much in demand, and there is much work for him to do. There is a large field, paying in every sense of the word, open to him. Who, then, shall enter the field and labor in it? Any one who is ' fond of music '? By no means. The whole world is, or ought to be, fond of music; but only a few are called, and still fewer are chosen. A real musical talent should not only be a reason for becoming a musician, but should impose an obligation to do so.

" When Nature provides a talent, it is a capital which she intends shall bear interest, and woe to him who goes contrary to her mandate.

" Unfortunately, conditions in America have, till recent years, militated against any but practical development.

" Music, while looked upon as a good accomplishment for girls, was considered not worth while wasting a boy's time on. He had to get to ' real work ' in commerce, factory, or the scientific professions. How many talented geniuses in art were thus killed in the bud will never be known. Certain it is that a musical talent cannot easily develop out of nothing. The boy must at least have an opportunity to hear good music and have a rudimentary knowledge of musical self-expression either through his voice or on an instrument. Time thus spent is not lost. Even if he develops but moderate ability, he will at least learn to listen intelligently and to appreciate good music.

" If he shows talent, he should first of all get a thorough academic education, for a musician must be a true and cultured gentleman. Simultaneously he must acquire an all-round musical education, — technical, theoretical, æsthetical, and historical. Then he must specialize either as performer or teacher. Thus equipped he may go forth, sure of success in so far as a congenial, honorable, and sufficiently remunerative calling can give it.

" Under the conditions outlined above, I can conscientiously recommend young men to enter the profession of music. It means hard work and what many call drudgery; but the true musician is so interested in every detail of the work, in its development and its results, that he feels not the drudgery, and his work is his pleasure.

"Best of all, he feels that when he has succeeded, he has brought beauty into people's lives and happiness to their hearts. He is the friend of thousands whom he does not know, but who speak his name with admiration and gratitude. While he is never adequately compensated for what he gives, for the true musician gives his heart's blood, yet his work is its own reward, and he would not exchange with the king on his throne or with the richest man on earth.

"For the true musician can give more real and lasting happiness to the world than can any millionnaire.

"There are, of course, many disappointments and failures to overcome, but not more so than in other walks of life. Sincerity in the work, perseverance, high standards and ideals, and abnegation of self will win out in the end.

"America needs composers, conductors, singers, instrumentalists, such as pianists, performers on stringed instruments, wind instruments for high-class symphony orchestras (a great field), organists, etc., church musicians, directors, teachers, etc.

"There is room even on the bottom rungs of the ladder for true musicians, but there is room and to spare on top.

"Have you real musical talent, young man? If so, do not hesitate, but come and we will all help you to mount on the musical ladder."

THE MERCHANT

THE merchant, commercially speaking, is the keeper of a great store or the proprietor of a large buying and selling business.

By common custom we call the owner or manager of a country store, or of a small city establishment, a storekeeper, and entitle the more extensive storekeeper, or large buyer and seller, a merchant.

The manufacturer may or may not be a merchant. The merchant and storekeeper are, more than any other class of men, truly representative of business. They buy and sell, they maintain stores or selling headquarters, and do business, either over the counter or by the other usual methods of selling.

The successful merchant is a tradesman, a shrewd buyer and a profitable seller, just as is the horse-trader or the market-wagon vender. That which makes one makes the other, except that the merchant possesses these trading qualities in a higher and more developed degree.

The merchant may or may not manufacture. The average merchant does not, but purchases his products in large quantities from the manufacturer, and sells these goods directly to the consumer, — and by consumer I mean the public, — or sells them to the retailer, who, in turn, sells them to the public.

The commission merchant differs from the regular merchant in that he does not own the goods he sells, but retains them upon consignment, and sells them upon commission.

Merchants are in business for themselves, and it is therefore impossible to state, with any degree of accuracy, their maximum, minimum, and average incomes.

Some merchants receive an annual profit in excess of one million dollars, but the number of such is naturally small. Probably the average metropolitan merchant does not make more than ten thousand dollars a year. Perhaps ten per cent enjoy annual incomes exceeding this figure, and among them are not a few netting a profit of over one hundred thousand dollars.

The merchant is in every way a business man, and professionalism never enters into his vocation. His success depends almost entirely upon his buying and selling capacity, and upon his mastery of details and discipline.

Probably not more than twenty-five per cent of our leading merchants have received more than a high school education. Education, no matter how extensive, will not make a merchant. Education never has, and never will, teach one how to trade. Book-knowledge, in itself, is worthless. Book-knowledge, in connection with experience, produces a result which experience alone refuses to produce. Experience, however, is the head-instructor, but has never succeeded in

making a merchant, unless its possessor had, in the first
place, some natural trading ability. The merchant with
a liberal education, all things being equal, stands a better
chance of success. A common school education is essential, and a college course, although not necessary,
will probably be of value.

There is a popular notion that if one intends to enter
business, the college years are wasted; and that the boy,
or young man, can use his time to better advantage by
entering the counting-room directly from the common
school; and the voice of experience says that the college
or higher education is in no way essential and makes
for wasted time to the boy whose ambition is directed
to money-getting.

If one desires only to make money, it is obvious that
a college education is not only non-essential, but posi-
tively harmful, — harmful in the sense that it is likely
to instil into the boy an ambition not represented by
cash results.

It must be admitted that a very low order of intellect
can earn money, and that the development of the finer
senses, and the rounding out of respectable manhood,
are not necessary to the making of financial profit.

He who cares nothing for mental growth and for
the upbuilding of manhood, and whose only desire is
to make money, and who never wants or expects to
receive anything else, would better get to money-
making as soon as he is through with the common
school. As a money-making merchant he may be a
success, but he can never be a responsible and honored
citizen of any city, whether he is worth one dollar or a
million dollars.

The merchant of true success is an honorable man,
a man of reputation beyond that of money-making. He

is an educated man. If he is not college-bred, he has, by observation and application, mastered the knowledge of essentials. He is fairly well-read, and not ignorant of current events. If he is not a college graduate, he may have regretted it, for he may realize that a classical education would have probably strengthened his self-respect and his confidence.

The great merchant is a leading citizen, and occupies a high and honored position in his city or town, often in his state, and sometimes in the nation.

The boy of mean, grasping instincts, who is legally honest and morally dishonest, if he be a shrewd manipulator of money, may, without education, and certainly without conscience, become a merchant of great money-success, but never a *great* merchant.

The great merchant comes from the boy of character, the boy with a steady willingness to learn, and who seldom has an idle moment. This boy has an ambition, and most everything is set aside for the realization of that ambition. He is an economical boy, and seldom spends a dollar without first weighing it. He is not mean; he is ¬aving and just. Life to him is a serious undertaking. He does not underestimate obstacles, but is willing to overcome them by the strength of his labor. He neither lags nor jumps; he walks with steady tread. He may or may not be at the head of his class at school, but he gets out of his studies all that they are worth to him. He makes a business of his school-time. He puts his time against his teacher and his books, and makes a profitable trade. He is not a loafer. When he plays, he plays; and when he works, he works; but his time is under some sort of regulation.

Occasionally a wild boy develops into a successful merchant, but those who have studied that boy carefully have undoubtedly observed that his dissipated moments are not his real moments, and that the evil and the consequent carelessness and thoughtlessness are but transient enemies.

The great merchant may almost always be traced back to the boy of thought, energy, and work, and of continuous work. He realizes that time is money, and if he is late he is seldom responsible for his tardiness. He is systematic. What he does, he does as well as conditions warrant. In fact, he makes a trade with everything he does, and attempts to make the trade a profitable one to himself, at least, and generally to the other party as well. The boy profitably handles himself, even at an early age. He approximately knows his own value, the value of others, and of things in general. He is a master of detail, and this is one point that must not be quickly passed over. It is true that the great merchant, in the inner office of his palatial counting-room, may have forgotten how to properly wipe a pen, or to blot his letters as he signs them. He may have lost the power of successfully handling the active part of detail. But when he was a boy, he did poorly nothing worth doing. As a boy, he was a master of every detail which led to business. If he kept account of his school expenses, his accounts balanced. If he had charge of anything, whether it was a church fair or a skating party, he knew where he stood.

No one ever became a merchant who was not able to, and who did not, master details in his youth.

The boy fitted to become a merchant is master of himself when a boy, and master of everything he touches. Whatever he does, he does systematically and well. If he is careless, he is only temporarily so; if he is thoughtless, he gets back to thoughtfulness.

The great merchant is a big storekeeper; that is to say, he is made of the kind of stuff, and has the same characteristics, as does the storekeeper, only he is broader and grander in his ability.

The boy destined to become a great merchant possesses the material which would make a success of anything, save that of the purely professional. If he chooses to become a great merchant, he should reach that end through natural changes, and yet he should attempt to control those natural changes.

The chances of becoming a great merchant are very small, because not one boy in many thousand is competent to become one. Therefore, it is well for the boy not to expect too much, and to feel reasonably satisfied if he does not reach the top of the mercantile heights.

The city will offer him greater opportunities than the country; that is, if he has the necessary ability; but if he does not have that ability, no matter what he thinks he has, all the opportunity in the world will not suffice.

Therefore, I would not advise the country boy, who wants to be a great merchant, and who believes that he is competent to reach that point, to come to the city at the start. He would better stay in the country store, and there learn the rudiments of business, and besides, discover whether or not he has the capacity which the realization of his ambition demands. The chances are that, no matter how great he may think he is, or will be, he will fall far short of the goal. Therefore, he would better protect himself along the line, and not allow his ambition to rise beyond reason and to drag him out of the track of his possibility.

Mr. John C. Juhring, vice-president and secretary of the Francis H. Leggett Company, of New York City, in a letter to the author, says:

" I would recommend a young man of ambition, who was endowed with energy and had the desire for a commercial life, to strive to become a merchant, for the reason as set forth by the late Herbert Spencer, who said, ' Leaving out only some small classes, all men are employed either in the production, preparation, or distribution of commodities.'

" It is therefore obvious that the two real kings are the farmer and the merchant. The one is a great producer, while the other is the distributer. When we consider that the distribution of farm and manufactured products represents the bulk and backbone of the business of a nation, it can readily be understood that the position of a merchant is one of dignity and the highest calling of any of life's walks.

" But a successful career calls for earnestness of purpose and hard work, as well as for the application of the law of economy, for it must be remembered that waste of energy, time, and money, carelessness in credits as well as investments, injure many a man's career.

" The law of success calls for concentration of mind and effort and steady devotion to the interests involved.

" As Daniel Webster said to the young law student, who complained that the profession was too crowded, ' There is always room at the top.'

" If a young man lacks the desire for a commercial life, and the qualifications necessary to successful merchandizing, such as inclination for hard work, the rudiments of financiering, as well as the art of tact, which represents judgment and wisdom not to antagonize — then I would advise such a one to bend his talents and efforts in the direction of some other calling."

Mr. John R. Ainsley, president of John R Ainsley Company, of Boston, in a letter to the author, says:

" You ask me to point out the advantages to a young man in becoming a merchant, and place me in rather a grave and responsible position, for to act as monitor or guide to young men in a matter pertaining to their future career is a serious affair.

"Of course it is absolutely necessary that a young man should select the line of business that he would prefer, and then to give his whole time and strength in securing every detail connected therewith.

"The advantages offered are the opportunities given of learning business customs, system, discipline, neatness, and punctuality, of securing the knowledge of materials, styles, and qualities, of studying human nature in its many phases, for there are many different specimens in the mercantile profession; and of acquiring information and experience, which will pave the way to positions of influence, honor, and responsibility, for, on the merchants of the country the success of the nation depends, and the business man is a controlling force in the world's markets.

"At the same time, these advantages are of no use to the young man unless he has health, ambition, energy, and persistence, and shows a determination to grasp and improve every opportunity.

"In our country, to-day, the advantages exceed those of any previous generation. Every success is possible, provided the right sort of activity and intelligence is given to the work, and a young man can make of himself just what he chooses.

"Employers are looking for bright, capable young men, to whom they are more than willing to intrust great responsibilities; and in this connection I will say that the question of price should never be considered. The young man should make himself valuable, should master every detail, remembering that the opportunity is worth more than a few dollars extra per week.

"With ambition, eagerness to learn, willingness to work, advancement is sure to follow, and sucess is its reward.

"The disadvantages of a young man entering a mercantile business are the small compensation, the natural competition where there is a large number of employees, the fewer opportunities for advancement, for out of the many a very few are drawn for the advanced positions, the necessity of nearly every one holding firmly to his position in order to secure his own bread and butter, and the lack of ambition and energy on the part of a large majority of young men."

THE ARMY

IN this chapter I shall consider exclusively the enlisted soldier and officer of the United States Army, and not the members of the State Militia and of other military organizations who do not depend upon their wages or rations for a livelihood.

The United States Army is recruited in two distinct ways: from the graduates of the United States Military Academy, at West Point, who begin as second lieutenants, and from the enlisted soldiers or men in the ranks.

The West Point Military Academy is the highest grade technical institute at which is taught everything which may have any bearing on the life and duties of the soldier, including engineering and all kindred sciences.

To become a West Point cadet it is necessary to receive an appointment, either from the President of the United States or from some member of Congress; but this appointment does not make one a student at West Point. It simply permits him to apply for permission to take the examinations.

It is a common custom for those having the power of appointment to require special competitive examinations, the appointment going to the one receiving the highest number of marks. From this examination, which is very severe, the appointee passes to the regular West Point entrance examination.

Thus it is usually necessary for the candidate to pass two sets of examinations, both made as difficult as requirements will allow. Besides being able to pass these two examinations, one of which is competitive and is likely to be very much more difficult than the other, the candidate must have the necessary physical qualifications. He must not be shorter than a specified height, weigh not less than a specified number of pounds, and all of his organs must be thoroughly sound. So difficult and strenuous is the life at West Point that a proportion of the students are unable to remain there more than a year or two.

Any one can obtain all the information desired in regard to examinations and requirements by addressing the Secretary of War, at Washington, D. C., or the Commandant of the West Point Military Academy, New York State. It is not necessary to enclose stamp for reply.

The private soldier of the regular army is recruited from men at large. He must be between twenty-one and thirty-five years of age, unmarried, of good antecedents and habits, and free from bodily defects and diseases. He must be a citizen of the United States, or have declared his intention to become one. No one who cannot speak, read, and write the English language is eligible.

The private soldier, in addition to his pay, is given what is known as rations; namely, clothing, fuel, bedding, medicine, and medical attendance. If he should become incapacitated during service, or be discharged on account of wounds received or sickness brought on while in the army, he is entitled to a comfortable home for life at the Soldiers' Home at Washington. For this last consideration he is assessed twelve and a half cents a month, which is taken from his regular pay.

He is allowed, while in service, one hundred and sixty dollars for clothing during his first three years. By care and economy, many of the soldiers are able to save from one-third to one-half of this amount.

The private soldier, after he has passed through his recruiting days, drills not more than two hours a day, Saturdays and Sundays excepted. He rises at about six o'clock, has breakfast shortly afterward, and is detailed for either guard or fatigue work. He assists in cleaning up and doing other work about the quarters. Dinner is served in the middle of the day, and supper about five o'clock, with retreat parade at sunset. From that time until eleven o'clock he may do as he pleases. He is liable to have considerable " off-time " during both the morning and the afternoon, which he may use for amusement, study, or for the cleaning and caring for his arms.

For about three months of the year he is at the target range, and while there, he practically attends to no duties other than those directly connected with the care of his arms and learning to hit the mark.

Any private soldier with a fair education, and whose work shows a persistency and faithfulness, is reasonably sure of being promoted to the position of corporal. This is the lowest non-commissioned office, the first step upward. Above the rank of corporal comes the office of sergeant, and next in line is what is known as first sergeant; then comes battalion sergeant-major, regimental quartermaster-sergeant, regimental commissary-sergeant, and sergeant-major of the regiment. The last three named are the highest regimental positions in probable reach of the private soldier. Although they are all non-commissioned offices, they are of much responsibility and require men of considerable capacity.

Theoretically, the private soldier may become a commissioned officer, and may even rise to the position of captain, major, colonel, or to be general in command of the entire army; but in reality his opportunities of being promoted to a commission, except in time of war, are very small indeed.

In any year, after all the cadets graduating from the West Point Military Academy have been appointed second lieutenants, which is the lowest commissioned office, the vacancies left, if there be any, may be filled by private soldiers, provided they are able to pass the examinations. When they once obtain a commissioned office, their theoretical opportunities are on a par with those of the graduates of West Point.

Nearly all of our United States Army officers are graduates of West Point. If they were not sound in body and strong in mind, they could not have been graduated. The fact that they have been West Point graduates is a guarantee of physical strength and mental attainment. They have successfully met educational difficulties; they have fought against themselves, and have become masters of themselves; they have something more than book educations; they possess a substantial knowledge of things in general and of army affairs in particular.

The cadet's education, after he enters West Point, costs him nothing in money; in fact, he is paid a salary

LEONARD WOOD

Major General United States Army; born in Winchester, N. H., 1860; graduate Harvard Medical School, 1884; assistant surgeon, U. S. Army, 1886; organized, with Theodore Roosevelt, and commanded the "Rough Riders" during the Spanish war; promoted to brigadier general, 1898; military governor Cuba, 1899; promoted major general, U.S. Army, 1903; on duty in Philippines, 1903-8

while being educated. He enters the army as a commissioned officer, lives in officers' quarters, and associates with officers. From the West Point Academy he
begins to command men. With all these advantages,
however, he is at one great disadvantage, for he cannot
choose a location for a home, nor is he ever sure of a
permanent residence. He may be stationed at one place
for a year or for ten years, and then moved to another
or to several others. But this constant moving, or the
liability of constant moving, need not interfere with his
having a family, for the government provides for such
exigencies, and in many of the stations suitable living
quarters for its married officers are maintained.

I would not advise any boy of only ordinary ability
to attempt to enter the West Point Military Academy;
first, because there is little chance that he can pass the
competitive examination; and secondly, because it is
doubtful if he can pass the regular West Point examination; and thirdly, because he may not keep up with
his class and be graduated into the army, even if he
is able to enter the Academy.

If the boy is sound of body, of good mental capacity,
and is willing to work hard and to be faithful under
army discipline, which is to some very obnoxious, there
is no reason why he should not consider the army. To
become a soldier by enlisting as a private is an entirely
different matter from entering the army as an officer.
Rightly or wrongly, the lines of army caste are finely
drawn between the West Pointer and those who have
risen from the ranks; and the commissioned officer who
has not graduated from the Military Academy will find
that he is not considered on the same social par with
those who are regular graduates. This condition of
social affairs began with the establishment of the Mili-

tary Academy, and the feeling will probably remain for many years to come.

Although the man in the ranks is not likely to rise higher than the position of a non-commissioned officer, I am persuaded to believe that a large proportion of our under-clerks, our common laborers, and many of our servants, would be better off, financially and otherwise, in the regular army than in doing what they are now unsuccessfully attempting to accomplish. Success in the ranks does not depend upon more than ordinary capacity. Any physically sound man, with a little education, and with a moderate amount of intelligence, can successfully hold the position of private soldier. He is under the discipline of a great system, and becomes a part of a machine, — a machine so perfectly regulated and so carefully run that it will successfully carry him, provided he is not a shirker.

Loafers and lazy boys and men are not wanted in the army, and they will not succeed in it. The army is not, and never should be considered, an asylum for worthless boys and men. It is an institution necessary to the maintenance of our government. What it offers is worthy of the consideration of the ordinary man of good bodily health, who has no special ability in a given direction, for in the army he may expect to obtain more comfort, and certainly a greater lack of care and responsibility, than in the ordinary walks of subordinate life.

Each Congressional district and territory, including the Districts of Columbia and Porto Rico, is entitled to one cadet at the West Point Academy; each state is entitled to two; and, in addition, forty are allowed from the United States at large. Congressional district appointments are made upon the recommendation of

Congressmen, state appointments upon the recommendation of Senators, and territorial appointments upon the recommendation of Congressional delegates. It is necessary that each appointee be an actual resident of the district, state, or territory from which the appointment is made. The appointments at large, and for the Districts of Columbia and Porto Rico, are made by the President of the United States, and the appointees may reside in any part of the Union. The appointment must, by law, be made a year in advance of the date of admission, except where a vacancy occurs by reason of death or other causes.

Appended is a scale of emoluments paid to members of the United States Army:

COMMISSIONED OFFICERS

General	$13,500	ron Adjutant, Engineering, Cavalry, and Infantry [1]	$1,800
Lieutenant-General	11,000		
Major-General	7,500		
Brigadier-General	5,500	Battalion and Squadron Quartermaster [1]	1,600
Colonel [1]	3,500		
Lieutenant-Colonel [1]	3,000	First Lieutenant, mounted [1]	1,600
Major [1]	2,500		
Captain [1]	2,000	First Lieutenant, unmounted [1]	1,500
Regimental-Adjutant, [1] mounted [1]	2,000	Second Lieutenant, mounted [1]	1,500
unmounted [1]	1,800		
Regimental-Quartermaster [1]	2,000	Second Lieutenant, unmounted, [1]	1,400
Regimental-Commissary [1]	2,000	Chaplain [1]	1,800
Battalion and Squad-		Cadet, Military Academy	540

[1] After 5 years' service an increase of 10%; after 10 years' service an increase of 20%; after 15 years' service an increase of 30%; after 20 years' service an increase of 40%.

Non-commissioned Officers

	Per month		Per month
Electrical Engineer	$75	Sergeant, — Engineers, Ordnance, Signal Corps	$34
Head Musician	60		
Battalion Sergeant-Major, — Engineers	36	Company Quartermaster-Sergeant, — Engineers	34
Battalion Quartermaster-Sergeant, — Engineers	36	First Sergeant, — Engineers	34
Regimental Sergeant-Major, — Infantry, Cavalry	34	First Sergeant, — Artillery, Cavalry, Infantry	25
Regimental Quartermaster-Sergeant, — Infantry, Cavalry	34	Corporal, — Engineers, Ordnance, Signal	20
Senior Sergeant-Major, — Artillery	34	Cook, — Engineers, Signal	20
Battalion and Squad Sergeant-Major, — Infantry, Cavalry	25	Company Quartermaster Sergeant, — Artillery, Cavalry, Infantry	18
Color-Sergeant, — Infantry, Cavalry	25	Private, first-class, — Engineers, Ordnance, Signal	17
Junior Sergeant-Major, — Artillery	25	Corporal, — Artillery, Cavalry, Infantry	15
Sergeant, first-class, — Signal Corps	45	Private, — Artillery, Cavalry, Infantry	13

Laborers, from $10 to $12 per week. Hostlers, from $480 to $600 per year; teamsters, from $480 to $840 per year.

Draftsmen, clerks, stenographers, messengers, $1,200 to $2,000.

The above pay is for first two years; for third, fourth, and fifth years, add one dollar a month per year.

An increase of two dollars per month is paid after five years of continuous service, and an additional one dollar per month for each five years of continuous service thereafter.

Thirty years' service entitles one to be retired on three-quarters pay, with an additional allowance of $9.50 for clothes, fuel, food, etc., and transportation and subsistence to place of enlistment.

The late General Joseph Wheeler, of the United States Army, in a letter to the author, said:

" In answer to your first question, I will say that for a brave, determined man of singleness of purpose, the army offers great possibilities, in the event of war, during the ages from twenty-five to fifty years.

" Of course, only a comparative few can rise to win national distinction, but the prize is so great that it is well worth the effort.

" In answer to your second inquiry, I will say that the disadvantages of the life are, that unless the country is involved in war during the period above mentioned, the opportunity for advancement is very limited."

General Henry C. Corbin, of the United States Army, in a letter to the author, says:

" Only those predisposed to a military life should think of following the army as a profession, particularly in time of peace. This applies to the enlisted man, as well as to the officer.

" The requirements of the service are in a way exacting and tedious.

" The compensation, though more liberal than in any other army, does not offer material advantages at all tempting, when compared with the rewards for like ability, energy, integrity, and sobriety in civil life.

" A young man not yet established in business or employment can very well serve an enlistment in our regular army with profit to himself and to the service.

" One can with reasonable care and prudence save $10 a month, — $120 a year, — amounting to $360 on a three years' enlistment. I mean by this that he can reach home with this amount. I have known instances where men have saved $500, at the same time providing themselves with every need.

" The government is in many ways more liberal to the enlisted men than to officers ; their pay is supplemented by everything necessary in the way of subsistence, also a very liberal clothing allowance, from which careful men make some saving, which is paid them on their final settlement.

" Medical attendance and medicines are furnished, and without cost to the soldier. So that all in all a young man, with character and determination, can in one enlistment make provision for a start in life. The increase of pay for non-commissioned officers is always open to the ambitious and competent.

" Again, if he gives attention to his duties, he gathers a knowledge of a soldier's duties that will enable him, in the event of war, to serve his country well. Again, the opportunities to obtain personal knowledge of different parts of the country are good, and have, to my personal knowledge, in many instances been of great advantage to the men.

" These advantages come only to those who are frugal, sober, of clean morals, and strength to resist temptations.

" Much that I have said and intimated applies with even more force to those who aspire to be officers.

" Unless one can subscribe fully and without reservation to every one of these conditions, and at the same time bring to the service that superior intelligence and training so long characteristic of the American officer, I advise him to keep out of the service.

" One seeking a commission should not only be duly

qualified, but should be prepared to meet cheerfully a life of sacrifices and often barren of rewards. He must be busy in making ready for the emergencies of war, which may never come, and which every man fit for a commission earnestly hopes will never come, understanding well, while war may be to the advantage of the army officer, it is hurtful and hateful to every one else.

"Those worthy of their cloth feel that it is their business to aid in building up an efficient army, which is always a preventive of war. Only comparatively few ever gain distinction, and the very few achieve fame. In our entire history but two, Washington and Grant, can be said to have achieved lasting fame.

"And yet, if with these things well in mind young men feel that they can freely give their services to their country, they can be happy in the life, and have the comfort that comes to those possessed of a consciousness of duty well done. After all, this is the best compensation that it is possible to obtain."

General George L. Gillespie, chief-engineer, United States Army, and member of the Army War College Board, in a letter to the author, says:

"In giving advice to a young man in whose future life one takes a particular interest, the desire is to do by that young man what is deemed best for his future welfare and success.

"If the career of arms be selected by him the advice given him would be to enter the army through West Point, knowing that in this way he will be able to start upon his career on graduation with that equipment best fitted to enable him to do his whole duty to his country with credit and honor to himself.

"Preliminary preparation is necessary in all branches of competitive civil service, but especially is it necessary in the military service, — and the best, if not the only, school for such preparation is West Point, whose course of instruction includes the highest standards of morality and integrity.

" For a young man of culture and ambition, the only justifiable reason for entering the army as a soldier, in time of peace, is the hope that after good service as an enlisted man he may reach a commission. Many sons of educated parentage, failing to secure appointments to West Point, or to be directly appointed a commissioned officer in the army, enlist with the object of attaining a commission by passing the examinations required of an enlisted man. This preparatory service is very valuable to the future officer, and increases his future usefulness by the intimate knowledge he acquires of the duties, obligations, and needs of a soldier.

" The position of a soldier, without the incentive of a commission, has nothing to commend it. The life is an extremely hard one, and the benefits hoped for can be more readily gained by engaging in civil pursuits, which elevate the character and incite the ambition of the individual to become a good citizen and the head of a household.

" In time of war, the position of the soldier, whether enlisted or commissioned, is most noble and patriotic, and the services rendered cannot be measured in terms of rank and pay, but only by the gratitude of the nation."

General Theodore A. Bingham, of the United States Army, retired, and police commissioner of New York City, in a letter to the author, says:

" 1. Because he will obtain a splendid education, not in books only, but in character. The physical, mental, and moral training there is not exceeded by that of any other school in the country. Also, because he will obtain a more thorough training as a soldier, enabling him to do better work in the world, and a training which will always be missed if not secured.

" 2. I would not advise him to enter the army except through West Point, unless the West Point course cannot be had and he is determined to be a soldier. He may be promoted as high, but it will require harder work, and work against many disadvantages and even obstacles.

" 3. I would not advise a boy to enter the army as a common soldier, except as just stated under ' 2.'

" 4. I would not advise a boy to enter the army at all, unless he had a strong leaning that way, in which case he should make every possible effort to enter West Point. Failing in that, enlistment as common soldier will lead to a commission by very hard work.

" If a boy wants some years of adventure, and has a good constitution, it will not hurt him to soldier for three years; but it is not a free life, and he cannot with honor quit when he gets tired.

" But the right kind of boy, in these days, does not want to be a soldier. He should be a good, honest, truthful, hustling citizen. He can then have a settled home, friends, a name in the community; and in our peaceful nation there is no chance for an ambitious young man in the army."

THE NAVY

SO far as opportunity for advancement is concerned, the United States Navy offers neither more nor less than is presented by the United States Army; consequently, any general advice for or against the army would apply with substantially the same force to the navy. The principal difference between these two great national departments is in the fact that the field of the one is upon the land, and the life of the other is upon the water.

Neither the army officer and soldier, nor the naval officer and sailor, have any dependable permanent home, for they are under the orders of their superiors and may be moved from point to point at hardly a day's notice.

From a home standpoint, the army offers more than does the navy, because, while the army officer or soldier is frequently transferred, he may under certain conditions carry his family with him; the naval man is seldom allowed to live with his family, except under furlough or unless stationed at some quite prominent land point. Neither wife, nor any member of the family, nor any outsider, is allowed to live on shipboard, unless actually enlisted in the service, and women are not permitted to enlist.

The soldier is much more likely to remain within the boundary of the United States than is the sailor, who perhaps, during the greater part of his enlistment, will be entirely outside of American waters.

One must enter the navy either at the bottom as a common sailor or workman, with little opportunity for advancing beyond a non-commissioned officer's berth, or he must enter as a graduate of the United States Naval Academy, at Annapolis. This institution is to the navy what the Military Academy is to the army, and its graduates enter the navy as midshipmen, which places them in the direct line of commissioned officer's promotion. They are officers at the start, and never serve as common sailors or hold positions below that of a commissioned officer.

The common sailor enlists for a period of four years. The enlistment of minors, however, expires at their majority. Boys under the age of eighteen cannot enter the navy without the consent of their parents or guardians. All candidates must pass a severe physical examination, which is substantially the same as that required for enlistment in the army.

Enlisted men, who serve continuously and earn the grade of petty officer or first-grade petty officer, are eligible for appointment to warrant officers, and are paid from twelve hundred to eighteen hundred dollars a year.

Warrant officers of four years' service are allowed to take the examinations, which may place them in the regular line of commissioned officer promotion. Twelve are appointed annually.

It will be seen that the ordinary sailor is not likely to become more than a petty officer, although he has some chance of obtaining a warrant berth, and that he has even less opportunity of reaching a commissioned officer's position. Theoretically, he has every opportunity; practically, his opportunity is quite small. Even when he becomes a commissioned officer, he is, to an extent, a naval outcast socially. If questioned, comparatively few naval officers will admit this to be true, for it certainly would not be ethical or in good taste for them to do so, and it would materially discourage enlistment. However, this condition exists, because the social lines of naval caste are as closely drawn as those of the army.

The student at Annapolis begins as a naval midshipman, and is a naval officer. The midshipman ranks as the lowest commissioned officer, but because he is commissioned he is in the line of promotion and may reach any height, even that of admiral.

Although at school, these midshipmen are in the navy, and are required to sign articles binding them to service for eight years, including the time spent at the Naval Academy.

While at the Academy, as students, and at the same time as officers, they receive five hundred dollars a year, dating from their admission to the Academy. This amount is sufficient to maintain them in comfort, and by economy a part of it may be saved.

I certainly would not advise the bright, energetic, ambitious, and educated boy to consider entering the navy except through the United States Naval Academy.

If he is not at all domestic, and prefers a roving life with congenial companions, and an opportunity to visit the ports of the world, the navy certainly offers exceptional opportunities.

Naval officers are not only school-trained men, but

they are almost invariably men of character and of the highest intelligence. They are in every sense gentlemen and enjoyable companions. The life of the naval officer is ideal, provided one does not care for business and can be happy without a permanent home on land. He is removed from care and worry, and his livelihood is secure. He cannot pass through financial troubles. He is given time for reading and study. Barring the family and business sides of life, he occupies a most enviable position.

Most emphatically would I advise any bright and ambitious boy to keep away from the navy, if he must enter in any other way than through the Naval Academy, although as a naval man his livelihood is secure and his old age is provided for. When once admitted to service in the navy, he is furnished with a free outfit of clothing to the value of forty-five dollars, and his pay and rations are sufficient for good physical comfort. He is entitled to a life pension after twenty years of service, and if he should become disabled by reason of age or infirmity, he may secure a pension equal to half pay or be admitted to the Naval Home.

NAVAL EMOLUMENTS

	Active	Shore
Admiral	$13,500	$13,500
Rear-Admiral, first nine	7,500	6,375
Rear-Admiral, second nine . . .	5,500	4,675
Brigadier-General-Commandant, Marine Corps	. . .	5,500
Captain	3,500	2,975
Commander	3,000	2,550
Lieutenant-Colonel, Marine Corps .	3,000	3,000
Lieutenant-Commander	2,500	2,125
Major, Marine Corps	2,500	2,500

	Active	Shore
Lieutenant, Navy	$1,800	$1,530
Captain, Marine Corps, Staff . . .	2,000	2,000
Captain, Marine Corps, Line . . .	1,800	1,800
Lieutenant, Junior, Navy	1,500	1,190
Ensign	1,400	1,190
Second Lieutenant, Marine Corps . .	1,400	1,400
Midshipman		500

Chaplain . . . $2,400
Professor . . . 2,400
Constructor . . 3,200
Gunner, active . . 1,200
   " shore duty 900
   " on leave or
waiting for orders 700
Mate, active . . 900
   " shore duty . 700
   " on leave or
waiting for orders 500
Electrician . . 360 to 720
Warrant machinist 1,200
         to 1,250
Machinist . . 480 to 840
Warrant carpenter
      1,200 to 1,800
Carpenter . . 360 to 600
Coppersmith . . 660
Boiler maker . . 780
Blacksmith . . . 600
Shipfitter and plumber
      480 to 660
Sailmaker . 480 to 1,200

Painter . . . $360 to 480
Shipwright 300
Fireman . . . 360 to 420
Coal-passer . . . 264
Cook . . . . 300 to 660
Steward . . 420 to 600
Chief-Commissary . 840
Commissary . . . 720
Mess attendant 192 to 288
Baker . . . 420 to 520
Hospital apprentice
         240 to 360
Steward 720
Chief petty officer . 840
Seaman, first enlistment 168
Ordinary seaman . . 228
Apprentice seaman . 192
   and $1.36 per month in-
   crease in pay for reënlist-
   ment for four years.
Rations and medical attend-
   ance free. Privilege of re-
   tirement after thirty years
   on three-quarters pay.

Admiral Royal B. Bradford, of the United States Navy, in a letter to the author, says:

"I would advise a boy to enter the navy through the Naval Academy; or, in other words, I would advise him to become a combatant naval officer, who is patriotic, and who desires to be in the service of his country during his entire life, and is willing to make reasonable sacrifices in order to do so.

" No boy who is not of good physique and of strong will should attempt to enter the navy under any circumstances.

" It must be understood that to graduate from the Naval Academy requires an intellect above the average.

"A boy who decides to devote his life to the navy, as a profession, must understand that he will, at times, be obliged to undergo hardships and encounter dangers which members of the ordinary professions on shore know little of.

" Perhaps I ought to add, that boys who are fitted for the navy are brave, determined, and possess what is sometimes called ' sand.' There are boys who shrink from danger, from hardship, and from undue exertion, and who prefer ease to manly exercise; such boys would be out of place in the naval service.

" Notwithstanding the hardships, the navy presents many advantages; it is one of the most honorable professions known to men; it offers a fair salary for life, a pension on retirement at the age of sixty-two years, and a pension in case of injury incurred in line of duty.

" Young officers are given an excellent education at the Naval Academy; their services afloat take them to every part of the world, and they usually become broad-minded and accomplished. They should be, and generally are, frank, manly, honest, trustworthy, and jealous of the reputation of their profession.

" The navy is essentially democratic in its constitution; the uniform of a naval officer, however, takes him into the best society of the world, and no officer must forget for a moment that he wears the insignia of his country.

" As an officer advances in age and rank his position is one of great responsibility and frequently requires the exercise of abilities of the highest order.

"I would not advise a boy to enter the Naval Academy who is physically or mentally weak, or who has not probably inherited good health, good sense, and a reasonable amount of pluck and ambition.

"A boy who is fond of ease, luxury, and wealth, or one who shows a predisposition to engage in trade or other special lines of business, or who has a strong inclination for any specialty such as art, literature, law, politics, etc., should not be encouraged to look for a career in the navy.

"In general, I would advise a boy to enlist in the navy when by so doing his surroundings are improved. If he is worthy, he will rise, the way now being open for an enlisted man to reach the grade of commissioned officer. Many reach the grade of warrant officer, which is a good life position, especially for those who would have had nothing but daily labor to which to look forward.

"It is very common to find a boy who expects to adopt the trade of his father, often of a confining routine nature from morning to night, from one year's end to the other and from boyhood to old age. Sometimes among this class are sturdy boys who rebel at their inherited tasks and wish to learn something of the world and to strike out for themselves. If they are strong, of good physique, intelligent, and above all are fair-minded, honest, and without vicious tendencies, they can do well by enlisting in the naval service.

"Under no circumstances would I advise a boy to enlist in the navy who believes that he can do better elsewhere; he would not be contented.

"If a boy is inclined to vice, either by inheritance or cultivation, if he has not that quality which makes men interested in their work and sufficient ambition to desire to excel and to receive the praise of his superiors, or if he aims at nothing but clothes to wear and bread to eat, the navy is no place for him.

"The navy is not a reformatory institution, and boys and

GEORGE DEWEY

Admiral, hero of Manila, born in Montpelier, Vt., 1837; graduate U. S. Naval Academy, 1858; participated in the naval fights which gave Farragut possession of New Orleans; Jan., 1898, assumed command of Asiatic squadron, and on May 1st entered Manila Bay, annihilating the Spanish Asiatic squadron. Made a rear admiral immediately; returned triumphantly to the States and promoted to Admiral of the Navy, 1899

men who enlist with the hope of being cured of bad habits are out of place.

"The best of treatment is accorded good boys and good men; when ill or injured they are carefully attended by skilled physicians and surgeons and are excused from work; they are well-fed, and well-clothed, and they are well-paid. They may place their money on interest or send it to their families. Their necessary expenses are small. They are given proper recreation and leave. With occasional exceptions, the work is light, but implicit obedience is demanded and enforced. Punishments are mild and regulated by law; they can only be assigned by a captain. Thousands of men pass through years of service without committing a single offence.

"No boy or man should enlist in the navy unless willing to keep his contract with the government and serve out his full enlistment, or until he is honorably discharged. A deserter from the navy or army is a most contemptible person. Under the law of the land he loses the rights of citizenship; he is a man without a country; he cannot hold any office of profit or trust; and he cannot exercise the right of suffrage."

Admiral Albert Sydney Snow, of the United States Navy, and Commandant of the Charlestown Navy Yard, in a letter to the author, says:

"Should any American boy be able to secure an appointment to the Naval Academy, I would certainly advise him to do so, esteeming it one of the most honorable of professions, and one in which a boy can secure an education which will fit him, not only for the navy, but also for many outside positions, should he ever leave the service.

"For boys not sufficiently educated to enter the service as midshipmen, and who desire to follow the sea, I would advise, conditionally, that they enter the service by enlistment as apprentices, or landsmen for training.

" Bright boys, who are willing to take advantage of the many opportunities afforded to qualify themselves for special positions in the service, may rise quite rapidly to positions of trust, importance, and responsibility, as petty officers. Many of these petty officers are further advanced, after passing the examinations required, to the position of warrant officer. A few of these warrant officers are given commissions, under the regulations and the laws pertaining to the navy. A commission, however, is not held out as an inducement for enlistment, as it is the idea to train boys of the class who enlist for the subordinate positions on board ship.

" Information as to the requirements, either for the Naval Academy or for enlistment, may be obtained by application to the Navy Department, Washington, D. C.

" For enlistment, only boys of good character are desired, and who have a common school education. They also must pass a rigid physical examination."

THE CLERGYMAN

THE terms "clergyman" and "minister," by common acceptance, are synonymous, as both apply to those who, by ordination or by other official act, are authorized to preach the Word of God, to officiate at certain Church functions, to wed the living, and to bury the dead.

Considerably more than a majority of ordained or licensed clergymen are graduates from some theological school; probably two-thirds of them attended some college or high-grade institution of learning, and undoubtedly three-fourths of this two-thirds are college or university graduates. However, notwithstanding that more than one-half of our clergymen, and particularly our leading preachers, are liberally educated, there are by no means a few brilliant pulpit orators and thoroughly efficient ministers who have not passed beyond the high school, and who have received no theological training other than what has come from self-teaching. But none of these clergymen will claim to owe any part of their success to a lack of higher education, and probably all of them, if it had been possible, would have graduated from a high-class university, finishing with a course in a good theological institute.

The clergyman assumes, by virtue of his office, a responsibility of the most vital character. It is for him professionally, officially, and profitably to connect the Material with the Spiritual, for the benefit of humanity and to the glory of God. To him, more than to any one else, is given the opportunity of doing immeasurable good or unlimited harm. If the clergyman cannot properly sustain this position, he is most unfortunate. If he realizes that his inability is sufficient to make him entirely incompetent to meet the conditions, and then knowingly accepts the responsibilities, he is a criminal before Heaven, and certainly he should be prevented from performing his official duties by the common law of humanity with or without the interference of a higher law.

The Church is supposed to be, and should be, Christianity's earthly headquarters, and the clergyman, the working-head of the Church, is rightly considered the professional exponent of spiritual things.

The clergyman is human. He cannot, by any method of procedure, make himself into the perfect man. He was human before he became a minister. It is not probable that ordination will materially change him; but, nevertheless, he voluntarily assumes a position which the world has a right to construe as a literal dedication of his life to things above the material, and as a promise, or guarantee, that he will, so far as he can, live a virtuous and spiritual life and devote every energy to the propagation of Christianity and to all that Christianity stands for.

The minister, then, although a man, and more or less subjected to the temptations of the world, is under official obligation to be less worldly than those who are not of the cloth. Because he assumes this position, because he publicly takes the vows of the Church, both the Church and the world have a right to hold him to account, and more to account than either have a right to hold those who are not ordained clergymen.

Let me make myself perfectly clear. I am not saying that all men should not be so good as all ministers. He who does not pretend to be good, and is not good, is not a hypocrite. He who pretends to be good, or rather, he who takes the vows of the Church, and does not, so far as he can, live up to those vows, combines with his sin the great sin of hypocrisy.

The desire to enter the ministry, and the deepest piety, in themselves, do not constitute the right to preach. Many a pious mother has unconsciously injured her son, and wronged the community and the Church, by forcing her boy into the ministry. Because the boy was good, or she thought he was good, she has, in ignorance, done immeasurable harm.

The theological school does not and cannot make a minister. The man must, in the first place, be naturally adapted to the ministry. He must be a leader of men, a skilful teacher, and should have experienced the important phases of life, that he may know life, and know men, and know things, not in their exceptions, but in their averages. Without this every-day, all-around experience, he may become a great and learned teacher of the techniques of theology, but he will never actually accomplish much in the way of distributing the Bread and Milk of Religion.

It is unfortunate that many a clergyman who ought

to know the most about his work knows the least about it. Because he is educated, because he is more book-learned than experienced, — an improper balance of inside and outside facts, — he makes a theory of life from the guess-work of theology; and thus equipped, he attempts to reach the people, and to assist them in their material and spiritual upbuilding. In his ignorance of the real, and in the preponderance of his devitalized learning, he misrepresents both God and man. His ignorance may exempt him from punishment, but it does not lighten the harm that he does.

The call to preach, as preaching is now professionally done, may not occur half so often as is popularly supposed. A selfish desire, backed by a parent's unholy ambition — and all ambition born of selfishness is necessarily unholy — has been the substance of many an alleged call to the ministry.

From every standpoint, from that of Heaven and that of earth, no boy has a right to consider the ministry unless he is reasonably sure of his ability and adaptability.

No boy has a right to enter the ministry, nor has he any right seriously to consider it, unless he has thoroughly and completely experienced active religion, and by active religion I do not mean the irreligion of sentiment, but the deep emotions of real Christianity, which always include an absorbing love of humanity. To this must be added ability and adaptability, and the necessary educational preparation; and, further, a practical experience in real life.

Books alone will not prepare one to preach; studying will not equip one for the pulpit; but study, experience in the world at large, and adaptability with ability, produce the Earthly Trinity absolutely essential to good pastoral work and profitable preaching.

I want to speak particularly about adaptability. Adaptability is close to essential in every calling, whether it be farming or preaching; but adaptability is more necessary in the ministry than in any other profession. Without adaptability one cannot successfully preach, nor can one do profitable ministerial work. Without that something, which permits him properly to use his ability and his religion, a clergyman, unless in ignorance of his lack of capacity and of adaptability, commits a crime which certainly should be condemned by the Church; and I am constrained to believe that common humanity, irrespective of the Church side of it, should exercise its right of intervention, and prevent, should the Church fail to do its duty, the unfitted from assuming the highest, the greatest, the grandest, the noblest, and the most sacred responsibility, — that of teaching and preaching the essentials of eternal life.

Without learning, the minister is not fully fitted to handle his responsibility. He needs the knowledge and discipline of a liberal education. He cannot become familiar with men and things in general until he has learned how to handle himself. While a college education may not be necessary, it is by many considered most important. It certainly makes one the better able to know and to handle himself.

Graduation from a theological school may not be essential, although most clergymen would recommend a theological course. Theology is not necessarily a part of Christianity, and I am willing to admit, for argument's sake, that theology is unrelated to Christianity. The theology of the Bible should be known to every preacher. Certainly, he should be well trained in everything pertaining to Holy Writ. The theological school gives him this information.

The more education the young man can get, the better preacher he may make, and the better clergyman he may become, even though he may make use of but a small proportion of what he learned in college or school; but a big heart and less learning make a better minister than much learning and no heart. The discipline is what he needs, and by discipline I mean that school-training of the mind which makes the mind pliable and able to properly grasp the situation.

The boy who has not the energy to get the right kind of an education, whether or not his parents are able to support him, has not the stuff in him for the making of a clergyman.

There are altogether too many weaklings in the Church, altogether too many characterless men, altogether too many men who would not have become ministers if they had not been helped and pushed into it.

The Church, to-day, needs the aggressive Christian, the man with physical and mental power, the man who can strike a physical as well as a mental blow for good.

But let it be understood that education, in itself, no matter how broad it may be, unaccompanied by common sense, ability, adaptability, and experience, is worth substantially nothing in any market, and next to nothing in the pulpit.

Many a man possesses inventive talent, and is able to approach close to actual creation. His ingenuity is marvellous. He can do things which no one else has done, and things which show an enormous inventive genius; yet this man, through lack of adaptability, may produce absolutely useless inventions, and his discoveries may be worthless to him and to the world. A man may be learned in theology, and filled with every class of education; he may be a human encyclopedia; and yet, through lack of adaptability, he is unable to distribute that which he has. He has the power of loading, but not that of discharging. Such a man is unfitted to the ministry. On the other hand, adaptability without experience, without the necessary education, may be as impotent as ability without adaptability. The great professional man is likely to be deficient in business, and the great business man may know little of the things which make for success in professionalism. Still, there is no reason why proficiency in one direction should entail ignorance of the conditions in another. While the business man may succeed, to almost any extent, without possessing many of the mental equipments of professionalism, the professional man is likely to make a sad financial failure if he knows nothing of business.

The great proportion of men are in business or trade, and these men constitute the bulk of the congregation and represent the male majority in every church membership. The minister, in the pulpit and in his pastoral calls, comes face to face with business and trade, because he comes in contact with these conditions. If he does not know what business is, even though he may be unable to practise it, he is not fitted to any modern congregation.

Churches are business institutions. The Church appears not to have a sufficient hold upon the people to make them voluntarily support it; consequently seventy-five per cent of our churches are supported only by strenuous and continuous labor. The necessary money is not easily obtained; and frequently it comes only by force. The Visible Church has a material side, a house requiring maintenance and a pastor who must live. Under our present form of civilization, the Church cannot be maintained without money, and money is a part of business.

I believe that every minister should be trained to business; or, at least, that he should come sufficiently in contact with business to know what constitutes business. I do not believe that he can properly lead modern men, or properly administer to their wants, unless he understands men from men's standpoint, not wholly from the ethical view-point of the clergy.

It may be said, with some degree of truth, and perhaps with all truth, that ninety per cent of our ordained clergymen lack ninety per cent of the experience necessary for the proper fulfilment of their duties. In no other walk of life is lack of experience so tolerated. Nobody would think of hiring a bookkeeper to assume a responsible position unless that bookkeeper had had experience and could prove it. No one would engage a doctor who had not had the experience necessary to properly handle the case. Every physician has practised under the direction of regular physicians before he is allowed to practise by himself. Every lawyer must prove himself before he can be admitted to the Bar. No man is allowed to handle the throttle of a locomotive until he has gained the right to drive an engine by working up to it as wiper and fireman, earning by actual experience the right to assume responsibility.

The minister will not be the power he should be until he earns the right to preach, — earns it as the bookkeeper earns his right to keep books, as the doctor earns his right to practise, and as the salesman earns his right to represent his goods. It is the duty of every embryo minister to gain experience before he dare to stand in the pulpit.

No man can teach successfully anything which he does not understand; and I believe that he can never teach successfully anything to any one whom he does not understand. Familiarity with the subject taught is almost useless unless the teacher understands his pupils. The successful minister, the man who has a right to preach, should possess four essentials: first, ability; secondly, adaptability; thirdly, education; fourthly, an experience with men and things which will enable him intelligently and profitably to work the good which his vows require him to perform. Without this experience he is sure to fail, even though he may continue his pastorate. But above everything else the minister must be a man, a man in the truest and highest sense of the word.

Commercially speaking, the ministry is not remunerative. Comparatively few clergymen receive as much as ten thousand dollars a year, and the fifteen thousand dollar mark is rare indeed. There are several thousand earnest preachers, of some ability, whose clerical incomes are hardly more than three hundred dollars a year, a sum altogether insufficient for the support of a family under the most economical conditions. These men, if married and without property, are obliged to work upon the farm, or to do other outside work, to make both ends meet. The average salary of an ordained and settled clergyman is not in excess of eight hundred dollars a year.

Outside of the large cities few clergymen enjoy salaries of over three thousand dollars; and the leading country town churches seldom pay more than fifteen hundred dollars a year. In the average city few clergymen can expect to receive salaries much above two thousand dollars a year. Many bright, able, and competent ministers successfully labor, even in cities, on salaries not above a thousand dollars a year.

The average country church does not give its pastor more than twelve hundred dollars a year, and probably the majority of self-supporting village churches pay not much over six hundred dollars.

The pastor of a church of any size usually finds his time completely occupied by pastoral duties. If he has literary ability and the time, he may increase his income by writing books or other literary matter. The receipts from wedding fees are very much smaller than they are popularly supposed to be, and they are seldom sufficient to meet the calls of charity and the cost of books, which a clergyman cannot very well be without.

The financially successful clergyman must be an able preacher, an orator of the first rank, a possessor of unusual magnetism and prodigious power; and, further, he may think it expedient to sacrifice the better part of his manhood; that is to say, he may feel obliged to preach to his congregation what his congregation wants, more than what his congregation ought to have. He may dally with the truth, not necessarily to outrage it, but so as not to offend the policy of his constituents. I do not claim that all, or nearly all, of our high-salaried preachers are slaves to their congregations, nor do I feel that all of them sell out to their salaries; but I do believe that a proportion of these clergymen accept these positions more for the salary, and for the notoriety and prominence that they will gain, than they do for the good they may do. These high salaries are almost invariably paid for magnetism, brilliancy, and pulpit-power, and not often for the truth which is in the preacher, or is supposed to be in him.

Few churches, unless endowed, or with wealthy congregations, can afford to pay large salaries; and the rich church seldom wants more than a semblance of truth. The endowed church is frequently a one-man-power affair. Consequently, its clergyman may not hope to retain his position if he preaches according to his conscience and according to his light. He becomes a slave to policy and to expediency. He makes a business of his profession. He is not a clergyman, except officially. He is simply a business or professional man, using the pulpit for a means of livelihood and as an instrument of notoriety.

No earnest Christian minister, from his own effort, ever received more than a competency. It is utterly impossible for any Christian minister, — and, mark you, I emphasize the word *Christian*, — to make more than a comfortable living and to save more than a moderate amount from his salary, if he has a family or others dependent. All clergymen of wealth either sold themselves to their congregation, or received their money from inheritance, or from gift, or from outside work. I am speaking plainly. I am not attempting to varnish or to paint. The truth is what the reader wants, and so far as I can tell it, he shall have it.

Of all callings, professional and business, there is none which offers so little financial return as that of preaching. There are comparatively few rich or endowed churches. Most churches are struggling for existence, and each year show a financial deficit, which must be met by fairs and other schemes. Even if a man will sacrifice his honor, he stands a very slight opportunity of making the pulpit commercially profitable. The man with sufficient ability to command a large church salary can make from twice to ten times as much money by using his ability in some other direction.

Only those who believe that they are called of God, and who have reasonable evidence that they are adapted to preach, have any right to enter the ministry; and every effort should be made by Church, school, and community to keep its members from becoming clergymen, unless they show both heart-and-hand proof of their ability, adaptability, earnestness, and Christianity.

The boy who wants to do good in the world, who would be ever faithful to God, should hesitate long before entering the ministry. As a layman, unfettered by professional assumption, he can do probably more good than he could in the pulpit.

The minister by no means has the monopoly of Christian directorship. If he is adapted to his profession, his calling offers him a better chance to work for God and for man than is given him by any other profession; but if he is not adapted to it, there is no profession which gives him so good an opportunity to do the wrong thing and so little opportunity to do the right thing.

The boy fitted to become a clergyman is equipped with something besides piety and a desire to preach. Piety itself, without the power of distribution, is worth little in the pulpit, or anywhere else, for that matter. A desire to preach may be absolutely worthless, for while desire is the first indication of adaptability, in itself it is of no consequence.

The boy adapted to the pulpit is not only a Christian, but he is a Christian of reason. What he does he does conscientiously; and his conscience is regulated, not altogether by sentiment, but by the reason of solid sense. His sense of right and wrong is acute and safe.

He always exercises his reason.   He has reason for his faith, and his faith is reasonable.   He wishes to preach, and his desire carries with it ability and adaptability. He is faithful.   He is studious.   He does not refuse to look into the clouds, but he remembers that his feet are on earth.   He knows books, but he is not a book-worm.   He is a student, but he does not forget to fill himself with the exhilaration of the open air.

The boy who has a right to enter the ministry shows, even at an early age, unmistakable manly qual-ities.   He is a manly boy.   From manly boys spring manly men, and only from the ranks of manly men come the men fit to preach.

The head of the class of the divinity school may be at the very foot of the ministry.   The boy who knows how to absorb theology, and who has an appetite for history, may not possess one single drop of the oil necessary to light the roads of the world.   The faith-ful boy, although faithfulness is one of the essentials, may be unfitted to preach.

The boy fitted to become a minister wants to be a minister with his whole heart and soul.   He believes that God has called him, and he furnishes evidence of his belief.   He not only assumes that he has been called, but he gives his reasons why he felt that the sound he thought was a call had the genuine ring to it.   Nothing can stop him.   He would stand any hardship, suffer any sacrifice, to attain his end.   If you ask him how he knows he should become a minister, he will tell you. If he cannot tell you, he has mistaken his calling.

This boy loves his fellow-men next to his God.   He loves Nature.   He loves the open air.   He realizes that book-learning, in itself, is as valueless as air without motion.   He is a boy of action, but he does not forget to think. He is a boy of thought, but he does not forget to act. In other words, the boy fitted to be a minister is a manly boy, a boy who takes life seriously and yet joyfully, a boy who does things, a boy who understands how to lead his fellows, and who knows how to talk to his schoolmates, — an absorber and a distributer of the things of life.

The boy fitted to be a minister practises his ministry, save that of preaching, before he enters the theological school. He is his school-fellow's pastor, not in theology, but in the things worth living for. He begins to do good long before he takes the official obligation which ordains him as a professional clergyman.

He who would preach must be great in greatness, great in ability, great in adaptability, great in experience, great in sense, — great enough, and good enough, and broad enough, to see the truth, and honestly to distribute it.

In the ranks of laymen there is room, and room enough, for those who would minister unto men, but who are not fitted by Nature to act as professional leaders.

The parent can do no greater harm to his boy, to the Church, and to the community, than to attempt to make him a minister unless he is fitted for the ministry.

There is no reason why the parent should not suggest to the boy that he, the parent, would like to have him become a minister; but it is criminally wrong to make this suggestion, and to force it into the boy's mind, unless the parent has positive proof that the boy has ability and adaptability.

The Christian parent will use the utmost care, and the chances are that he will not find it necessary to suggest the ministry to the boy fitted to be a clergyman, because that boy almost invariably makes the discovery himself, and when he has made it, nothing can stop him.

The Right Rev. David H. Greer, D.D., LL.D., Bishop Coadjutor, of New York City, in a letter to the author, says:

"The Christian ministry does not so much offer advantages as opportunities, in connection with which strong and devoted men can serve God and humanity. It is, in my judgment, the highest and noblest of all callings, and one which yields the greatest satisfaction.

"Of course, if one's object in life is to make money, he would better stay out of the ministry, although he will receive enough for a sufficient support for himself and family — and what more does any man want, if he is the right kind of person?

"Your second question, 'What are the particular disadvantages in the ministry?' I cannot answer, for I have never found any."

The Rev. Robert S. MacArthur, D.D., pastor of Calvary Baptist Church, of New York City, in a letter to the author, says:

"We are all familiar with the fact that in several denominations the supply of young men for the Christian ministry, in the technical sense of that term, has fallen off considerably in recent years. In some other denominations it has increased during the last few decades, taking one year with another. It is now clearly and rightly felt to a greater degree than was formerly the case, that men can efficiently serve God as laymen. The attractions of business and politics keep some men out of the ministry, and the opportunities for Christian work in Y. M. C. A. organizations, and in other Christian bodies, keep many more out of the ministry, in the technical sense.

"I still hold to the old-fashioned idea that the ministry is a vocation rather than a profession. The recent trend of thought is in favor of regarding it simply as a profession, to be adopted or rejected as are other professions in the light of a man's qualifications and predilections. The matter of qualifications and tastes must not, of course, be neglected; but I still believe that the summons to the Gospel ministry is a special calling, under God's providential guidance, to a special work for the good of men and the glory of God.

"I should say that no boy ought to enter the ministry unless a consciousness of this call be the dominant and resistless conviction of his life. The moment men enter the ministry, under the impellent force of any other motive, they degrade the ministry, dishonor themselves, and lessen their own possibilities for a useful and joyful life.

"In determining the reality of the Divine call to the ministry, due weight ought, of course, to be attached to physical health, literary tastes, elocutive expression, and spiritual attainment and character. The presence or absence of these qualities will assist in determining the reality of the Divine call. But the significance of that call no young man ought to depreciate; it ought not to be considered as synonymous with any professional duty. It will be a sad day for the cause of God and man if the old-fashioned idea expressed in the phrase, 'Woe is me if I preach not the gospel,' be obliterated from our Christian literature and be not dominant in deciding the question of entering the ministry."

The Rev. R. Heber Newton, D.D., formerly rector of All Souls' Church, of New York City, and Select

Preacher to Leland Stanford, Junior, University, California, in a letter to the author, says:

" What are the principal advantages offered by the ministry to a young man seeking a life work?

" A stated income, relieving him from the anxieties of bread winning, thus releasing his energies for better things. A work which calls upon him for all possible self-culture, and compels him, if he is to fill it worthily, to keep abreast of all thought and in touch with all truth, — the broadest intellectual work known to me among the professions. The high joy of teaching men intellectually and inspiring them morally and spiritually, — the divinest work that a man can do upon earth. The privilege of ministering in consolation and comfort to the sorrowing and suffering, of succoring the tempted, and of making himself generally helpful to man individually in the most sacred of all ways, the sacred service of all the friends and helpers of mankind.

" What are the principal disadvantages to the ministry as a life work?

" Upon the material plane, the scantiness of the income likely to be assured, united with the necessity of carrying on self-education, — always an expensive work, — and of keeping up social appearances, — also always an expensive task. In this connection the certainty that, if he steps out of a parish after he has passed fifty, there is not a human probability of his being asked into another one. Coupled with this, the shameful attitude of the Church toward its aged parsons, who are turned out after their working days, in many of our denominations with no sustentation fund to support them, with small savings to fall back upon, and with the usual ingratitude of the usual congregation to a man who has served them till he can serve them no longer.

" On the intellectual plane, the false position which the clergyman must occupy, very frequently if not customarily, as he is seeking to be free in his own thought while true to the creeds or confessions of faith to which he has vowed allegiance in his earlier days, before his intellectual development really began. The bondage of creed subscription and the false intellectual attitude in which this places most men, — one of the worst objections to the ministry to-day. In connection with this the tyranny of the pews over the conscience of the pulpit, — the unwillingness of the average layman to have his thought disturbed by the advancing conceptions of his minister, and his equal unwillingness to have his vested interest disturbed by the moral earnestness of his minister seeking to apply the Golden Rule to every-day life."

THE STREET RAILROAD

PROBABLY no industry so suddenly began to be, and so rapidly assumed gigantic proportions, as has what is known as "trolley transportation."

Within a few years from the introduction of the first trolley or electric car,— and this event is within the memory of most of our young men,— the horse-car and cable car seemed to disappear in a night. There are, outside of New York City, comparatively few horse-cars now in existence; and, barring the few cross-town "boxes" at the metropolis, they may be considered obsolete.

For some years the operation of the trolley lines was confined to cities, the trolley car simply taking the place of the street-car; but within the last ten years trolley roads have been built from city to city and from town to town, running through the woods and across the farms, and are opening up territory which without them would have remained almost uninhabited.

There are comparatively few towns of any size in the East through which a trolley line does not now pass, and this condition is rapidly becoming chronic in the West.

A few years ago the trolley became an open competitor with the steam railway. Long-distance electric lines were established, and cars were run at the rate of from twenty to thirty miles an hour, making, in some cases, not far from regular steam-railroad time.

As a rule, the trolley fare is about one-half of the steam-railroad rate; and this condition, in itself, gives the trolley an opportunity to enter into successful competition with the steam railway, except for long distances.

While there are no trolley lines with a mileage or operating department like that of the great steam railway, the trolley company in its management is not materially different. Like the former, the trolley company is a corporation, working under state charter, its affairs being managed by a board of directors elected by the stockholders, the directors choosing the president, vice-president, secretary, treasurer, and other leading officers, and being responsible for the appointment of the department heads.

The president, if active, is the financial head of the company.

The general superintendent is responsible for the running of the cars.

The office of chief electrician, in a way, corresponds in importance to that of chief engineer of the steam railway.

Practically all that I have said in the chapter entitled "The Steam Railroad," so far as the general management is concerned, applies to street railroading, and need not be more than mentioned here.

The officers of a large trolley company are paid salaries

not much lower than those enjoyed by steam-railway officials; and those connected with the smaller companies, although receiving lesser sums, are by no means poorly paid.

Street-car conductors and motormen are paid, on an average, two dollars and a quarter per day of ten hours; switchmen receive about eleven dollars a week; starters, from two dollars and a quarter to two dollars and a half per day; mechanics, in the repair shops, from eleven cents to twenty-nine cents per hour; linemen, who repair the trolley lines, from twenty to thirty-two and a half cents per hour; car-cleaners and ordinary car-barn helpers receive the same as commercial houses pay for that class of work.

Conductors, motormen, repair-shop men, linemen, and those directly connected with the operating department, unless holding the position of foremen in charge of some department or section of a department, are paid by the hour or day, and receive nothing while not actually at work or on duty.

Street railroading has' hardly begun to attain its maximum. Its rapid increase, and its necessity, make it a great commercial institution, presenting splendid opportunities for young men.

From a clerical point of view the street railway offers little or nothing more than is presented by the mercantile house; but in the operating department are positions of more than ordinary opportunity.

The business is a growing one, and is growing rapidly; and any growing business, provided its growth is healthy, invariably possesses opportunities far in excess of those offered by any business or trade at a standstill or progressing moderately.

In the actual working of the road is the chance of

advancement. The motorman is reasonably sure of a position; and although his hours are long and his work tedious, he is not likely to be out of work, except through fault of his own.

Many of our best street railroad officials began as motormen or conductors, and worked up to their present positions.

While it is obvious that not one motorman or conductor in a hundred is likely to rise above his present position, because the number of better positions is limited, and because the average motorman and conductor, like the average man in every other calling, is of little capacity and of not much more than ordinary ambition, the fault, in most cases, lies with the man himself and not with his position or opportunities.

The man of ability and of character, who knows himself and has himself well in hand, will not indefinitely remain a motorman or a conductor. Sooner or later he will be at the head of a department or an official on the line.

I would advise the would-be street railroader to begin in the operating department, or to do some of the actual running work of the road, that he may understand the action of the road from every side save the purely clerical side. Emphatically would I advise him to obtain, if possible, a broad technical education at some institute of technology or other training-school. Fortified with this school-training, a training which he cannot possibly obtain in the same length of time from actual experience, he will, in the end, all things being equal, outstrip the boy who began with no other education than that obtained at the common school.

Of course I am well aware that the capable boy, without the technical education, will win against the boy of less capacity with a sound school-education; but this is not an argument against a technical school-training, which I consider the greatest investment a boy can make.

This technical education not only trains and disciplines his mind, but gives him an understanding of the fundamental principles of mechanics necessary to the quick and profitable handling of mechanical conditions.

While it is true that the boy can learn these things, or most of them, while on the road and in actual work, he cannot learn them so readily, or so quickly, or so well, as he will if he is trained to learn them in an institution, whose prime object is not only to teach facts, but to teach how to learn, to observe, to absorb, and to use the information needed for one's best development. I believe that, in every mechanical business, including that of the street railway, the two, three, and four years in a technical school will contribute, in the end, more to one's success than can double this number of years in actual working experience apart from the training-school.

Street railroading is certainly worthy of the boy's attention and his investigation. The work in every department, save of the clerical, is much harder than in a mercantile business. The hours are longer, and there is much exposure to weather; but no boy of character will ever refuse to enter a business solely because of the difficulties of the work chosen, provided he has the physical and mental strength to withstand the strain.

I would not advise any boy who has not a mechanical bent to consider street railroading as a business unless his ambition goes no further than the position of motorman or the clerical side of the road. Without more than ordinary mechanical ability, he will find it difficult to rise from the ranks.

The operating department of a street railway requires a combination of mechanical and business ability — mechanical ability, that one may understand the actual working side; business ability, that one may be able to profitably utilize his mechanical capacity, — and, further, the successful street railroader and operator must be a disciplinarian, be able successfully to manage men, and to meet quickly, and yet with sound judgment, the emergencies which are continually rising and which usually come without warning.

The street railway man, like the steam railway man, is said never to sleep. He is a servant of activity and is always in motion. This business is one which the lazy boy, and the boy without ambition, will do well to avoid.

Mr. Herbert H. Vreeland, president of the New York City Street Railway Company, in a letter to the author, says:

"It has long been my opinion that most of the advice given by men of achieved careers to young people about how to start in life has been wasted. It has been addressed to the wrong party. Advice of this kind should be adressed to the guardians and not to the wards.

"Young men are without the experience necessary to estimate accurately either their capacities or their tendencies. An intelligent estimate of both, however, can be made by an observing, enlightened parent or guardian. To them, therefore, this advice is addressed concerning the choice of street railroading.

"It goes without saying, that no youth, with strong literary and academical tendencies, should be urged to this course. Such youths usually lack the physical, as well as the mental, temperament to make a success of it. The last thing this business tolerates is theorizing.

"Its very basis is the ponderable and obvious, and it requires, for its successful prosecution, one whose temperament delights in the handling and adjustment of mechanical means and the solution of problems that arise out of physical conditions.

"If the youth under your charge shows an aptitude and inclination for practical work, if he wants to handle things and displays an aptitude for making easy exit from his besetment, he is indicated as a developable street railroader.

"The work in a career of this kind is forever changing. Nothing remains settled. What you plan to-day, for the use of all time, is made obsolete to-morrow by a new invention, the completion of a new public work, such as a bridge, a tunnel, a terminal, or a highway. Where the crowds swarmed yesterday, and clamored for accommodation, is now a deserted square, and the quiet byway of yesterday is invaded by an army of men and women seeking means to get elsewhere.

"You must adjust what means you have to meet these sudden tidal changes with economy and effectiveness, and such a boy as I have indicated gives promise of being the man for such emergencies."

Mr. T. E. Mitten, first vice-president of the Chicago City Railway Company, in a letter to the author, says:

"I might say that 'Street Railroading' means more and has a much wider scope than formerly. This, on account of the adoption of electricity as the motive power and the subsequent building of high-speed long-distance interurban lines in connection therewith·

"The methods in vogue with steam railroads are closely followed by the electric street and interurban railroads, so that perhaps the qualifications necessary for a successful steam railroad man are also applicable to the street railroad man.

"To answer literally the query, 'Why would you advise a boy to take up street railroading as a means of livelihood?' is a difficult matter. As in other fields, there are arguments for and against it. I will say, however, that a boy entering the railroad field may eventually reach a very high and influential position and be of great benefit to the community at large.

"The essential qualifications for a successful railroad career are, perhaps, the same as for any other; namely, good health, a willingness to work hard, with, of course, some natural ability.

"I would advise the boy who considers seriously taking up the work, to start at the bottom and to learn the business in all its many branches in a thorough and practical manner.

"It is the practical man who is wanted at the top to-day. There are thousands of capable office men, but the number of really capable practical men is in the minority.

"Learning the business in the practical way may not be so pleasant as office work. At first the work would be hard, the hours long, and the pay small; but unquestionably this is the proper way to begin."

THE TEACHER

IF the good of a thing is to be reckoned by what it does or may accomplish, then the profession of teaching is the most honorable, the most responsible, and the most indispensable of all human callings.

The clergyman is a teacher, and so is the lecturer, the philanthropist, the reformer; and so are also all kinds and classes of men and women who distribute knowledge. But the teacher, technically considered, is one who makes a profession of teaching as a means of livelihood, and who usually performs his duties within the school or other institution of learning.

Probably ninety per cent of our teachers, college professors excepted, are women. The reason for this is obvious. Comparatively few teachers receive more than a moderate income; and men, with present or prospective families to support, shun any calling which offers limited remuneration.

The strength of the nation is more in its schools than in the homes of its people. The influence of the teacher has more to do with the progress of civilization, with the building up of character, than has any other factor in our country. I am placing the home as it is beside the school as it is, comparing the two as they present themselves,— not through sentiment, not through prejudice, not through the suggestion of preference, but through their actual conditions when seen under the searchlight of truth. And I am convinced that the school of to-day is a greater factor in the development of the young than is the present home, and most of our boys and girls owe more to the school than to parents or any other influence.

The child's first view of real life is in the schoolroom. At school he begins to realize what there is in the world, what has been, and what probably will be. In the home there is rarely opportunity for the child to see what living really means. It is the teacher who introduces the child to life, who brings him into contact with the vital forces and principles of living.

The germ of the child's education is first developed in the school. There he first realizes what he is and what his relations to others are. Whether or not this awakening should have begun in the home, it is not the province of this chapter to discuss. It is a fact, and no student of human nature and of live conditions will take exception to it, that the school has a stronger influence and brings more pressure to bear upon the child than the child's home or anything else that the child comes in contact with.

The school is composite. The teacher represents, with some degree of correctness, the great standard principles of life.

The teacher is educated and trained for his work. He is a part of a great, long-established, and organized educational body, a reflector and distributer of a planned and accepted policy.

The parent is an individual. He is seldom trained to perform the duties of parentage. He brings up his child as he will, subject to no rule but his conceit, his knowledge, whether great or small, and the few laws of the state which aim to protect the child, but which rarely invade his home castle.

The parent is virtually in complete control of his child. So long as he does not appear to violate the law, he may do as he pleases with his offspring. He may give it advantages or disadvantages. He may properly nourish it or slowly starve it.

A law of conventional custom has magnified parental rights, and has given to the parent powers which no individual has a right to assume and exercise over another, and of which no parent, fitted to be a parent, ever takes advantage of.

But as the majority of human beings are selfish, conceited, or ignorant, and, voluntarily or involuntarily, are without discipline or training, the average parent is frequently incompetent intelligently to manage or raise his children; and the exercise of this legal prerogative is one of the stumbling-blocks in the progress of civilization.

The teacher, whether or not he is more efficient than the parent, is not allowed to follow his own ideas. He must, of necessity, teach the child as the great universal board of education elects.

The teacher is an agent of a system, of an imperfect system, but one as perfect as present conditions may permit, and which is the outgrowth of the best thought on the subject by the most eminent educators of present and previous generations. Because he is the servant of that system, the teacher obeys its commands, although he may at times diverge from them.

Neither the individual parent nor the composite teacher is perfect; but an organization of imperfection, striving for perfection, is far greater, far grander, far more proficient, and far safer, than individual ignorance at a standstill.

Unfortunately, many teachers do not realize the height, depth, length, and breadth of their eternal responsibility, for their responsibility is everlasting.

Few teachers receive from the parent the co-operation and support they deserve, that aid which would be of incalculable benefit to them. On the contrary, many a parent at home, from wilfulness, conceit, or ignorance, counteracts the work of the school.

The teacher and parent not only should be friends, but they should be collaborators, working together for the benefit of the rising generation, the one in the school and the other in the home; and there should not be, and there could not be if we were civilized, that strong dividing line between the home and the school.

I would magnify the teacher's position. I would place him upon a pedestal as high as any other erected to human endeavor.

From a financial point of view, teaching can hardly be considered a remunerative profession. Comparatively few teachers earn more than a living; a lesser number obtain a competency; and none of them, unless they are owners of institutions, ever become rich from the harvest of their planting.

College presidents occasionally draw salaries of ten thousand dollars, but the average salary is not in excess of four thousand dollars a year, and many presidents receive less than three thousand dollars.

College professors and instructors are seldom paid more than four thousand dollars a year, and the average salary is much less than twenty-five hundred dollars, not a few receiving as small a sum as a thousand dollars.

Proprietors of some private schools, which cater to the wealthy, have large incomes and pay good salaries to their instructors; but as a class, the principals of academies and seminaries receive less than three thousand dollars a year, and some of them do not net much more than one-half of this sum.

Principals or head-masters of high and Latin schools, in the large cities, are paid from thirty-five hundred to four thousand dollars a year, a very few receiving as much as five thousand dollars. Masters in high and Latin schools, in large cities, receive from twenty-five hundred to three thousand dollars a year. Ordinary high and Latin school teachers, in our large cities, of the grades below the master, receive anywhere from eighteen hundred to twenty-five hundred dollars a year. Head-masters or principals of grammar schools seldom earn more than thirty-five hundred dollars a year, the average being about twenty-five hundred dollars.

Masters in grammar schools, located in large cities, are paid from one thousand to twenty-three hundred dollars a year. Ordinary teachers in these grammar schools, who hold positions below the master, receive salaries ranging between eight hundred and twelve hundred dollars a year.

Principals or head-masters of high schools, in cities with populations of from fifty thousand to one hundred and fifty thousand, are paid from twenty-five hundred to three thousand dollars a year; masters, from two

thousand to twenty-five hundred dollars; ordinary
teachers, from seven hundred to twelve hundred dollars.
The head-masters of grammar schools receive from
eighteen hundred to twenty-five hundred dollars; masters, from one thousand to sixteen hundred dollars, and
ordinary teachers from six hundred to seven hundred
and fifty dollars.

Principals or head-masters of high schools, in cities
having a population of less than fifty thousand, are paid
from eighteen hundred to twenty-five hundred dollars;
masters, from twelve hundred to two thousand dollars;
and ordinary teachers from six hundred to seven hundred dollars a year. In such a city the principals or
head-masters of grammar schools receive from fifteen
hundred to eighteen hundred dollars a year, and ordinary teachers from four hundred and fifty to seven
hundred dollars.

Head-masters or principals of high schools, in towns
of less than ten thousand inhabitants, seldom earn in
excess of twelve hundred dollars a year, the minimum
being about one thousand dollars. Masters, who are
usually women, are paid from five hundred to seven
hundred dollars a year, and ordinary teachers from five
hundred to six hundred dollars. Head-masters or
principals of grammar schools, in towns of this size,
receive from six hundred to a thousand dollars a year,
and ordinary teachers from five hundred to five hundred
and fifty dollars.

In towns of less than five thousand population, the
principal or head-master of a high school is paid about
eight hundred dollars, ordinary high school teachers
receiving about six hundred dollars a year. Head-
masters or principals of grammar schools, in towns of
this size, generally women, earn from five hundred to

CHARLES W. ELIOT

Foremost educator and for 40 years president of Harvard University; born
in Boston, 1834; graduate Harvard College, 1853; assistant professor of
mathematics and chemistry, Lawrence Scientific School, Harvard, 1858–
63; studied abroad, 1863–5; professor analytical chemistry, Massachusetts Institute Technology, 1865–9; made president Harvard University
in 1869, and retired with honor in 1909

seven hundred dollars, and ordinary teachers receive about four hundred dollars a year.

Teachers in small country towns are seldom paid more than four hundred dollars a year, the average salary being about three hundred.

Music teachers in our large city public schools are paid from five hundred to thirty-five hundred dollars, the average being about fifteen hundred dollars. Drawing teachers earn, on an average, fifteen hundred dollars a year, with a minimum of five hundred dollars and a maximum of thirty-five hundred dollars. Teachers of chemistry in the public schools in the largest cities receive from five hundred to twenty-five hundred dollars, the average being somewhat less than fifteen hundred dollars.

Superintendents of schools receive anywhere from three thousand to six thousand dollars a year in the large cities and towns, but as little as five hundred dollars in the smaller places. The custom of uniting several districts or towns under one superintendent makes it possible for him to receive a salary much in excess of what he could hope to obtain from any one town or district.

So-called "room-teachers" in large city schools, these positions being occupied almost entirely by women, receive from five hundred to fifteen hundred dollars a year; and less in country centres. Many a country school-teacher is paid but a few hundred dollars a year for her work.

New York City pays its public school-teachers higher salaries than are enjoyed by any other teachers in the world; Boston and Philadelphia come next. California and Nevada have the distinction of better remunerating their country teachers than other states.

Massachusetts, Pennsylvania, and Indiana follow California and Nevada.

Possibly one educational worker in five hundred, in schools and colleges, gets more than three thousand dollars a year; one in five hundred of the remainder more than twenty-five hundred dollars; one in five hundred of the remainder more than two thousand dollars; one in five hundred of the remainder more than fifteen hundred dollars; and probably four hundred of every five hundred receive less than four hundred dollars; three hundred of every five hundred get less than three hundred dollars a year; and two hundred less than two hundred dollars.

Some teachers, particularly the instructors in the higher branches, are authors of text-books, the sale of which often materially adds to their incomes.

The good teacher is reasonably sure of a living, provided he does not carry too heavy expenses; but the profession does not offer financial prizes.

No money-worshipper wants to teach, and it is a very good thing that he does not, for such a person would not be sufficiently broad-minded or able to instruct properly the young or anybody else.

The profession of educator or teacher is filled with the noblest class of men and women, those of the highest aspirations, seekers for the truest success, and possessors of genuine high character, with the unselfish and loving spirit of the missionary,—for what cause is grander or nobler than that of forming character? The teacher is honored and respected, but he does not receive half the honor, respect, or remuneration that he deserves.

The profession should be recognized more than it is. It should be publicly lifted to a higher plane. It should be given greater opportunity to perfect itself.

Every effort ought to be made by the nation, state, city, and town to bar from its ranks those who are unfitted to impart knowledge.

Learning does not make a teacher, nor does adaptability without learning give him the right to teach. No one should teach, no one should be allowed to teach, who does not possess the right combination of ability, adaptability, and actual knowledge.

Our national policy, not the individual, is to blame for the large number of incompetent teachers. We cannot get the right kind of teachers, and we cannot expect such to remain in the profession, until we offer them more remuneration and opportunity than we are now giving them.

The teacher is certainly worthy of his hire, and nothing but an imperfect civilization allows him to suffer for the comforts of life.

Unless we offer the proficient teacher somewhere near what he deserves, we shall never raise the grade of teachers, nor shall we be able to place in the teacher's chair many of our ablest and best men, who, instead of teaching, enter other professions which offer more in the way of fame and fortune.

To-day there is little demand for the male teacher who is not a graduate of a college or some other high institution of learning; and comparatively few school boards, even in the country districts, will engage any woman teacher who has not passed through a seminary, or a college, or a normal school, or at least a high school.

The male teacher is seriously handicapped if he is not a college graduate. He may rise to the top without this education, but the chances are against more than ordinary advancement.

An education at an institute of technology or other high-grade technical school is essential to the rapid rising of any one who would teach the sciences.

But let me say here, that all this learning in itself, no matter how carefully obtained, is substantially worthless without that ability and adaptability which allow the teacher to impart to others.

The book-worm seldom makes a good teacher. He may become a learned professor, and, in a way, be fitted to teach teachers; but he is not likely to be of any use as an all-around instructor.

One criticism against teachers, which unfortunately is true to a certain extent, is that they, like clergymen, confine themselves to theory more than to practice. They are likely to consider learning, and the theory of learning, of more importance than the actual application of it. Consequently, many of our teachers who live outside of the world of their pupils do not render to their scholars half the helpfulness which they are capable of giving, and would give, if they only realized that no one can teach effectively those whom he does not understand. The great teacher almost invariably springs from the hard-working, thoughtful student at school, who may or may not be at the head of his class.

Comparatively few boys at the foot of their class ever become good teachers or teachers at all. The boy who has not ambition enough to get above the foot of his class generally has not enough ambition to make much of himself. Yet some of our best teachers were not star students, simply because they did not study for the sake of the class-rank, but strove to obtain only what they could properly utilize.

It is a fact, that, while those who graduate with the highest rank are seldom failures in life, our greatest men, whether educators or not, are those whose class rank was somewhere in the upper half. These men considered the school a practical institution, something from which they must obtain something; therefore, class rank was of little consequence to them. They strove to get out of the school all that they could utilize, and they did, irrespective of their rank or position in the class.

Our best teachers were real boys, who played when they played with all their hearts; who studied when they studied with all their minds; who possessed, even at an early age, the power of imparting their knowledge to others. At school they were known as "helpers." They had the faculty of "coaching" their fellow-students. They began to teach while they were being taught.

The natural teacher cannot help distributing his knowledge to others. He teaches whether he is in school or out of school. He has not only the faculty of absorption, but the power of distribution. The one is worthless without the other.

The boy who cannot reason, and who cannot distribute what he learns, even though he may be a close student and letter-perfect at school, is unfitted to teach, and can never make any kind of success. The boy competent to teach, and who will probably become a proficient teacher, wants to be a teacher, and wants to teach long before he finishes his common school. At an early age he shows an ability to instruct others, to teach his schoolmates; to absorb, and to impart. This boy never considers teaching as a makeshift, unless it may be as a means of earning money to pay his college expenses. When he decides to become a teacher, he does so with his whole heart, and dedicates himself to his work.

No boy who did not want to be a teacher ever succeeded as a teacher. No boy who was not a fair scholar
at school ever became fit to teach, barring exceptions
too few to be considered. No boy who did not, and
could not, instruct his fellow schoolmates ever made a
good teacher, even under favorable conditions.

In the first place, the boy fitted for teaching must
want to teach. He must have an education, and a long
and thorough school-training, that his mind may become
properly disciplined; and, above all, he must have that
peculiar power, without which no one can successfully
teach, — that of knowing how to distribute what he has
received.

Albert E. Winship, Litt.D., editor of the *Journal of
Education*, author and lecturer, in a letter to the author,
says:

" Teaching can be attractive to a man capable of success
in some other occupation, trade, profession, office, or calling,
only when he has a mission to or a message for young
people. To such there is no other field in which his life can
be so completely given to the unfolding and developing of
the mind and character as in teaching. The position is
ordinarily secure for life; it provides a good living; it
makes no outside demands upon his time; does not intrude
upon his home life; leaves him free to do the utmost in his
power for his students.

" Teaching is a noble, uplifting, glorious life for the one
who accepts it as a mission to young people.

" Teaching offers no opportunity to a young man to do
more than make a good living out of his life work. It removes him from the field of political activity; it places
limitations upon his social privileges; it confines his thought
and energies largely to immature minds; it tends to magnify

unduly the minor details of knowing and doing ; it lacks the
stimulus that comes to most professions.

"Unless one appreciates his mission to young people,
teaching may be irksome, vexatious, tedious, and belittling."

Mr. Stratton D. Brooks, superintendent of the Boston
public schools, in a letter to the author, says:

"There are several reasons why teaching as a life work
offers few attractions for young men of high ability.

" 1. Even the highest compensation is scarcely sufficient
to enable a man to live as one in his position is expected
to live.

" 2. Promotions, except in large cities and universities,
can be secured only by moving from place to place ; this
prevents the building of a home, the establishing of life-long
friendships, and the growth of a feeling of permanency of
position and influence in community life. On the other
hand, in the large cities and universities, the rate of promotion is so slow that the number of men who can hope for
better positions is very small and the period of waiting is
very long.

" 3. The time required for preparation for higher positions in the teaching profession is as long, and frequently
longer, than that required in other professions.

" 4. In most professions the compensation increases with
years of experience. The competent lawyer or doctor cannot
be driven from his position by any mere caprice or public
whim. With a teacher, however, it is quite otherwise.
Because he works for the public, his position is always
semi-political and subject more or less to local political and
religious influences, and even the ablest are liable to be
asked to resign. When this resignation comes after a
teacher is fifty years of age, there is small chance of his
securing another position, and the teacher is compelled to
seek employment in some other business.

" 5. The business of school-teaching is passing rapidly into the hands of women ; even the higher positions are now being held by them. If the present trend continues, school-teaching as a business for men will almost cease to exist.

" 6. The same amount of preparation, the same ability in scholastic or executive lines, the same industry and application, will bring vastly higher results in a financial way than can be expected from teaching.

" These and many minor drawbacks are sufficient to cause a young man, even though possessed of the missionary spirit and high ideals of public service, to hesitate before setting himself seriously to preparation for teaching as a life work."

Professor J. M. Green, principal of the New Jersey State Normal and Model Schools, in a letter to the author, says:

" The principal advantages to teaching as a profession for the young man seem to me to be :

" First, that pleasure which comes from the dissemination of truth. While this reward may at first seem rather visionary, it will appear upon second consideration to be very real. Throughout all the ages nearly every one has devoted some time to this purpose, great numbers have fully devoted their time to it, while many have given their lives for this end alone. There must, therefore, be in it a very gratifying return.

" Secondly, teaching opens the way to the extended pursuit of knowledge and investigation.

" Thirdly, it gives an opportunity for a very fine class of writings.

" Fourthly, it is a calling in which efficiency always commands respect.

" The disadvantages of teaching are :

" The work is not sufficiently remunerative to permit of

any considerable accumulation of wealth. The teacher must, therefore, from the first, be limited to a very modest mode of life. He cannot provide himself with an elaborate home, surrounded by beautiful lawns and furnished with costly libraries and choice works of art, nor can he travel extensively.

" While he may enjoy a high degree of respect, his social circle is more or less limited by the lack of means.

" He is practically shut out from any large participation in the affairs of public life.

" While teaching has been a stepping-stone to many positions of prominence in state and nation, it does not merge directly into these positions, as does law, medicine, engineering, architecture, and a number of the other callings."

THE STOREKEEPER

ECHNICALLY the terms "storekeeper" and "merchant" are analogous, but commercially and practically speaking they are somewhat different. In trade, the wholesaler and great retailer are commonly known as merchants, while the owner or keeper of a retail store of moderate size, located either in the large city, in the small city, or in the country town or village, is commonly known as a storekeeper.

The storekeeper's business is not extensive. When it becomes extensive, he is known as a merchant. As his trade is local, and comparatively small in volume, he is naturally his own buyer and manager. In fact, he is about everything in the store except the clerk, and he frequently adds a clerk's duties to his own.

The successful storekeeper must be a natural trader and a master of detail, even though he may not be competent to handle large propositions. If he does not possess native shrewdness, he will buy against the market and pay more than he receives. He is virtually a trader, a direct buyer, and a direct seller, who meets face to face both the man who makes the goods for him or sells them to him and the man to whom he sells the goods.

There are few callings more certain than that of the storekeeper. If he understands the fundamental principles of business, is shrewd, a good buyer, economical personally and in business, he is almost certain of a livelihood, and is reasonably exempt from failure, provided he is satisfied with a moderate income and does not overspread in business or in living.

Most of the storekeeping failures are due to marked inability, extravagance, carelessness, inattention, or an attempt to do a larger business than the field warrants.

Almost any boy of average ability and of good habits, who is willing to work, and is reasonably cautious, can become a successful storekeeper.

The storekeeper almost always begins at the bottom. He was a boy before he was a salesman, and from salesman he became head-clerk or head-salesman, and from that he jumped into proprietorship, as partner in, or owner of, the store he worked for, or of a store he purchased or established.

The storekeeper should be an all-around man. He can use a knowledge of bookkeeping, although he need not be a professional bookkeeper. He should understand buying as well as selling, and it is absolutely necessary that he know how to meet his customers. He should, above all, be a good calculator and be able to financier for the future.

The boy best fitted to be a good storekeeper shows, even at an early age, a natural trading propensity. The sharp boy is likely to fail. No matter how much dishonesty pays, or seems to pay, in general business, it is absolutely essential that the storekeeper be at least reasonably honest. The customer he makes to-day is the customer he has to-morrow. The bulk of his trade is permanent and not transient.

Sharp practice of any kind, although it may pay under certain large city conditions, is sure to be fatal to the success of local storekeeping.

The storekeeper comes in direct contact with most of his customers. He knows them socially as well as in a business way. His personality counts as much as does his store. He is therefore a part of the goods he sells, and he must keep himself, as well as his goods, in good condition.

Success in local trading is based upon the fundamental principles of honesty. The successful trader gives value for value; that is, he sells something that is worth more to somebody else than it is worth to him, for a proper consideration. If the boy successfully trades a jackknife for a kite, he really sells a jackknife which is worth more to the owner of the kite than to himself, and the kite is worth more to him than to the other boy. The trade is an equitable "swap," each party being the gainer, each party receiving something he wants by giving for it something which he does not want as much as he wants what he receives.

Success in local store-trading does not consist in getting the better of the other fellow, but in making a mutual exchange. The boy who gets the better of his fellows every time he trades will not be a successful storekeeper, but may make a success somewhere else, because it cannot be denied that sharp practice sometimes pays financially, and produces, for the one who understands its manipulation, financial success; but mark you, it brings only financial success, for no success other than the success of honesty is real. The owner of all the financial success in the world, if it is not the result of honesty, has the quantity and not the quality of success, and will, when he realizes his condition, envy the bootblack who honestly earns his living.

In this chapter, however, I am attempting to give the reader the facts about leading trades, businesses, and professions, and to handle these facts without gloves. I do not propose to deny that dishonesty, provided it keeps within the law, often succeeds financially, but it never made a successful man; for although he may count his wealth by millions, he is not worthy of the name of man unless he obtained honestly what he has.

The successful storekeeper develops from the natural boy-trader. This boy instinctively puts a value upon everything he has, and when he gets something which he does not particularly want, he looks around for an opportunity to legitimately get rid of it. He is continually trading, and is satisfied with a reasonable profit. He is in the stores more or less, not as a loafer, but as a watcher. He instinctively appraises everything, that is, he seems to have set a value of his own on almost everything he sees.

While many a successful storekeeper has not shown these characteristics as a boy, the chances are that he expressed a distinct preference for storekeeping when finishing school and ready for work.

If a boy exhibits trading instincts more than he shows any other characteristics, opportunity should be given him for their development. He should be allowed to buy his own clothes and other things, or to have a voice in their purchase, long before he is out of his teens. Responsibility should be thrown upon him, so that he may come in contact with trading in general. But let me say here, that there is no good reason why responsibility should not be placed upon every boy worthy of confidence, whether he is going to be a storekeeper or not.

A common school education is essential, and the boy should graduate from a high school if possible.

A college education will do no harm. Such a training is likely to do him lasting good, but it can hardly be considered necessary.

The storekeeper is not likely to become a rich man, but he is reasonably sure of a comfortable living, and probably the average storekeeper is better off than is the average merchant or manufacturer, who, with all his wealth, is living over a mine of uncertainty.

Many of our great merchants began as storekeepers.

Storekeeping is often the stepping-stone to greater things.

The storekeeper lives a contented life at the minimum of worry.

While I would not advise one to curb his ambition and to permanently let well-enough alone, because ambition is necessary even in the most conservative walks of life, I would suggest that the ambitious storekeeper, who has definite plans for becoming a great merchant, and who is working to this end, pause, and continue to pause, until he receives positive evidence that a rise commercially is worth the price he must pay for it.

Financial success is not so much a question of income as it is the difference between income and expenditure.

The storekeeper in a progressive country centre, earning a few thousand dollars a year, is often far better off, financially, than is the proprietor of a great city establishment.

This rush to be great, particularly to be financially great, is injuring the world more than we realize.

Mere financial ambition is not born of the best that is in man.

A desire to do well, and to live comfortably, is to be encouraged; but this struggle to reach beyond the line of comfort, and to be master of more wealth than any one can intelligently handle, is detrimental to the spirit of progress.

A man's business should not be his chief end in life. It should simply be a means to an end. He must work, and he must work to live, but when he has realized a reasonably permanent and comfortable income, it is time for him to be of some service to his community. He can become a far greater man, socially and in every other way, by having an ambition outside of trade, than he can by the exclusive acquirement of wealth.

The world never forgets the good citizen. The world immediately forgets the man of money only. Go through our "Who's Who in America," and other books of men of mark, and not one-tenth of one per cent of those registered as worthy of having their names printed there are men who are known for their money.

Storekeeping should be encouraged. We need more small stores and fewer big ones. We need more men in business for themselves and masters of themselves. We need fewer salaried men and wage-earners, and more men who, although at the head of their business, do a part of the active work themselves.

I do not believe there is any other calling so good and so beneficial to the people at large as plain, every-day storekeeping, chiefly because it gives broad opportunity to ordinary men, and ordinary men are in the vast majority.

The calling of the storekeeper, then, is along the lines of progression; and I would advise every boy, whether he be of the city or of the country, who does not have a pronounced love and a recognizable ability for some professional calling, seriously to consider becoming a storekeeper and adding himself to the ranks of common responsibility and respectability.

Mr. Humphrey O'Sullivan, proprietor of the Merrimack Clothing Company, member of the firm of O'Sullivan Brothers, and treasurer of the O'Sullivan Rubber Heel Company, of Lowell, Mass., in a letter to the author, says:

"You ask me to designate the traits of character in a young man that would prophesy success for him in the retail business.

"First and foremost, it all depends upon the young man himself. The ideal young man for such a career is one who is born to succeed, who reads, and believes that nothing can prevent him from attaining success. His motto is success, not money, — that comes of necessity, and is a secondary consideration. Such a man you cannot hinder.

"Given an average education, not necessarily an academic one, he will do any kind of menial work, perform it well, and bide his time. He will be patient. Seeing the stream of affairs flowing in the wrong direction, he will still be patient, set his teeth, and say within himself, 'Some day I will change the current of that stream.' When that day comes he needs a big amount of practical information, an humble spirit, and a level head, because then, for the first time, he really begins his difficulty.

"A young man may inherit wealth and education, possibly a business. If I were he, and wished to succeed, I would first get in touch with the smallest details of the business, and work up to the office, if I deserved it; and after I had worked in the office, I would wait until the cleverest man in the business was unable to attend to some particular duty. Then I would happen to get beside it, do it so much more satisfactorily to the firm, and do it unostentatiously; then relegate myself back to my ordinary seat in the background.

"In the course of time, the young man who could thus act in an emergency would be required to do it again. The next time he would perform the duties as satisfactorily as before, or more so; and again he would retire to his place as a subordinate. But when an opportunity of that kind occurred again, he would undoubtedly be given an appointment to take charge of the position.

"This is simply a case of keeping yourself in the background, and performing your duties so conscientiously and so successfully that the firm who employed you, for their own protection and for their own benefit, will give you preference.

"The next proposition that appears to my mind is that of the young man who falls into active business by inheritance. I pity him, whatever his education, whatever his ambition; the fact of preferment places him at a disadvantage; he has prejudices to overcome; he has precedence to make good. Unless he is guarded and prepared with indomitable courage he will fumble and shirk the responsibility.

"I have seen success offered to such young men, assured success (I am talking actual facts, not momentary obligations), and they have simply shrunk before the magnitude of the enterprise, because they had not within themselves resourcefulness.

"What shall I do with my boy? First give him an ordinary common school education. Do not deprive him of a high school course, but before he is through with that, we can determine of what mettle he is made. All that is needed to-day in business is a knowledge of a few things that are taught in the high school and in polite society, an even temper, courteousness under all provocation, a thorough knowledge of commercialism, bookkeeping, arithmetic, and grammar. History is a good auxiliary; the knowledge of the languages, poetry, and music, while they are not necessary, sometimes come in very handy.

" Give me a young man who is a good judge of human nature, with a high school education and a determination to be a leader, and ultimately I will show you the young man who will be a success in the retail, wholesale, manufacturing, or financial world. It does not make any difference to what field he devotes his energy, except politics, and if you ask me to pass my opinion on politics — I simply do not know anything about it."

Messrs. Augustus and Horace Bacon, members of the firm of W. and A. Bacon, of Boston, in a letter to the author, say:

" The storekeeper has before him a larger and broader field than is offered by any other calling. His training from boy to proprietor is a broad education. His acquaintances are in every walk of life, and his influence grows every year. Next to the judge and minister his advice is most sought. He is a real power in the community. The rich man comes to him about investments, the poor woman to ask if the bank is all right or if her interest is correctly calculated; the young man and young woman also consult him.

" It is easy to understand from this why the storekeeper seldom makes a failure. Statistics show that the fewest failures are among them.

" The successful storekeeper often becomes the influential man in some large retail establishment, his early training fitting him for just such an exacting position."

THE JOURNALIST

THE depàrtment of journalism, or what is commonly called newspaper work, is distinct from that of literature.

The newspaper editor or reporter is a writer of transient matter, of something presumably of the life of a day or of a week. His reputation and commercial value are not determined by the quality of any one article or report. He is reckoned by his collective ability, and known for his capacity continually to do one thing well, or for his versatility in all-around work.

The literary man often gains a reputation by the writings between two covers, and many a brilliant literary light has become fixed from the reflections from a single book or from two or three books.

Literature, theoretically at least, is supposed to have long-time value. The higher grade of literature may never die, although the best authors are read more at one time than at another, each literary star being in the ascendant for stated periods. The modern and popular novel, however, representing as it does every grade of literature except the highest, has a life of hardly a year; and its author, unlike the writers of quality, must produce at almost newspaper speed, if he would keep in the public eye. The book author is not a journalist.

Newspaper work, like yeast, is good only during the state of ferment, and the best of it may dry as quickly as the ink that prints it.

There is not a more honorable profession or business than that of journalism.

The newspaper is the mirror of its city or town, and its editors and reporters are truly representatives of the people, and almost invariably of a grade higher than their constituents.

There are wolves in editorial clothing and there are black legs on the newspaper staff the world over, but the men who make the newspaper, unless they represent the over-colored side of journalism, are superior to the majority of their readers.

The filthy sheet, with every column a typographical gutter for the sewerage of sensation, bad as it is, is a peg or two ahead of its support.

While I have no respect for the yellow journal, or for its editors and others connected with it, I do not believe, as many do, that the immoral newspaper contributes much to public immorality.

The newspaper is better than its readers. The reader, more than the editor, is responsible for journalistic degradation. The newspaper is, and in these days cannot often afford to be other than, a business institution. If it were not a business affair, it could not live unless endowed. It must make money or die; therefore, it gives its readers what its readers want. The reader, not the yellow journalist, needs reformation. The good newspaper, and the good newspaper is in the vast majority, is the foundation stone of civilization, upon which is built and kept in repair the monument of progress.

Great editors, if they be owners or part owners of their newspapers, have amassed much wealth; but it must be admitted that the journalistic land is not a field of gold. Still, in these days of warlike competition the man with journalistic instincts stands as good a financial chance in journalism as in any other profession. The good newspaper man is reasonably sure of a living. The poor newspaper man, like any other poor professionalist, will certainly have a hard time of it.

The editor-in-chief, as his name implies, occupies the highest editorial position. He is supposed to have complete control of every department of his newspaper, except the business one. It is for him to decide the policy and to maintain it, to engage and discharge the members of the editorial staff, and to be responsible for everything that appears in the paper outside of the advertisements.

The theoretical power of the editor-in-chief is absolute. Practically, however, only a small proportion of so-called editors-in-chief control the right of policy of their papers, as this is established by the owners, the editor-in-chief being virtually only an employee.

Years ago, great editors were known by name. To-day, editors of fully as much ability as then, and with much broader experience, are seldom recognized outside of their own circle. They are the important parts of a great machine; in fact, they are the spring of the journalistic watch, and, like the spring, make the watch go as the maker designed that it should.

The editors-in-chief of newspapers in large cities

draw salaries of from three thousand to ten thousand
dollars a year, and a few are paid twice as much; but
the twenty-thousand-dollar men can be numbered on
the fingers of one hand with the thumb left out.

Probably the average salary of the large city editor-
in-chief is not far from five thousand dollars. The
editor-in-chief may or may not actually do editorial
writing; but most of these editors write some of the
editorials known as leaders; in fact, I think that the
majority intend to produce not far from a column
a day.

In salary the managing editor is next to the editor-
in-chief. He may or may not be a good editorial writer.
The chances are that he is not. He is the executive
officer, and, under the editor-in-chief, actively carries
out the policy of the paper. To an extent he is a
superintendent, assuming the responsibility for the
newspaper's active work. Managing editors receive
annual salaries of from ten to twenty-five per cent
less than those paid to the editors-in-chief. Comparatively few managing editors on large city newspapers
draw less than two thousand dollars a year, and very
few, if any, reach the ten-thousand-dollar mark. The
average yearly salary paid by a first-class daily to its
managing editor is probably in the vicinity of four
thousand dollars.

Editorial writers are those who do the bulk of the
editorial work of the paper, and who write all the
editorials except those furnished by the editor-in-chief
himself. A large city newspaper employs anywhere
from two to a dozen such writers, who are graded
according to their capacity and responsibility. The
head editorial writer composes the leaders not written
by the editor-in-chief, and the other writers prepare

the rest. Some editorial writers do their work at home, giving only a part of their time to the newspaper. These are paid by a salary, or by the column.

It is quite common nowadays for a great daily newspaper to have a number of editors-at-large, each a specialist in some one department. These writers are usually paid by the piece, although some of them draw salaries. When a matter of any special importance, requiring expert opinion, comes up, the editor familiar with that kind of work is ordered to prepare an editorial, which he does in the time allotted.

Editorial writers in large cities may hope to draw salaries of from fifteen hundred to five thousand dollars a year. Probably few ever receive more than six thousand dollars. Special editorial writers, who give but a part of their day to the newspaper, if they do not work at space rates or by the column, draw stated salaries of from two hundred and fifty to two thousand dollars a year, the average probably not exceeding seven or eight hundred dollars.

The city editor has charge of the local reporters. He is responsible for obtaining the city news. He may or may not be a good writer. Most city editors, however, are fluent writers, and are graduates from the reportorial ranks. The city editor must understand men and things, so that he may know how to use them to the best advantage. He must also hold a finger upon the public pulse, that he may give the readers what they want in the way of local happenings. The city editors of large papers receive anywhere from fifteen hundred to four thousand dollars a year, a few salaries reaching five thousand dollars. The average city editor of a great newspaper earns not far from twenty-five hundred dollars a year.

Telegraph editors are editors or readers of telegraphic copy. The telegraphic news passes through their hands, and is edited or rewritten by them. They are responsible for the headings of such matter in the newspapers, and the writing of these head-lines is really very important work. A telegraph editor of a great paper receives anywhere from one thousand to three thousand dollars a year, the average salary probably not being in excess of two thousand dollars.

The musical and dramatic editors devote their time exclusively to music and the drama. Some papers employ both a musical and a dramatic editor, but usually these duties are combined in one office, one man being responsible for everything dramatic and musical. The dramatic and musical criticisms are supposed to be written by the dramatic or musical editor himself. They are certainly written under his direction; but it is obvious that with a dozen, or several dozen, dramatic openings on a single Monday night, no one person can personally write all of the criticisms. The dramatic and musical editors of large newspapers have one or more assistants, who aid them in attending the prominent openings. The other openings are covered by members of the newspaper staff.

The dramatic or musical editor is a very consequential personage, and his position is growing in importance. The ordinary editorial writer is not fitted for this position. It requires not only a special training, but natural ability in criticising. Any one can find fault, and any one can praise a performance. It takes one of the keenest judgment and of a broad mind to understand what a performance means, to realize the period, the country, and the life depicted, and to properly criticise, weigh, and appreciate a play or other performance. These editors, if on a great newspaper, draw annual salaries of from fifteen hundred to five thousand dollars. Comparatively few receive more than three thousand dollars a year, the average probably not exceeding twenty-five hundred dollars. The dramatic editor may or may not have other connections, and if he does, he has the opportunity to increase his income.

Literary editors are responsible for the book reviews and literary matter. As a rule, they work away from the newspaper office, and most of them do not devote their entire time to any one publication. Their stated salaries run from one thousand to three and four thousand dollars a year, the average being not far from two thousand dollars. Many of them work by the "piece."

Desk-editors are readers and correctors of manuscript of every kind and class. They must, first of all, be good grammarians and users of pure English, and also possess much discretion. On great dailies these men draw salaries of from fifteen hundred to three thousand dollars a year. The small city newspapers, as a rule, do not employ such editors.

The big papers carry a number of other editors or heads of departments, but I have given the principal ones, and the others may be reckoned, so far as income or opportunity is concerned, upon a par with the editorial writers, excepting the sporting editor, who is in most cases a man of large salary. The sporting editor has charge of the sporting events, and personally writes all the important reports, including many of those received by wire. He is paid a salary of from fifteen hundred to five thousand dollars a year, the average being not far from three thousand dollars.

Space-writers, those who write by the column and are

paid for what is printed, receive from four to fifteen dollars a column, eight dollars being the fair average. Comparatively few of these so-called space-writers devote their time to any one publication. They may write for a daily newspaper to-day, for a magazine to-morrow, and fill in their odd time on book work, either in actually writing a book of their own or in reviewing books for the newspapers or magazines. A first-class space-writer has the opportunity of earning not far from three thousand dollars a year, although the average income is much less. A very few may receive in excess of five thousand dollars per annum.

Reporters on great newspapers are paid from ten to one hundred dollars a week, comparatively few earning the higher figure, the average remuneration probably not being in excess of twenty dollars a week, although a first-class, competent reporter may obtain as much as fifty dollars a week. The majority of editors, even editors-in-chief, were originally reporters. In no other way can one so easily obtain the knowledge and practical education necessary for editorial writing. The reporter, at the start and for several years, is virtually a member of a training school. For a while, at least, he probably learns more about men and things than would be possible in any other walk of life. So varied is the reporter's experience, and so much does he come in contact with everything from the highest to the lowest, that I have even suggested that a reportorial training be made a part of the curriculum of the divinity and law schools.

The real journalist never reaches the top by beginning in the editorial room. Before he can tread the quarter-deck of journalism, he must begin before the mast, and master each step as he rises. He must be

trained in the hardest school of knowledge — life itself. He must tramp the streets by day and by night.
He must write, and be able to write well, under the most
exasperating difficulties. He may never know an hour
that is exclusively his own. He is under the editor's
blue pencil, and he must be strong enough to stand
almost daily discouragement.

The city reporter's daily life is hard, and it never
becomes easy. The life of the employees of a great
daily, from the editor-in-chief down to the city editor
and reporter, is strenuous and nerve-wearing, and many
run the pace that kills. Their opportunity for doing
good is almost as broad as the land itself.

It is a pity, indeed, that so many editors, trained to
do the highest and greatest work of civilization, are,
for bread and butter reasons, obliged to die in harness,
when they are needed as leaders in every movement for
the upbuilding of the race.

The country editor is no less an editor than his city
contemporary, yet he lives in an entirely different
atmosphere and works under conditions impossible for
the city. He is the great big toad in the little puddle,
and the prominent man of his locality, with every opportunity for the realization of ordinary ambition.

True, the country editor may not climb to the pinnacle of journalism, but to be at the top of a country
monument is more remunerative, and far more pleasant,
than it is desperately to cling half-way up the shaft of
national fame.

There is nothing happier and surer than the life of a
country editor. His income is small, but so are his
expenses. If he is a decent fellow he is respected, and
nobody in town is too good for him.

The influence of the country press, in its aggregate,

is the greatest power for good which the past has ever seen, which the present has ever experienced, and the future has ever dared to suggest.

The country newspaper has done more for progress, and has pushed civilization farther to the front, than have all other influences for good combined, save that of religion.

The life of a country editor is as close to the ideal as civilization has yet permitted.

The average income of a country editor is from one thousand to fifteen hundred dollars a year. The maximum income of a country editor and proprietor does not exceed six to seven thousand dollars, except in very exceptional cases, and comparatively few go beyond the five thousand dollar mark, but quite a number get from two to three thousand dollars annually, usually with the assistance of the printing office connected with the newspaper.

Most country editors are proprietors, few country newspapers being edited by salaried men.

The country weekly newspaper, as a rule, has but one editor. Usually the bulk of the work is done by the editor himself, or perhaps by his reporter, if he hires one, with the exception of the out-of-town news items, which come from various correspondents, few of whom receive any money for their services.

There is no sharp line drawn between the country weekly newspaper editor and reporter, as they do similar work, the editor doing more editing than reporting, and the reporter more reporting than editing.

During the last fifteen years the country daily newspaper has been very much in evidence, and in many localities has supplanted the weekly paper, but most of these dailies also run weekly editions. Their editors are almost invariably owners of the whole or a part of the paper, and therefore are not salaried men.

Many daily newspapers, outside of the largest cities, are enormously profitable, and the owner of a leading paper in a city which has at least one hundred thousand inhabitants is likely to be one of the richest men of the town. The life of these daily newspaper editors is similar to that of men on the large city dailies, but not so strenuous.

Many of the dailies in large cities have both morning and evening editions, consequently the majority of the men connected with the editorial and reportorial departments work until midnight every day, including Sundays.

In the smaller places, more than one-half of the daily newspapers issue only evening editions, but this does not exempt the editors and reporters from night work, although their night work is very much less than upon exclusively morning papers.

Some of our greatest editors and most capable editorial writers are not found in the larger cities, but confine their labors to the smaller places, where they undoubtedly have more opportunity, and certainly live much happier lives.

Any bright boy with journalistic ability, who starts right and works faithfully, if he sticks to the country, is pretty sure to arrive at the position of country editor or proprietor, and may hope to build up a competency.

The city boy, of the necessary ability, may feel reasonably sure of earning his livelihood on a great daily, but the chances are that his country cousin will be gaining more in the aggregate and have a much happier life than is possible under great city environment.

A good position in society and a comfortable living are almost certain for the country boy of ability who is satisfied with country journalism.

In the great city there is a higher goal to strive for, with very little chance of reaching it; first, because only those of the greatest ability can ever hope to obtain the highest honors; and secondly, because there are altogether too many contestants in the race.

There are many schools of journalism, some of them financially successful, but I very much doubt if any school can properly impart the knowledge necessary for the making of an editor or a reporter. A classical education may or may not be essential to journalistic success, but the college-bred man has a better chance than has the man of only common-school education.

Generally speaking, the more broadly educated a man is, the better equipped he is. The would-be journalist needs all the education he can obtain. If he expects to rise from the ranks, and to be other than an ordinary reporter, he must have a mind filled with general knowledge, he must know both the world of books and the world outside of books, and he cannot know too much about men and things.

A liberal education is the best preparation for journalistic life. It fits one to make better use of the practical things of life.

The country editor should be a printer, — not a theoretical one, but a practical printer, familiar with the whole art and practice of type and press.

Nearly all country newspapers, even those issuing dailies, maintain printing establishments, and comparatively few could exist without the printing office.

From this office the embryo journalist should begin by writing reports of local events, and after he has done

EDWARD W. BOK

Editor Ladies' Home Journal; born Helder, Holland, October 9, 1863;
came to the United States at the age of six; educated in the Brooklyn
public schools; stenographer with the Western Union Telegraph Company; in the employ of the publishing house of Henry Holt & Co., 1884–5;
and Charles Scribner's Sons, 1888; editor of the Ladies' Home Journal
since 1888

so for a year or more, he would better give a part of his time to producing special articles, — a sort of compromise between a report and a story. He should write up some industry, or description of something, or an argumentative article on some special, business, or educational affair, or he should put upon paper his ideas of some needed reform, and at the same time keep up his reporting.

The city journalist need not necessarily understand typesetting and printing, but a knowledge of the "art creative of all arts" will not come amiss, and he is better off if equipped with it. He would better begin by writing reports of local events, and by attempting to produce descriptive articles of things which he thinks will interest the public.

All good reporters do not make good editors, but there are very few good editors who have not been good reporters. It is better to stay in the reportorial ranks too long than to leave the nest before the wings are strong enough for editorial flight.

The next step upward for the reporter is to become some class editor, like a city editor, a desk editor, a literary editor, a general news editor, or a telegraph editor, and success in all these departments may depend upon the experience gained while in the ranks.

The boy most likely to make a good journalist possesses, among other things, great chunks of old-fashioned horse sense. He is naturally observant, and can readily put his thoughts upon paper. Quite likely he inclines toward the printing office, even at an early age, and likes to see the printers at work, and wants a few fonts of type and a printing-press of his own. Perhaps he starts an amateur paper, occasionally he writes little squibs for the local paper, or is sought after by reporters for news. He may not know how to express himself well verbally (very few editors are good talkers), but as a boy he can express himself in writing. Probably he begins by writing to his friends interesting letters, descriptive of a vacation trip, or about something else. His school compositions, although they may be ungrammatical, and may show a great disregard for rhetoric, are likely to contain the meat of his subject understandingly presented.

When this boy goes anywhere, whether he intends to write a report of it or not, he instinctively carries away with him a fairly correct résumé of the event. He likes to read, but his reading is not confined to the novel, to the story, or to the poem. He is anxious to be the first reader of the local newspaper, and he reads the news conscientiously. He may be conventional and unskilled in his writing, but the chances are that there is vigor in his conventionality and a completeness in what he writes.

So far as I know, there has never been a successful journalist who did not, at an early age, instinctively turn in this direction, and involuntarily show a preference for type, ink, and paper. Unless the youth shows these characteristics, the chances are that he will make a poor journalist, and parents should not attempt to push their son newspaperward unless they discover in him unmistakable inclination and ability. They would better take the doubtful boy to some good editor, show him around the office and the printing shop, and ask the newspaper men and reporters to talk with him. If the boy has the spark of the journalist fire in him, it will not be a week before the journalistic flame is sufficient to draw him back to the newspaper office, that he may again watch the activity and talk with the men.

Upon general principles, I advise the country boy who wishes to become an editor to remain in the country, to begin on a country newspaper, either daily or weekly, and to stick to the country. Later it may be advisable for him to move to a larger town, and even to a small city, but in ninety-nine cases out of a hundred he will be better off in the end if he gives the smaller place the preference, provided it is large and prosperous enough for a reasonable amount of growth.

Upon the same general principles I would advise the city boy who wishes to become a journalist to begin in the city; but after he has been in the city a year, and has discovered that he is fitted for his work, I would suggest that he seriously consider moving to some smaller city or country centre.

In no other profession would I so strongly advise the boy to give the country and the country-city the preference, and I would apply this advice to the city-bred boy as well as to the country-grown boy.

General Charles H. Taylor, editor and manager of the *Boston Globe*, in a letter to the author, says:

"In a general way, if a boy has ambition, industry, and brains, which are the microbes of success, he will succeed in a newspaper office or anywhere else. There is no advice which will change a lunkhead, and the average boy must, of course, take his chances.

"The only rule for success in a newspaper office or anywhere else is for a boy to do a little more than is expected of him every week, every month, and every year. If it is in him, he will go to the head of the class."

Mr. Herbert F. Gunnison, manager of the *Brooklyn Daily Eagle*, in a letter to the author, says:

" A young man who has aptitude and ability and a fondness for printers' ink will find the business of making a newspaper one of the most delightful occupations in the land. Next to the satisfaction which comes to the successful orator, who is able to sway multitudes by his spoken words, comes the thrill of delight to the newspaper writer, or to the author who sees his thoughts in print and knows that they are read by thousands of people.

"Journalism is a growing profession. There is a demand for the daily paper. The reading of newspapers is universal. The profession is not overcrowded with good men; it is growing in importance every day. As papers become larger and more profitable, salaries increase, and the demand for greater ability grows. Unlike other professions, there is a great variety of work in journalism. When the young man tires of reporting, there is a field of special correspondence or copy-editing, and there are many departments of editorial writing.

"It is a work that brings forth a man's best energy. He feels that his paper is a vital force in the community. He is dealing with the live issues of the day. He is giving people something that they want. He is in the most alert and up-to-date institution in his community. He is a part of an enterprise that has power and influence in the land.

"What are the compensations? First, if he is a born newspaper man, he enjoys his work; he likes the excitement of his labor. He is able, at the very beginning, to obtain a compensation sufficient to meet his immediate wants. The law, medicine, and the ministry would require years of preparation, without compensation.

" The average salary of the newspaper editor is much larger than that of the minister, fully equal to that of the average lawyer, and probably larger than that of the average doctor, though it is true that in the case of the medical and legal professions there are larger rewards in exceptional cases, and more of such cases than in the newspaper field.

" Oftentimes newspaper work leads one to the field of literature and the writing of books. It is often, too, the preparation for entrance into politics. Some of the best statesmen in our country came from the newspaper offices. Some of the best business men, successful bank presidents, and others notable in various important walks of life, have had their early training as newspaper men. The experience of the reporter and editor are exceedingly valuable to a man no matter what line of work he may subsequently enter.

" The only reasons I can see why a man should not enter the profession of journalism are that he does not have natural aptitude and sufficient education and ability for the work; or that, having these qualities, he has other qualities which would make him more successful in some other field of effort.

" It is useless for one to go into journalism unless he has a passion for the work and knows that he has sufficient education to enable him to meet the requirements of the profession. He must also, in addition to these things, have that element which is hard to describe, but which is known in the business as a ' nose for news.'

" It is difficult for one to tell a young man whether he has these qualities or not. He must be the best judge himself. Unless he is pretty well satisfied that he has the necessary qualifications, he would better not attempt to become a newspaper man, because he will find it one of the hardest and one of the most exacting of professions, and without success in it and without satisfaction in his work, he will become a drudge and his life will be one of disappointment and of hardship."

Mr. Walter Williams, editor of *The Herald*, of Columbia, Mo., ex-president of the National Editorial Association of the United States and Missouri Press Association, in a letter to the author, says:

" What are the principal advantages offered by country journalism?

" Aside from the advantage common to all journalism, city or country, country journalism affords social position, moderate but comfortable income, recognition, leadership, and independence. The country journalist usually owns as well as edits the newspaper. He is never bossed by others except when he willingly permits it. He has opportunity for large public service. He may lead opinion. He has power circumscribed only by the field in which his journal circulates. He may, if he will, be the chief citizen of his community.

" What are the principal disadvantages of country journalism ?

" The principal disadvantages of country journalism, aside from those common to journalism and leaving unconsidered those which exist for all the professions in country towns, are few and arise merely from limitation. The largest power and wealth cannot be his. He cannot amass riches. He cannot mould the opinion of the state. His horizon is too near at hand. He must ever be regarded as a country editor."

THE ADVERTISING MAN

WHILE advertising was born the day following the birthday of business, commercial advertising was not recognized as a business necessity, nor as an accomplice with business, until about half a century ago.

When twenty-five years of age, advertising was, by common acceptance, taken into business partnership and acknowledged to be as much a commercial commodity as flour or any other manufactured product. Then, business accepted advertising as an investment, and not as a trade-making expense. Before this it had been considered more or less of an experiment, and invariably as an expense, a sort of business luxury or a side-issue.

These quarter-of-a-century-ago advertisers advertised, or seemed to advertise, under a more or less pronounced protest, looking upon advertising as a something which for some unexplained reason they did not dare not to use, but did not want to use, and were not by any means sure of being able properly to utilize.

To-day advertising is a business necessity and a trade commodity, and is so recognized.   It is no longer looked upon as the fifth wheel of business, but as one of the four wheels, and by many as one of the two driving-wheels.

Substantially every North American publication carries advertising.   The total number of copies of these publications issued annually in North America, including dailies, weeklies, monthlies, and all others of regular appearance, may exceed thirty-five hundred millions. Assuming that there are one hundred advertisements — a very conservative estimate — in each issue of each publication, there would then be not far from an aggregate of more than three hundred and fifty thousand millions of impressions of advertisements during a single year.

Two hundred and fifty clipped advertisements, piled together, would equal an inch in thickness; consequently, a year's advertising placed sheet upon sheet would make a pile nearly one hundred and seventeen millions of feet high. If we were to clip all of the advertisements appearing in all of the North American periodicals during a single year, and place them end to end, we would have an announcement-ribbon of advertising fully one hundred and eleven thousand miles long.

These figures are unverified, but they are the result of careful and conservative investigations upon my part and consultation with others competent to estimate the magnitude of advertising.

North American progressiveness gives to our country an advertising value proportionately greater than that of any other civilized nation. Probably a multiplication of the foregoing figures by three or four, as well as of the following ones, will not fall short of the statistical truth of the world's publicity.

The one hundred thousand or more printing offices in North America are producing matter, in the way of catalogues, circulars, and other things, which amounts to a sum not less than that consumed by periodical and newspaper advertising.

A most conservative and composite estimate shows that the business men of North America expend annually more than one hundred and fifty millions of dollars in newspaper and magazine advertising alone, and undoubtedly a sum equal to this for advertising printed matter in the form of circulars, catalogues, posters, flyers, etc. The grand total of money spent yearly for North American advertising, including commercial printing, but exclusive of all books and the product of the press, which is not pure advertising, cannot be far from three hundred millions of dollars.

If my figures are correct, the application of printers' ink annually costs the whole civilized world, including the expense involved in the printing of books and all other matter, whether it be advertising or other literature, and also including lithography, an annual aggregate of about two thousand millions of dollars.

I assume, and this assumption is sustained by many more competent than I am to estimate in the premises, that the world, exclusive of North America, uses somewhat more than three times as much printers' ink and paper as is consumed by the nations comprising the North American continent. Upon this hypothesis, which I believe to be a thoroughly reasonable one, I present my estimate that the world's use of printers' ink consumes an annual expenditure of not far from two thousand millions of dollars.

A statistician with plenty of leisure has calculated that the annual circulation of all the periodicals in the world exceeds twelve thousand million copies, and that these combined editions would consume seven hundred and fifty thousand tons of paper ; and, further, if spread out, would cover an area of ten thousand five hundred square miles; or, if piled one upon the other, would reach a height of five hundred miles.

Truly, it may be said that the path of progression is paved with printers' ink.

Twenty-five years ago comparatively few advertisers expended more than fifty thousand dollars a year in advertising, and probably not more than sixty paid out as much as twenty-five' thousand dollars annually. To-day there are hundreds of advertisers expending each year more' than one hundred thousand dollars, and thousands of business concerns annually advertise to the extent of from twenty-five thousand to fifty thousand dollars.

Probably the largest sum of money ever expended by any advertiser in any single year was paid out some years ago by an English soap house. The advertising covered the civilized world, and was supposed to have cost not far from two millions of dollars annually.

In the United States to-day there are a few advertisers expending upwards of half a million dollars a year, and quite a number pay out half of this sum.

Nearly ninety-nine per cent of all publications, whether daily or weekly papers, or monthly or quarterly magazines, carry advertising.

Few people realize that the advertising, as much as and more than the subscription, pays the expenses and makes the profit of the periodical publication, and that few of our periodicals could live, and fewer make a profit, if it were not for the income derived from advertising.

If it is true, as is claimed by many, that to the press of the world is due in large measure the progress of civilization, then advertising may be considered as one of the main-trunk progenitors of the diffusion of literature and knowledge and of those things which are the natural pushers of progress.

Advertising, then, has become a distinct business or profession, requiring specially trained men and women for its proper manipulation.

Advertising men may be divided into the following classes: the advertising solicitor; the advertising agent; the advertising manager, both for the advertising and the advertising medium; and the advertisement writer.

The advertising solicitor is the most in evidence, and there is "more of him" than of all other classes of advertising men combined. As his name implies, the advertising solicitor is a solicitor, or a drummer, or a salesman of advertising. His work is largely outside; that is, he calls upon those he would have advertise, because advertising, barring the classified wants in the newspapers, is seldom bought or sold over the counter. Substantially all of it is obtained by direct or indirect solicitation. Every daily newspaper, and some of the country weeklies, employ advertising solicitors, men or women, but usually men, who devote their entire time to calling upon advertisers to solicit their patronage.

All of the general publications, and I classify as general publications the magazines and other periodicals which are not newspapers and have more than local circulation, employ one or more solicitors, who may or may not be known as advertising managers. These men are either local or general solicitors. If local solicitors, they confine their work to city business and to that in nearby towns and cities. If general solicitors, they travel all over the country, visiting the offices of general advertisers, even though they may be located hundreds of miles from the base of publication.

The great daily newspaper employs both local and general solicitors, but generally the latter is what is known as a special agent, one who is located in some large city and handles nothing but the advertising space in a stated number of newspapers.

A few great advertising publications establish offices in the larger cities, but, as a rule, this is not done.

Newspaper advertising solicitors are usually paid salaries ranging from a thousand to five thousand dollars a year, and a few enjoy incomes exceeding the larger amount. The average salary, exclusive of country paper solicitors, is probably not far from two thousand dollars a year.

Solicitors for general periodicals, like the standard magazines, fashion papers, household publications, and religious papers, are usually paid salaries seldom less than fifteen hundred dollars, and from that up to ten thousand dollars, a year; the average salary which a first-class periodical pays being not far from four thousand dollars a year.

A high-class advertising man, employed upon a large newspaper or magazine, or other well-known publication of general circulation, invariably commands a salary of not less than five thousand dollars a year.

Comparatively few periodical or newspaper advertising solicitors work upon commission, but depend upon their salaries for their incomes.

A low grade of advertising solicitor, one who gives the

whole or a part of his time to obtaining advertisements for cheap programs and questionable advertising mediums, may work upon commission.

Soliciting advertising is extremely difficult work, and is considered the hardest kind of drumming. While to-day advertising is usually recognized as a business commodity, its position has not yet become sufficiently established to have determined for it a definite standard of value. It is not so easy for the buyer of advertising to decide in advance whether or not certain advertising will pay as it is for the buyer of flour and fabric to decide beforehand the quality and probable profit of these commodities ; consequently, the advertising solicitor, while usually not handicapped by the necessity of being obliged to argue the value of advertising, may be seriously hampered because of this lack of standard of values in buying and selling advertising space.

It is not particularly difficult for a first-class drummer to sell the goods which he has represented for years, and to convince the buyer that such goods are salable and profitable; but it is often extremely hard for advertising solicitors to prove to the buyer that the advertiser's business needs the particular kind of advertising which the solicitor has to offer. For this reason the successful solicitor has to be a salesman of the highest order, a man of great selling ability, and one able to overcome difficult obstacles.

While the solicitation of advertising is purely and simply an art of salesmanship, one may succeed as a general salesman and fail as a seller of advertising.

Careful investigation among advertising men has shown that advertising solicitors are obliged to make between twenty-five and fifty calls to obtain a single order. This means that an advertising solicitor may not close even one contract in an entire week of hard work.

I would not advise any boy to aim at the career of advertising solicitor, either of a daily newspaper or a weekly or monthly periodical, unless he is prepared to do the most strenuous kind of work, and unless he can show evidence of more than ordinary ability in salesmanship. His position in business and society is dependent upon his expertness and success, more so than is the case in almost any other calling. The incompetent advertising solicitor has little business or social recognition, and is, both in business and in society, rated below a man of his capacity in other callings.

An important class of advertising men is represented by the advertising agent. His name is a misnomer. He is not in any sense an agent, either for the buying or selling of advertising space. He is, in fact, a wholesale dealer in advertising; and, further, he is a solicitor either personally or by proxy.

Practically all of the periodicals pay a commission for business which does not come directly to them through their regular solicitors. They give the advertising agent a commission, ranging from ten to twenty-five per cent on all the business he brings them, ten per cent being the lowest rate of commission paid, fifteen per cent the average, and twenty-five per cent the maximum. Few publications of a large circulation, however, allow more than fifteen per cent, and those of the largest circulation seldom give more than ten per cent.

The agent, therefore, in the capacity of advertising solicitor, either himself or through the men he employs, visits the advertiser and endeavors to sell advertising space. Usually the advertising agent offers space in a certain number of publications, known as a "list," for a lump sum, which sum is apt to be less, and sometimes considerably less, than that which the advertiser would be obliged to pay for the same space if buying it directly from the various publications.

The advertising agent works in the interest of both parties; in the advertiser's, for he saves the advertiser's money; and also renders certain services in the way of clerical and other work which the advertiser may not so economically perform ; and he is of service to the periodical, because he reduces the periodical's expense of soliciting, simplifies accounts, and brings to it business which the periodical might not otherwise obtain, and certainly not so easily.

Advertising managers are of two classes, — the advertising manager of a newspaper or other periodical and the manager of an advertiser's advertising. The former may or may not be an advertising solicitor. The chances are that he is, and that he personally solicits the business of his largest customers.

Many periodicals combine the office of business manager with that of advertising manager, for the two are closely allied.

The advertising manager of a great daily paper seldom receives a salary of less than twenty-five hundred dollars a year. Many enjoy incomes of five thousand dollars, and occasionally they are paid somewhat more. The average, however, is probably about thirty-five hundred dollars.

Advertising managers of leading magazines, and of other general publications of standing and of extensive circulation, receive from twenty-five hundred to five thousand dollars a year, with ten thousand dollars as a maximum, and with an average of about four thousand dollars. This average, however, only applies to advertising managers of the leading periodicals, those of the second class in circulation receiving salaries of from twenty-five to fifty per cent less than the amounts just mentioned.

In many cases, even among the leading periodicals, the advertising manager, whether or not he is the business manager, is the head-advertising-solicitor and spends the greater part of his time on the road or at the offices or stores of his advertisers.

When the office of advertising manager and business manager is combined, the salary, in some cases, is increased to the extent of as much as twenty-five per cent.

The advertising manager of an advertiser's advertising is in every way different and distinct from the advertising manager or solicitor of a periodical, for the former is in no sense a solicitor. He is a buyer of advertising space and generally a writer of advertising matter. As a rule, he is as independent as the manager of any other prominent department of a business concern, taking orders only from some member of a firm, some officer, or from the board of directors. It is his business to buy the advertising space and the printed matter; and further, to prepare, or have prepared, the advertisements and advertising matter. He is as much a professional as a business man, — rather more so, in point of fact.

Business ability alone is not sufficient for the success of an advertiser's advertising manager. He need have no selling ability whatever. He may not even understand bookkeeping or the clerical side of business, so long as he knows how to buy advertising, how to write advertisements, and how to obtain general publicity.

To be successful, and to reach anywhere near the top

this advertising manager must be a composite man of high grade, with a knowledge of the principles of business and a practical experience in the methods or usages of business; and, further, he must be enough of a writer, and have a sufficient education to give him a command of language, so that he shall be able to write properly about that which his firm has for sale.

The successful advertisement to-day, the one that brings business, is a work not only of art but of literature, even of the upper grade of art and of a high class of literary quality.

The expert writer of advertising, with a record of success back of him, is, or could be, a literary man. If this were not so, he could not possibly have gained the success which is his.

The public to-day, educated by periodical and book, and by increasingly higher quality of advertising matter, demands in the advertisement the highest grade of art, both in illustration and in composition.

True, many advertisements show genius in no other direction than in a literary way; but the advertisement which pays is the one which brings the business or assists in bringing the business, and which helps to build up our largest mercantile establishments. This advertisement is undoubtedly prepared by a man or woman of strong mental capacity, with some mastery of the principles of art and literature, one who would have been a success as a writer had he or she taken up literature instead of advertising.

Many an advertisement in the leading magazines shows more art and more literary talent than some of the stories or articles billed in the table of contents. Frequently the reader finds more healthful reading, more that is worth reading, and more usable knowledge in the advertising pages of a great magazine, than he can hope to discover, even with double glasses, within the reading pages.

Many of our greatest artists, some even of our portrait painters, to-day work for advertisers.

Not a few of our famous authors are quietly preparing advertising matter, that they may receive a greater remuneration for their services than they can always obtain from the literary editor.

Advertisement writing has become so much of an art and so great a science as to require men and women of considerable artistic ability and literary attainment to produce matter of the required quality.

Substantially every general advertiser, and by general advertiser I mean one whose advertisements appear in the leading magazines and other periodicals of national circulation, employs an advertising manager, unless he himself assumes that position. This advertising manager may or may not devote his entire time to advertising, but if he does not give himself wholly to it he is none the less the advertising manager.

Advertising managers of the highest grade receive as much as twenty thousand dollars a year, although comparatively few enjoy salaries exceeding half this amount.

The average salary paid to a first-class man is probably not in excess of five thousand dollars.

Advertising managers for general advertisers, if of good capacity, are seldom paid less than a thousand dollars a year, and the average salary is about twenty-five hundred dollars.

The advertising managers of large retail stores receive from one thousand to ten thousand dollars a year, the average salary for the rank and file not exceeding fifteen hundred dollars a year, and that of the upper-grade man being about three thousand dollars a year.

The great department stores in our large cities invariably employ advertising managers, paying them from twenty-five hundred to ten thousand dollars a year, the smaller stores giving salaries ranging from five hundred to twenty-five hundred dollars.

The rapid increase of advertising, both in volume and in quality, has opened a new profession, or rather a business-profession, — that of the advertisement writer, or the advertising manager and writer. The newness of it, and the really high prices paid to those at the top, have drawn toward it hundreds and thousands of our young men and women, most of whom are without capacity and ability in this direction, and therefore cannot hope to rise beyond the second or third rung of the ladder.

One cannot learn to become an advertisement writer. True, the advertising school or the advertising book may teach the principles of advertisement writing. So can the school and book impart the principles of law and of medicine; but neither in itself can make an advertisement writer any more than it can make a lawyer or a doctor.

Unless one possesses a peculiar natural ability, advertisement writing offers to him little or no opportunity.

The boy who cannot compose, and compose decently well, or, in other words, cannot properly present himself and his ideas in writing, will never make an advertisement writer; and no amount of study, training, and experience will ever give him more than mechanical proficiency. He will never become a writer of real advertisements, advertisements with life in them.

The boy who does not observe things, and who cannot

carry in his mind the result of his observations, may not hope to become an advertisement writer.

The most successful writer of advertisements must have more than the usual power of observation and of concentration; and, further, he must possess the genius of contraction and of condensation, and be able to say much in little.

Any one who has a fair command of language, by the aid of a dictionary can properly describe things if he is given unlimited space for the description; but the advertisement writer must say all that it is necessary to say in the fewest possible words. He must describe a thing so that the reader will wish to see it.

The successful advertisement writer must possess the peculiar power of being able to put upon paper an accurate and brief description of what he seeks to present to his readers, and this peculiar talent is not common, and is never the result of any school or any kind of teaching.

As a rule, the best advertisement writers are those who have been newspaper men, who have been connected with some periodical, either in the business or the editorial or reportorial department, or in all of them.

Our most successful advertising men have gone through an apprenticeship that not one boy in a thousand is likely to experience, and which is beyond the reach of the majority of men.

Expert advertising men thoroughly understand the principles of the printing and the publishing business, from the setting of type to the running of a printing press. They are also familiar, from experience, with every class of engraving, from the photo-engraving process to the steel-plate, and understand the principles of lithography and of every kind of color-work.

They know how paper is made, and how to select it to the best advantage. They understand the newspaper business from the counting-room to the editorial chair. They know what the editor does and what the reporter does, usually from actual experience. They know at first hand the difference between newspaper work and magazine work. They know how to determine circulation, and, further, how to arrive at circulation values. Very often the publication having the largest circulation is not the best advertising medium for certain classes of goods.

I would not advise any boy to hope to become an advertisement writer or manager who did not understand, or who was unable to learn, the principles and practice of printing, and who had not, or who was unable to acquire, a substantial newspaper experience. Without a knowledge of printing, and without the experience of actual newspaper work, one cannot hope to become more than a fair advertisement writer.

The advertising school has its place, and the advertising book is of value; but neither of them, alone or together, are worth anything to the boy who has not the natural capacity at the start, — nor will they be of much use to him unless he combines with them actual experience covering printing and newspaper work in general.

The mere writer, no matter how proficient or successful he may be, cannot necessarily turn his attention to advertisement writing, for the advertisement writer, besides having literary ability, must possess some business capacity.

To summarize the qualifications for the successful advertisement writer: In the first place, he must know how to write. In the second place, he must understand the principles of display; and he cannot perfectly under-

stand these unless he has had practical printing experience. In the third place, he needs the reportorial
discipline and experience on some newspaper, where he
can learn concentration, and where he may obtain that
which is of the greatest value to him, — the knowledge
of men and things. It is necessary not only to describe
the goods or thing advertised, but they must be described so that they will appeal to the reader, and the
advertisement cannot be made to reach the reader unless
the one who writes it, or prepares it, is in close touch
with public requirements.

The advertisement writer, like the doctor, to be successful must know how to feel the public pulse and to
keep within hearing of the beatings of the public heart.
Unless he has the ability and the experience to do these
things, he never can become a good advertisement writer,
and the chances are that he would have better success
in other directions.

In short, advertising offers much to the competent,
something to those of some ability, and nothing to the
incompetent.

Mr. Robert L. Winkley, manager of the department
of publicity of the Pope Manufacturing Company, of
Hartford, in a letter to the author, says :

" If I advised a young man to try to become advertising
manager for a large concern, it would be for the wonder-
fully varied experience to be gained from such work when
done at its best. I would recommend it as a means of
advancement and not as an end to be attained.

" In successfully managing a large department of publicity,
a man gets a more varied experience than comes to one in
ordinary departmental work, because, if affairs are rightly
handled, the financial, mercantile, and literary training is

superior, and if he has the right make-up, it will fit him for a larger and more important field of activity.

"If I advised a young man not to hope to become an advertising manager, it would be because I feared, from his characteristics, that he would fail to get from it the maximum benefits, and, if fairly successful, might be satisfied to follow it for a life's work.

"Not every man can be a leader. Nevertheless, each one should be placed in a position where competition or ambition or some other good incentive would be constantly at work to draw out the best that is in him.

"Hence, the individuality must be carefully analyzed before a line of work is recommended.

"No one should be satisfied with his career, but should be constantly striving for something better."

Mr. Thomas Balmer, the late advertising manager of the *Delineator*, the *Designer*, and the *New Idea Woman's Magazine*, of New York City, in a letter to the author, says:

"The advertising solicitor should be a college graduate, who, if possible, in addition to the standard requirements, has taken a course in physiology, psychology, logic, political economy, and socialism, even if they are not included in the required course of his college.

"I say a graduate, because if a man has finished a college course, it shows that he appreciated the value of keeping at it and securing the confidence of his success in a diploma; and this experience should qualify him to do good, hard thinking and reach right conclusions.

"He should have good health, because one of the first qualifications of a good solicitor is the ability to stand the strain of getting around; he should be a quick thinker and a ready talker; if he is not ready of speech, it gives the impression of hesitation and creates doubt about the topic upon which he speaks. He should be pleasant in his manner, patient, and somewhat scrupulous regarding his personal attire; he should not be vain, but should always show that he takes pride in a presentable appearance.

"Such a young man as just described, from twenty-two to twenty-five years of age, if he believes that he would like to be in the advertising business, I should advise to get into it.

"I know of no career where brains alone, energy, honesty, truthfulness, and no capital or friends to help him, offer so successful a business from a pecuniary standpoint. He will acquire a personal reputation that is worth, and will be later capitalized into, a profitable salary, and distinction among his associates, if he makes use of all of his opportunities. Perhaps some day he may even reach a giddy eminence on the advertising ladder of fame.

"The man without these qualities would not receive much encouragement from me, because, in the next ten years in the advertising field none but the best of men need hope for much recognition from the advertising world, or for preeminence among his associates, or great money success."

PUBLIC SERVICE

EVERY public office-holder, and every one who devotes the whole or any part of his time to the work of the government, whether that government be of the nation, of the state, of the city, of the country town, or of the village, is a government worker, and a member of the public service.

Public service employees, commercially speaking, are those who work for the government as they would labor for a mercantile house, depending upon their salaries for a livelihood.

By those unfamiliar in the premises, the government clerk, or other employee, is often supposed to enjoy what our boys designate as a " snap," and to be overpaid for his service. This impression is somewhat founded on fact, but there is more apparent than real reason for its prevalence. A few government employees have an easy time of it, if one considers the small amount of clerical work which they do and their limited number of working hours. It is also true that there are a number of government clerks, but a much smaller percentage than is usually admitted, who could not actually earn the salary paid them if they received but twenty-five per cent of their present wages.

But the government employee, as he runs, is not overpaid, and is much oftener underpaid, although the government gives more on an average for the service it receives than does the ordinary mercantile house. If the government did not pay a little more than is paid by business establishments, it could not obtain other than the lowest order of clerical work, because the government position offers the minimum of opportunity, notwithstanding the well-established and generally executed Civil Service rules under which the promotions are made, or are supposed to be made.

The work of the government employee is of the routine sort, with little variation, and it seldom gives opportunity for the exercise of any talent save the practice of faithfulness and accuracy. He is a part of a great machine, and only a part. He cannot expect to be much more than an insignificant factor, one of a great army of similar factors.

Conversation with a number of government employees, representing every department in public service, thoroughly convinces me that more than nine-tenths of our government clerks who have held their positions for more than half a dozen years regret that they entered the government's employ; and that more than half of this nine-tenths would resign their positions if their experience were sufficient to give them fair opportunity of obtaining work in mercantile establishments.

The ordinary government employee, however, has one advantage over the clerk of commerce; for under the present Civil Service system he is likely to hold his position permanently. If he remains competent and faithful, he is reasonably certain of systematic promotion, but only up to a definitely defined point. Unfortunately the higher salaried governmental positions, although nominally controlled by the accepted rules of promotion, are frequently manipulated by influence and subject to political pull, and their incumbents are not certain of their positions, as they are likely to be transferred or thrown out altogether.

The boy with ambition, competent to do more than clerical work, should keep away from the government service.

The boy who is methodical, faithful, with some clerical capacity, and with little ambition, is, perhaps, better off in the employ of the government than he would be elsewhere.

Once in the government employ, always in the government employ, is a rule with few exceptions; for the government gives a kind of non-transferable experience, which, while it fits the boy properly to fill his governmental position, does not develop him along other lines; and, therefore, substantially every government employee who has been with the government more than a dozen years remains with the government as long as he lives. His training does not fit him to occupy many outside positions. This condition, to some extent, applies to all clerical workers; but the clerk of a mercantile house is better off if he loses his position.

The reason so many boys enter the government employ is because they are financially gainers at the start, the initiative government salary being in excess of that paid by mercantile houses, and because the hours are easier.

Sufficient-unto-the-day people are adapted to government positions. There are people who care more about

what they receive to-day than they are likely to fit
themselves to obtain to-morrow : who are better satisfied
with certainty's little than with opportunity's much.

The government-bred boy and man have grown up in
an atmosphere which may unfit them to live outside of
governmental walls. They have been steeped in the
policy of conventionality, at the sacrifice of their finer
ambitions and qualities.

The government office is something of an asylum. It
is seldom run upon business principles. The under
employee may overwork, — at least, he does the bulk
of the work, — while the upper employee, or head of a
department, often underworks. The work is not
balanced ; it is not fairly divided.

The majority of government employees are proficient
in only one thing, and many of them are noted for
doing the least possible work in a given time. The
whole tendency is against the development of ambition or of the finer qualities, because rewards are few,
none of the rewards have much value, and more than
ordinary faithfulness is not often recognized.

The objections I have presented do not apply to the
heads of great departments, for these positions are occasionally held by men of enormous capacity or of pronounced public spirit ; but, unfortunately, most of these
places are appointive, and are seldom held by the risers
from the government workers' ranks.

Take the post-office, for instance. Probably not one
per cent of the postmasters throughout the country
have had any practical experience along the line of their
work. They were appointed because they were good
business men, or for political reasons, generally for the
latter. Occasionally a head-clerk becomes postmaster,
but not often.

ROBERT E. PEARY

Arctic explorer, Commander Navy; born in Cresson, Pa., 1856; graduate Bowdoin College, 1877; entered navy as civil engineer, 1881; made reconnaissance, 1886, of the Greenland inland ice-cap; chief of Arctic explorations, 1891–2, 1893–5, 1898–1902, 1905, and finally in 1908, when, on April 6, 1909, he discovered North Pole, the goal of explorers for three centuries

Common sense, political economy, and the expediency of business unanimously demand that the governmental head of a working institution, like the post-office, should be filled by a man of actual knowledge on the premises, and not by one who knows nothing about its management, whether or not he is an able executive. But as all postmasters are appointed, and are not under the Civil Service laws, the assistant-postmasters or head-clerks, who have risen from the ranks and know the business of the mails, are seldom allowed to fill the position. In most cases the office of postmaster is given as a reward for political service, irrespective of one's special fitness for the office. In thousands of post-offices the postmaster knows little or nothing about the running of the mails, and depends entirely upon the assistant-postmaster or head-clerk; and yet this postmaster draws a salary double that paid to any one under him.

This same condition applies to the custom-house and to other governmental departments.

Therefore the faithful, industrious, ambitious boy who enters the government employ with the idea of being promoted to a responsible position is likely to be disappointed. All his faithfulness and hard work may amount to little after he has reached a certain point, unless he can bring influence to bear in his favor, or has actively participated in politics so that he can receive an office as a political reward; but no self-respecting man allows himself to be the recipient of a reward for the doing of his political duty.

The government employee is outside of the world of business. He does not come in contact with men, conditions, and things, except in a limited way. True, he has less cause for anxiety, but this advantage is offset by the loss of much which appeals to the ambition of manhood.

Young man, if you are ambitious, and if you feel that you have more than ordinary capacity, I would advise you to keep away from the government service. Do not sell your life's chances for a few extra dollars at the beginning of your career. You have many years to live. The importance of what you do to-day is largely in what it represents of to-morrow's opportunity. A small salary at the start, with prospects for the future, is far better than a good salary at the start, with limited chance of promotion.

The best that the government can give you, as a government employee, is not to be compared, from the point of view of fame or fortune, with what you may obtain in business or in a profession.

If you prefer a small present with a prospective certainty, rather than the greater reward at reasonable risk, then by all means obtain a government position, and stay there for life. But if you have in you the stuff that ambition is made of, strike out for yourself, and begin by following the road where individuality has opportunity, where ambition is limited to your capacity and is not under the standstill-will of an automatic master — your government.

A volume much larger than a good-sized book would be necessary to contain a complete schedule of the salaries and wages paid to United States Government officials and employees. I present a general table. Definite information may be obtained by addressing the proper departments at Washington, D. C. Unless otherwise stated, the figures given are the amounts received for a year of service.

President of the United States $50,000
 $25,000 additional for travelling expenses
Private secretary to President 5,000
Assistant secretaries to President 3,000
Clerks to President . . . . $1,400 to 2,500
Messengers to President . . . . . 900 to 1,100
Doorkeepers to President . . . . . 1,200 to 1,800
Members of President's cabinet:
 Secretary of State, Secretary of War,
  etc. 8,000
Assistant secretaries 4,500
Supreme Court Justices 12,500
Chief Justice 13,000
Messengers . . . . 720 to 1,100
Chiefs of Bureaus . . . . 1,500 to 2,500
Clerks . . . . 900 to 1,800
Ambassadors and Envoys Extraordinary 2,000 to 17,500
Secretaries of Legations . . . . . 1,500 to 2,650
Consuls General 5,000
Consuls . . . . 2,500 to 3,000
Consular agents . . . . . No stated salaries, but fees
Commercial agents . . . . No stated salaries, but fees
General superintendents at National
 Post-office . . . . 2,000 to 2,750
Chiefs of divisions, National Post-office . 2,000 to 3,000
Post-office inspectors . . . . 1,200 to 2,500
Superintendents of public buildings, at
 post-office, court-house, custom-house,
 etc., ... 540 to 1,500
Largest salary received by any postmaster . . . 8,000
Smallest amount received by any post-
 master . . . . 43 cents
Postmaster of first-class office . . . . 3,000 to 8,000
Postmaster of second-class office . . . 2,000 to 2,900
Postmaster of third-class office . . . . 1,000 to 1,900
(The postmaster of a fourth-class office is not paid a stated
 salary, but receives the entire amount of stamps can-

celled at his office, up to a certain sum, when he is allowed
to retain a proportion of the cancellations, and so on until
he becomes a third-class postmaster.)

Clerks in the post-office	$20 to $3,000
Letter-carriers at first-class offices, maximum	1,000
Letter-carriers at second-class offices, maximum	850

(Letter-carriers begin at a salary less than the maximum
salary, but reach the maximum salary after a few years
of service, and the majority of all letter-carriers receive
the maximum salary.)

Rural free-delivery carriers	$600
National bank-examiners	Fixed fees
Collector of Customs	$325 to 12,000
Custom-house inspectors, $3 to $5 a day (when working)	
Custom-house clerks	1,000 to 4,700
Custom-house appraisers	5,000

Custom-house packers, openers, deputy-collectors, surveyors,
storekeepers, cashiers, examiners, assayers, etc., $2.50 to
$5 per day, and $750 to $5,000 per year.

Marine hospital surgeon	$3,500
Assistant surgeon	2,400
Acting assistant surgeon	$500 to 1,500
Superintendent of life-saving service	2,000
Keeper of life-saving station	900
Surfmen at life-saving stations . . .	$65 per month.

The salaries paid to army and navy officers, and the
wages paid soldiers and sailors, are given in the chapters of
" The Army " and " The Navy."

The Hon. Edward A. Moseley, secretary of the Inter-
state Commerce Commission, in a letter to the author,
says:

" The principal advantage in entering the government
service in Washington is the opportunity it gives a young

man to obtain an education in almost any profession he may choose, as the sessions of our law, medical, dental, and other colleges are made to conform to the departmental hours, so that a clerk may perform his duties and attend lectures after office hours. Moreover, the great Library of Congress, the Public Library of the District of Columbia, and the many highly specialized libraries attached to the various departments of the government are accessible, and are rich fields for research on any subject.

" The debates in Congress are an education in themselves, and in its halls may be heard, without any expense whatever, some of our greatest living orators.

" The young man who is fortunate enough to obtain a situation here can support himself while acquiring a profession, and this is done by a great many. Some of our most successful men have held clerical positions here.

" As to the disadvantages: When a young man secures a position here, which gives him much leisure time, owing to the comparatively short hours, the knowledge that he is secure from dismissal, so long as he behaves himself and shows a disposition to perform work, rather tends to stifle ambition and to make of men naturally energetic mere machines, whose only hope is an advance in salary.

" The salary of the average government employee is inadequate to marriage and the support of a family, and if the married clerk is stirred to ambition and desires to learn some profession, he is very apt to find that all his earnings are swallowed up in the expense of maintaining his family, and he has nothing left with which to buy books and pay for tuition.

" I should hate to have any one belonging to me in the government service. The safety of the positions goes far toward deadening ambition and quieting desire for anything better."

The Hon. Carter H. Harrison, ex-mayor of Chicago, in a letter to the author, says:

"What are the principal advantages offered to the young man in public service, such service being either an appointive office or an elective one, but not in a clerical capacity?

"Political or public service appointments are usually, if accompanied with a salary, given to men who have interested themselves in practical politics, but rarely to very young men. Such appointments may be for a term of two to four years, or more. They give a man an opportunity for acquaintance, which may or may not be valuable, depending upon the use to which he puts it. Some of these positions may give to a young man a comparatively easy 'job' at a pretty good salary. If this is an advantage, he has it. As an opportunity for judging human nature, many of these positions afford splendid chances.

"Elective offices, as a rule, are not thrust now upon Cincinnatuses summoned from the ploughs. The average man elected to public service goes after it, horse, foot, and dragoons, and enlists all of his friends in his behalf.

"Elective or appointive office is, of course, sometimes a stepping-stone to higher official positions. Men have gone from the office of constable to that of governor. Everything depends upon the man himself, and there are no cook-book receipts for success.

"Public service has ruined some men and advanced others.

"Courage, honesty, faithfulness to duty — in a word, character — will inevitably tell, whether with advantages or disadvantages.

"Opportunities for promotion to young men in appointive public positions may result from good work, influence, caprice, or any other condition, the same as in a private business.

"What is the principal disadvantage to the young man in public service?

"The principal disadvantage to the young man in public service is the precariousness of his tenure of office. He must be ready to fold his tents like the Arabs, when a new administration steps in. Civil Service has, of course, made political situations more stable of late years, but Civil Service is not omnipotent.

"The average man, holding a political position, feels, when a new administration comes in, that 'the gobbelins 'll git him, if he don't watch out.' This feeling of insecurity is liable to have a disquieting effect upon his work. Then, too, whether appointed or elected, he must spend considerable money and time in assisting the political administration which placed him in power. He is bound to do this or be ungrateful. The result is, that the man who honestly saves money in a political job is a wonder. By reason of the numerous calls upon his time in a political way, such as campaigns, primary contests, balls, raffles, entertainments, ward-club meetings, funerals, etc., he rarely has leisure to get on much more than speaking terms with his family.

"As for leisure, that word is a stranger to his vocabulary. The opportunities for advancement are not better than in private business, if as good. If a young man is fond of seeing his name in the papers, he is liable to have that feeling gratified more often if he is in the public service than he would in private business. This may be claimed as one of the doubtful advantages, appealing more to youth than to the congealed wisdom of middle or old age.

"For the work done in public service, the criticism, the anxieties, responsibilities, and even great triumphs achieved, the legitimate pecuniary results are the poorest in any line of business on earth. It is almost impossible to combine business and politics successfully. If politics interfere with a young man's business, the only way to be successful politically is for him to give up his business. At the same time, politics is an exceedingly uncertain business.

"It is the duty of every man, young and old, to take an interest in politics outside of any question of preferment.

"The only way in which good government can be obtained

is by citizens of all classes taking an active interest in seeing that good principles and measures are upheld and honest officials elected to uphold those principles. The very fact that many reforms have been inaugurated and brought to a successful conclusion has been due, in great measure, to disinterested efforts of the good citizenship of the community, enlisted without any hope of pecuniary reward, but solely from patriotic motives. The man who merely votes a party ticket, right or wrong, is a very poor specimen of an American. He owes it to himself, to his family, to his community, and to his country, to interest himself actively in practical politics, and to do everything in his power to improve the condition of things from a political standpoint."

AUTHOR'S NOTE. — Mr. Harrison's reference to the uncertainty of permanently holding positions probably refers to political office-holders, and not to the rank and file of public service employees.

The Hon. George W. Hibbard, postmaster of Boston, in a letter to the author, says:

" I would say on the side of encouraging efforts in this direction that there is a free field for all in securing entrance to government positions through the competitive merit system of the Civil Service Law of our country. A certain satisfaction comes to the young man who enters a contest of this character and succeeds. His intellectual attainments, such as they may be, have stood the test of inquiry, and this step, if he will but take the lesson home to himself, will point out the way for future success in his chosen work. Competition will surround him in his many co-workers, and he must have the ambition, not only to do well, but to do better than others, if he would advance to the pay and responsibilities of the higher grades in the service.

" Any intellectual equipment, apart from the faculties which the ordinary work of the day bring into play, will be an advantage to the ambitious and secure for him more speedy promotion.

" Advancement is the handmaid of integrity and ambition, and the government employ may bring a sufficiency of success to those who desire to succeed.

" On the other hand, while the government, in its lower grades of employment, secures to the beginner a larger recompense for the work performed than private business will afford him, there is more or less dead-levelism about the duties, and a person content with his lot will not attain to much honor or emolument. Such a person, perhaps, would not succeed in any business, and the question of success in employment largely resolves itself into one of personal application and ambition of the worker.

" Trade and business activities undoubtedly call forth the characteristics of industry and mental direction to a greater degree than the ordinary government position; and there is, therefore, a larger field for the development of the individual."

CIVIL SERVICE EXAMINATION

THE term "civil service examination" applies to those written examinations given under the direction of the United States Civil Service Commission which one must take to obtain a government position.

One who wishes to take these examinations should write to the United States Civil Service Commission, Washington, D. C., for a blank form of application, and he should be sure to state in his letter the kind of examination he proposes to take. The application form should be carefully filled out in accordance with instructions and mailed as directed. The Commission will immediately notify the applicant of the time and place of the next examination. Examinations are held in all large cities, and in other places, at stated intervals.

No one is eligible to examination who is not a citizen of the United States, and who is not, on the date of the examination, within the age of the limitations prescribed (the age limit, however, is subject to variation), who is physically disqualified for the service he seeks, who is addicted to the habitual use of intoxicating beverages to excess, who is enlisted in the United States Army or Navy and has not secured permission for his examination from the Secretary of War or the Secretary of the Navy, who has been dismissed from public service for misconduct within a year preceding the date of his application, who has made a false statement in his application, who has been guilty of fraud or deceit in any way connected with his examination, or who has been guilty of any crime or notoriously disgraceful conduct.

There are three grades of examinations, the first grade requiring some educational attainment, the third grade demanding very much less. No one can hope to pass a first-grade examination who is not proficient in spelling, who does not understand the fundamentals of arithmetic, including fractions, percentage, interest, discount, analysis, and simple accounts. The penmanship must be legible and neat, and the applicant must write rapidly. A test will be made of the use of the English language for business correspondence and in copying from draft-manuscript with interlineations, erasures, misspellings, errors in syntax, etc.

The second-grade candidate will be examined in spelling and in arithmetic, including addition, subtraction, multiplication, and division of whole numbers, and common and decimal fractions. He will be tested in the use of the English language for business correspondence, and his penmanship must be legible, rapid, and neat.

The third-grade examination consists of spelling, arithmetic (including addition, subtraction, multiplication and division of whole numbers), a test in business correspondence, and the candidate must write legibly and rapidly.

Candidates for special subjects, requiring a knowledge beyond that which has been just described for the first, second, and third grades, must pass examinations covering the subjects a knowledge of which is required. For instance, an assistant-examiner in the Patent Office will be subjected to a rigid scientific examination.

I especially advise the reader not to be misled by statements made by schools and teachers, who may claim, or who may seem to claim, to be in a position to be of material assistance to the would-be candidate. I advise the candidate to get his information at first-hand, and to write directly to the United States Civil Service Commission, Washington, D. C., for information. If the general information sent does not appear to be sufficient, a second, third, or any number of requests may be made, each requiring a specific answer, which the Commission will gladly render.

With this information in hand, the candidate, if at all intelligent and if of capacity sufficient to pass an examination, cannot help knowing whether or not his education is sufficient for the passing of the examination. If it is not, I advise him to apply to some regular teacher, familiar with the studies in which he is deficient, and submit to this teacher the information he has received from the Commission.

It is far better for the candidate to study under the personal direction of a teacher than to attempt to teach himself by the help of books, or by taking a course in some of the so-called correspondence schools.

I especially caution the reader against believing any statement made by a teacher, or any one else, who claims to have inside information or pretends to be in a position more than educationally to aid the candidate. All the information desired can be obtained from the Commission, and information from other sources may more or less depart from the truth.

THE SAILOR

THE term "sailor" may include all those who follow the water as a means of livelihood, whether that water be the ocean, an inland sea, a lake, or a river; but the sailor, as commonly understood, is one who exposes himself to the dangers of a broad expanse of ocean or of a large inland body of water, and does not include those who sail upon rivers and lakes of moderate size.

Half a century ago the romance of the sea was at its height. In those glorious days sails instead of smoke obstructed the horizon, and many a skipper was owner of his craft and in command of both the navigation and business side of shipping. Now, seafaring is even more a business and trade, more closely allied than ever to cold-blooded commercialism and under the scourge of the fiercest competition. To-day our ship officers are, for the most part, hired men, having no interest in their work beyond their salaries and their duties, and few enjoy ownership in the vessels they command. They are employees, taking their orders from a master of finance, their work consisting of little else than sailing vessels safely from port to port.

The use of steam for all kinds of water transportation has become almost universal, and nearly all of the comparatively few sailing-craft are coasters or vessels confining their voyages between nearby ports, and seldom going more than a hundred miles from land.

Substantially all of the trans-ocean commerce is handled by steamers, either regular liners or " tramps."

The regular liner, whether she crosses the ocean or is a coaster, is usually a steamer or steamship which makes stated or scheduled trips between two or more ports, and carries both freight and passengers.

The " tramp " is a vessel subject to charter and having no regular port of clearance or of entry. She may sail from Boston to Liverpool one month, and the next from Liverpool to South American ports. She goes where she can get a cargo to transport.

There are comparatively few full-rigged ships and barks in commission. For the most part they cross the oceans or take other long voyages.

The coasting-trade is carried on exclusively by steamships, steamers, and schooners, and in recent years largely by barges in tow.

Steam-coasters are from fifteen hundred to six thousand tons' burden, averaging, perhaps, not far from three thousand tons.

Coasting-schooners carry either two, three, four, five, or six masts, the three-master being the most in evidence. These schooners have a carrying capacity of anywhere from four hundred to two thousand tons, the average of such vessels carrying between seven and eight hundred tons.

The schooner is a most economical vehicle for the

coasting-trade. She has the carrying capacity of a ship of the same length, beam, and depth, and is much more easily handled.

The coaster-passenger business is exclusively confined to steamers and steamships, the former handling the trade between two nearby ports, the latter running over routes of several hundred miles.

The steamboat, technically speaking, is a vessel depending exclusively upon her engine for propulsion and is helpless without this motor power.

There are two classes of steamboats, — side-wheelers and propellers. The side-wheel steamer is propelled by means of paddles, one on each side. The propeller may or may not be a steamship. She may be constructed on lines similar to those of the side-wheeler, although for her length and beam she invariably draws more water; that is, she requires deeper water to sail in than does the side-wheel steamer.

The steamship is a vessel built somewhat upon the lines of the regular sailing ship, with her main cabin within the hull itself; and she has, besides her steam-power, more or less sail-area, theoretically supposed to be sufficient to give her steerage-way should accident occur to the engine. Her engine may be of either the side-wheel or the propeller type. There are, however, comparatively few side-wheel steamships now in commission, as they have been superseded by the propeller.

The introduction of twin-screws has given the steamship greater speed and the maximum of safety, because these screws require two separate and distinct engines, and the vessel is navigable with only one engine and one screw in operation.

Briefly enumerated, the three classes of vessels are: the sailing vessels, which include the sloop, the schooner, the brigantine, the brig, the barkantine, the bark, and the ship, all propelled wholly by the wind; the steamboat, a vessel propelled entirely by steam; the steamship, a craft propelled primarily by steam, but with a sufficient number of sails to give her what is known as steerage-way.

The cabins of all steamboats are mostly above the hull, and therefore they are not so seaworthy; but their construction gives them more convenient cabin-room; and, for this reason, they are given preference for service on the waterways which are not particularly perilous.

Sailors — and here I am referring to those who take part in the active work of the vessel, whether it be of sail or steam — are divided into two classes: coasters and deep-water sailors.

Coaster sailors include those who do not sail more than a few hundred miles from shore, and deep-water sailors either cross the ocean or take long voyages, and sail, for the most part, out in the open sea.

The life of a sailor before the mast, that is, a fore-castle-hand, is one of the hardest and most unsatisfactory of callings.

The common sailor seldom has as much as a common-school education, and to-day the rank and file of them are foreigners, ignorant and unambitious men, who live from hand to mouth, with no thought of the future, and who work only under the command of discipline. They live in cramped quarters, are exposed to the elements, generally subsist upon the cheapest kind of food, whether or not it be wholesome, and receive comparatively little consideration and substantially no recognition.

Even the most humane captain dares not, for the safety of his vessel, become on much more than commanding terms with his crew.

One of the sharpest lines of caste is drawn between crew and officer. They have little or nothing in common, and are never on social terms, seldom on speaking terms, the one living the life of what may be considered a paid slave, the other being in command.

Sailors upon what are known as fishing-smacks, however, are more or less upon equality, the officers, to some extent, associating with their men; but here the work is not only continuously hard, but extremely dangerous.

It has been said, and not wholly without the semblance of truth, that every boy, at some time in his life, wants to be a sailor, and wants to go to sea with or without the ambition to become an officer. This is simply a passing fancy of most boys; or, at least, all boys have this or some other idiosyncrasy. More than half of us, when boys, became circus-struck, and wanted to perform in the ring or act as a clown. When horse-cars were first introduced, almost every boy wanted to be a car-driver; and to-day thousands of our boys, at a certain period of their lives, have a decided "leaning" towards the duties of the motorman. These preferences are always exhibited at an early age, and are soon outgrown. They are worthy of no consideration, nor should they be the cause of any anxiety, unless the boy's apparently unmatured desire seems likely to become permanent.

The sailor, no matter how low he may be in the social scale, and no matter how small are his opportunities for advancement, is reasonably sure of a livelihood.

The life of the sailor, if he be an officer, is one which appeals to many a man as well as to the boys, for besides giving a reasonable certainty of livelihood, it presents opportunities for honorable advancement, although it gives little promise of more than ordinary remuneration.

The erect, and frequently heroic, bearing of the cap-

tain, or of his officers, coupled with the display of gold
lace, often appeals with irresistible force to the boy, and
even the older ones look with admiration upon the
stately form of a commander who has earned his stripes
by study, training, and the hardest kind of work, and at
continuous exposure to danger.

The commander of a large vessel, whether it be of sail
or of steam, is one of civilization's best products. No
man can successfully occupy such a position without a
broad education, either from being self-taught or school-
taught, nor without a firmly set and well-balanced head.
He must be able to meet emergencies, and, in the main,
successfully to overcome them. He must have the
ability to command men, and to grasp all kinds of
situations and complications, save those of finance or
business. He is deserving of our admiration. He is, if
he be a successful captain, a man from head to foot.

But hold a moment. How did he obtain this position,
which attracts the admiration of boys, and of men too?
In the first place, he was years, perhaps as much as a
quarter of a century, earning his promotion; he went
through years of training, and was under the hardest
kind of discipline. Very likely he has been before the
mast and slept in the forecastle, and worked up, step by
step, to the commanding position he now occupies.

The ordinary man can never become a successful
commander of more than a small vessel. The majority
of mercantile successes do not possess that alert mental
power, that ability quickly to meet emergency, essential
to the successful sea-captain.

Captains of trans-ocean lines seldom receive more
than three thousand dollars a year, and probably the
average salary is not in excess of twenty-five hundred

charge of from a million to two million dollars' worth of material property, including the steamship and its freight, and from two hundred to four thousand human souls. And yet these men, able successfully to assume this great responsibility, are paid no more than some of our head-bookkeepers receive for clerical work.

Masters or captains of barks and ships seldom earn more than two thousand dollars a year, their average salary not being in excess of fifteen hundred dollars.

The first officers on ocean steamships, including the trans-ocean liners and coasters, are paid not more than one hundred and twenty-five dollars a month, the average wages being rather less than ninety dollars a month.

Second officers upon steamships receive, on the average, about sixty dollars a month, the maximum being not in excess of seventy-five dollars.

Watchmen on all classes of power-vessels, whether trans-ocean or coasters, are not paid more than forty dollars a month, the average wage being between thirty and thirty-five dollars.

Boatswains on some vessels rank as third officers, and receive anywhere from thirty to fifty dollars a month; quartermasters, about five dollars a month less; and ordinary seamen, that is, sailors, occupants of the forecastle, are paid not often less than twenty dollars, and not more than twenty-five dollars, a month.

Chief-engineers of large vessels, whether trans-ocean or coasters, are seldom paid more than two thousand a year, the average salary being about one hundred and thirty-five dollars a month; yet often these men are graduates of our institutes of technology and are in absolute control of machinery costing anywhere from two hundred and fifty thousand to a million dollars.

They are, like the captains, men of enormous brain capacity and able successfully to meet any complication or emergency ; and yet they receive no more than head-clerks in some mercantile houses.

First assistant-engineers of large steamers seldom earn more than ninety dollars a month, and from that down to sixty; second assistant-engineers are paid anywhere from sixty to eighty dollars a month; and oilers, or what are known as junior-engineers, receive from thirty-five to fifty dollars a month. Firemen on large steamers are paid from twenty-five to forty-five dollars a month.

Pursers and stewards draw salaries of from seventy-five to one hundred dollars a month, although possibly a few may be paid a little in excess of the larger amount. Assistant-pursers and stewards receive, on an average, forty-five dollars a month. Chefs, or head-cooks, on the largest trans-ocean liners, are paid as much as a hundred a month, but the average is very much below this figure. The wages of second cooks are never more than fifty dollars a month; assistant-cooks are paid from thirty-five to forty-five dollars a month; and waiters from eighteen dollars to twenty-five dollars a month.

The above figures are the salaries, or wages, usually paid for services on large steamboats or steamships, but apply, to an extent, to all smaller craft, the pay being anywhere from five to fifteen dollars per month less for the rank and file of employees.

The captains of small steamers seldom receive more than a hundred dollars a month, and their chief-engineers are not often paid over seventy-five dollars a month.

Commanders of sailing vessels making long voyages earn anywhere from a hundred to two hundred dollars a month, and their mates and crew are paid about the same as those upon the steamships.

These figures show conclusively that water transportation offers little financial opportunity beyond moderate salaries or wages, and much less than is paid to men occupying land-positions requiring not half so much hard work or such long hours and responsibility.

The management of all transportation companies, except the few which are owned by the officers in command, is similar to the direction of any mercantile institution, the president and other officers enjoying similar incomes.

Transportation business, in its purely business or clerical side, is much like that of railroading, although comparatively few transportation companies do the same amount of business as the average railroad, and consequently do not employ so many clerks or helpers.

I am inclined to the opinion that a clerk in a transportation office has a better opportunity than he has in a railroad office, but I am not disposed to make this a definite statement.

Returning to the water-working side of transportation, let me emphatically advise the boy who does not really love the water not to consider for a moment the sea-side of transportation.

If he loves the sea and seems born to command, if at an early age he has much mastery of himself, if he is able quickly to act in emergencies, the sea perhaps offers him good opportunity for the realization of his ambition.

The boy who cannot assume responsibility, who does not in his youth know how to act in an emergency, who never commanded anything, who is in no sense a leader among his playmates, is never likely to rise below a subordinate office.

No sailor-officer should begin on the quarterdeck, and fortunately conditions forbid it.

Rapid rising is almost unknown.

During the first years one is not likely to receive more than moderate promotion.

The ignorant man cannot become a commander of responsibility. He can never hope to be captain of other than a small vessel. It is necessary for him to know much more than how to navigate.

The successful captain of a large vessel is a man, a rounded man, a man who knows the world of water and of land and somewhat of books. He is in no sense ignorant. He is broad in his practical education, if not from the result of his book-studies.

I would advise any boy who intends to follow the sea, with the ambition of becoming an officer, to obtain a good, solid, common school education, and then to graduate from some nautical school, or from some high-grade technical institution.

This broad education, much of which he may not use, will nevertheless be of great value to him, for it will do much toward assisting him to become a master of emergencies and to meet complications and dangers.

If he prefers the mechanical side of the sea, graduation from the engineering department of a high-class institute of technology, or other technical school, is to be most strongly advised.

Although he may hope to reach the highest engineering position without this education, he will gain his end quicker, and be better prepared to hold his position when he does receive it, if he prepares himself at school to meet the exigencies of his work.

A few years ago this higher grade of school education may not have been necessary; but to-day our institutes are turning out so many well-trained men that the boy without this technical education is handicapped at the start, and meets obstacles all along the line.

Any comparison of wages between the sea-faring man and the shore-worker must recognize the fact that on shipboard food and sleeping accommodations are included, making the money received from wages or salary net, or nearly so, as against the land-scale, which seldom covers living expenses, unless one is a commercial traveller.

This saving in sleeping and food expenses, to other than a single man, may have more apparent than real significance, because the married man's absence from home may not materially lower the home-expense, — for it may cost him nearly as much for his family during his absence as it does when he is with them. The forecastle is not a desirable or attractive bedroom, nor is the sailor's mess-room particularly appetizing; but both of them, on a modern ship, are clean and reasonably comfortable. On the other hand, the accommodations for the officers are sometimes luxurious, and generally comfortable.

Water transportation will be as enduring as any other form of industry, but whether it will be extended along its present lines is doubtful. The coasting-schooner may become obsolete, although this condition will not be reached for many years to come; and certainly the long-distance sailing-vessel is rapidly going out of commission. Steam is taking the place of sail, and much of the coasting-trade is now confined to barges, — either barge-built barges, or old hulks made into barges, from one to a half dozen of which are towed by tugs.

Without doubt the best officers and seamen of to-day are graduates from the sailing-ship. Men thus trained seem to be better prepared for emergencies than those having only steam-vessel training; but as the opportunities for this training are growing more rare, it is evident that the supply must come from other sources.

It is not unlikely that sooner or later the demand for properly trained men will force the establishment of practical nautical schools, preferably afloat, where men will be taught, by book and by experience, the two together, that they may obtain profitable results at the minimum of time and expense.

Mr. William A. Fairburn, the naval architect, of New York City, in a letter to the author, says:

"Almost everything depends upon the personality and physique of the boy. It is useless for any boy to make up his mind to go to sea, and follow the sea for a livelihood, unless he has a good physique and is strong and rugged.

"The sea is no place for a weakling or any boy who is naturally unhealthy.

"The boy must also have grit, and be prepared to 'rough' it more or less. He must needs be a boy who will stand being disciplined, and take it in an optimistic way. He must also be respectful, and not be afraid of hard work and long hours.

"Many a boy who finds that school life and study are irksome may make a very good sailor. A higher education is not necessary; a fair public school education is all that a boy needs as a starting equipment, provided that he is intelligent and has the proper physique and personality.

"The sea offers a fairly good means of livelihood for the kind of boy who fulfils the above requirements and is not inclined to be homesick and discontented when away from his friends and relatives.

"To make a success of his calling, the boy will have to be very patient for many years, and although he may obtain a first mate's berth after six or eight years' service, it may be many years before he is given command of a ship. It is undoubtedly a big jump from the pay of first mate or chief-officer, at say about seventy-five dollars a month, to a position as master with the pay of two hundred dollars per month.

"Many a young man, after he obtains a position as first mate, becomes discouraged waiting for promotion to the command of a ship; and any young man following the sea to-day must make up his mind that he may have to work very hard, and exercise a great deal of patience, before the coveted goal is realized.

"For a young man who is determined to follow the sea the best means of attaining this end along successful lines is to ship as a boy on a sailing-vessel and obtain about two years' experience in such a craft. He would be classed as an apprentice, and be berthed in a boy's room away from the ordinary sailors; he would, however, work with the men before the mast, and at the same time would receive instructions from the officers.

"After about two years' service I should advise him to obtain a berth as quartermaster on a steamship, and after one year's experience on board a steam vessel, he will be ready to try for his second mate's license. After this license is procured, a first mate's and captain's license should be obtained, as soon as his sea-service will permit, and promotion will depend solely upon opportunities, environment, and the character and personality of the young man.

"If the boy is naturally weak or unhealthy, I should certainly not advise him to follow the sea for a living.

"If he is very studiously inclined, or a 'book-worm,' I should also suggest that he consider some other calling.

"If he is of a very affectionate disposition, desiring continually the comradeship of his family, friends, and relatives, I do not think the sea would prove very congenial to him.

"If he is color-blind, has poor hearing or poor eyesight,

he should never consider the sea; or else, after many wasted years, he will find that he is shelved and unfit for high responsibilities.

"If he is very reserved, and the opposite of a naturally robust good fellow, he will be handicapped as a sailor; for a man who follows the sea must needs be rough and ready, even though he be at heart a thorough gentleman.

"The sea pays well if a man gets the command of a ship. It pays very poorly if a man never rises to a position higher than that of a first officer.

"In these days the perils of the sea need not be seriously considered, but an officer of a vessel must be a man who can act quickly in case of emergency, and one who has personality to handle and control good men; and a good officer must have a clear head and a sound body."

Captain John G. Hulphers, of the Old Dominion Steamship Company, in a letter to the author, says:

"I cannot honestly advise boys to go to sea when starting out in life, unless in the navy, where they will be taken care of when their usefulness is over. Nor would I, on the principle that a good workman does not condemn his tools, say anything against it; yet I must perforce, to make myself plain, even though I may be thought a crank or a pessimist.

"Take two boys of about the same early advantages as to schooling, home training, and ability. On starting out as bread-winners, one elects to go to sea, the other enters some manufacturing industry. Admit that they are both successful. The one who went to sea reaches the height of his youthful aspirations, and eventually becomes master of a ship, valued, for instance, at three-quarters of a million dollars, and, when in commission, with a cargo of the same value, not to count the three hundred lives under his charge. The other is equally successful in his vocation, and reaches the superintendency of the manufacturing business, where the value of the plant is the same as the other, or, in figures, one and a half million dollars. Which of the two, do you think, is the better paid, or more highly esteemed man of the two, not taking into consideration the material comforts in life the one enjoys and the other does not?

" We on the water have to do our work and use our hard-earned experience among the dangers of the sea, exposed to the fury of the elements, when the superintendent, had he a decent dog, would not send him out of doors. We have no Sundays or holidays to look foward to; nothing but a continual tread-mill.

" But the worst feature is the rainy-day problem. As you well know, employers and corporations are not in the business for philanthropy, and do not pay us any more than they can help; yet from what we are paid we must try to save something, which brings our living down to a bare existence, both for ourselves and those dependent upon us. But I question whether one out of a thousand nowadays saves enough, even to exist, after our usefulness is gone.

" I know some commercial tourists, yclept drummers, who make twice the money a year that I do; consequently, with only the Sailor's Snug Harbor as a final reward for the boy who goes to sea, after a life of toil, deprivations, and exposures, thrown among a hard class of citizens, how can I recommend any one to go to sea ?"

Captain John S. March, of the Merchants' and Miners' Transportation Company, in a letter to the author, says:

" I may say that there is but little encouragement for a boy in the low state of American commerce; the foreign trade is very limited; the coastwise is confined to the coal and lumber trades; these vessels are manned mostly by foreigners, and in many cases commanded by men of foreign birth. There are many steamers running between ports; there is not much chance in them."

THE INVENTOR

BROADLY speaking, an inventor is one who invents, and an invention is the creation or discovery of something which before was unknown.

The inventor cannot be man-made. If a man is an inventor, he is born one, although his inventive faculties may not have been brought into play until most of his life had passed.

Inventors may be divided into two somewhat separated classes: the inventor who has made one invention and who gives little subsequent attention to inventing; and the man who practically makes a business of inventing, that is to say, is continually attempting to create something entirely new, or to improve upon something already in existence.

The inventor is a genius. Sometimes he is a genius and nothing else, and seems to have but one distinctive characteristic, that of originality, the ability to create; and often he does not even possess practicability, which is necessary to a profitable career.

Johnson said that " the true genius is a man of large general powers determined to some particular direction "; and others define a genius as one who has " an unlimited capacity for hard work."

The inventor certainly possesses some of the qualities which are popularly supposed to accompany a genius, and his success is due to those peculiar powers and to the most painstaking hard work.

But all the education, all the training, and all the inclination in the world will not make an inventor out of one who does not possess natural inventive ability. A crude ability by itself is likely to accomplish but little as compared with what would be possible with this natural capacity developed by an appropriate training.

The inventor is, and of necessity must be, an educated man, whether he be self-educated or school-taught.

It is true that some of our greatest inventors had little school-training, and some of them little or no book-knowledge, as school books go; but for all that they were educated men, educated along the line of their inclination and ability, for without this training it is probable that they would never have produced anything worthy of the name of invention.

Education, then, appears to be essential to the best inventive result. It may be self-education or school-education, or a combination of both.

No one can teach himself as well as he can be taught by others; therefore the more general school-education the would-be inventor receives, the more likely he is to invent something worth while. The college course may be of no material assistance to him, but a technical or scientific education, in some high-class institute of technology or other training-school, will prove of inestimable value to him.

While no one has a right to trust to what we call "luck," it must be admitted that invention is occasionally the result of accident, and we sometimes hear of discoveries being made by untrained men of ordinary capacity who have never before invented or discovered anything. But these occurrences are too infrequent for consideration.

Substantially all inventions are the result of intention, although occasionally the experimenter in his laboratory, searching for one thing, may, by apparent accident, discover another. It may be said further that the inventions which prove valuable are usually the result of years of continuous study, deep research, and investigation. Even the so-called accidental inventions would probably not have been made if their inventors had not been trained to look for the unseen and to be ever ready to take advantage of opportunity.

The inventor is a close observer, and his faculties are always alert. He has a lively imagination. Sometimes he is an idealist and a dreamer, like the artist and the poet, his work being the exercise of his imagination.

Nearly all inventors are impractical in matters of finance, and comparatively few of them understand the earning and saving of money.

A very large proportion of inventions lack finish or fulfilment; that is to say, the inventor has fallen short of perfection in his creation. He began with enthusiasm, but this soon cooled, resulting in a failure to complete the task begun; consequently the invention which might have been of some value eventually reaches the ash-heap.

Probably ninety per cent of the inventions are worth almost nothing, and not more than one per cent pay a substantial financial profit. By this I do not mean to

THOMAS A. EDISON

Electrician and inventor; born in Milan, Ohio, 1847; instructed by his mother; became railroad newsboy at 12; learned telegraphy and worked as operator at various places; invented many telegraphic appliances; established workshop in New Jersey in 1876 and has patented more than 700 inventions, including quadruplex and sextuplex telegraphic transmission; megaphone, phonograph, incandescent lamp and light system and kinetoscope

say that only one per cent of inventions are successful, because many an invention is successful and of great use in the world, and yet does not earn much money for its inventor or for anybody else.

While success in invention, as well as in art, should not be dependent upon financial returns, it is indeed unfortunate that the public refuses profitably to reimburse the inventor, either with cash or with credit, for the work which so greatly benefits the unappreciative world.

The financial value of an invention depends upon its usefulness and upon whether or not it is sufficiently new or different from any other to be properly protected by patent, and upon what it is worth in a purely commercial way. Will it make money or save time and money? If it will do neither, from a paying point of view, it does not make any difference how good it is or how marvellous must have been the genius who conceived it. The great law of commercialism, a law often working without reason, must decide upon the value of the invention, and its decision is final, being subject to no appeal.

Many an invention which would have made the world brighter and better, and would have done inestimable good, has never succeeded, simply because it would not pay commercially to develop it.

Frequently an invention is ahead of the times, and therefore its usefulness is postponed.

The commercial value of an invention is always dependent upon its promotion. If the inventor invents a good thing, a labor-saving machine for instance, and properly protects it with patents, and places it in the hands of honorable and competent men, he is likely to realize some profit from it. But if he attempts to handle his invention himself, his chances of success are not one in a hundred, irrespective of the real worth of the invention.

Probably three-quarters of the inventions, although patentable, are so nearly similar to something else as to be hardly worth development.

Unfortunately, and wrongly too, the present condition of civilization is opposed to always giving credit where credit is due, and the inventor often mortgages his body and pawns his mind in an attempt to make a great utilitarian discovery, and for his work and sacrifice receives little or nothing, and seldom anywhere near what he deserves.

For financial profit, a combination of invention and business promotion is necessary. It is not an unusual thing for the inventor to be paid a small sum and then to be frozen out altogether, partly because it is very easy to cheat the inventor, who may be practically defenseless.

Most inventors are cranks, and many of them are obstreperous. Because they have invented something, they seem possessed with the idea that the development of their invention is impossible without their constant aid and attention. They demand a commanding position in the company reproducing their inventions, and interfere with their manufacture. It is often necessary to get rid of them by the use of heroic treatment, and this gives the capitalist or developer an excuse for cheating them out of a part of what really belongs to them.

Comparatively few inventors are capable of successfully manufacturing their own inventions. The inventor naturally attempts to improve upon his invention, and therefore is not likely to establish a standard of manufacture or to turn out uniform goods. He is seldom a good disciplinarian, and cannot usually properly handle men.

Notwithstanding the danger of receiving unfair treatment, the inventor's safest course is to place his invention in the hands of men he thinks that he can trust, and depend upon them to treat him fairly and honestly. He is more likely to cheat himself than he is to be cheated by others.

While good inventions are always in demand, the inventive field is filled even to overcrowding. The shelves in the Patent Office contain thousands upon thousands of models of the value of junk, and yet many of them represent new ideas and years of painstaking work and brain-labor.

Many of the worthless inventions are made by those who have little or no knowledge in the premises. For instance, the carpenter, unfamiliar with machinery, invents some machine or part of a machine ; the engineer, whose experience is limited to the engine-room, invents a spoke for a racing-sulky.

It is almost axiomatic to say that substantially all inventions of value come from men who are familiar from actual experience with the conditions surrounding their inventions, and that most inventions are the product of necessity. And it may also be considered an axiom that the realization of the possibility of a thing first comes to the one who most needs it, and the one who most needs it is likely to be the one who works along the line the invention would cover. It is absurd to suppose that an outsider, with no knowledge of conditions, could readily and personally feel the necessity, or could discover by accident, that which is not conceived by those who are looking for it.

Comparatively few people possess any genuine inventive talent. The genius is not necessarily an inventor, although the inventor may be a genius. No copier, no matter how skilful, will discover anything or invent anything. The trained 'mechanic may possess no inventive qualities. The inventor who really does valuable work is a creator. He does not depend entirely upon what others know. He takes the knowledge of others and adds to it what he knows or can discover, that he may produce something not already made by some one else.

The true embryo inventor will show unmistakable inventive talent at an early age. Frequently he displays it when hardly out of the primary school. This quality naturally increases as he grows older.

The real inventor cannot help showing his talent. As a boy he is generally studious, and a good scholar in a few branches, if not in all of his studies, — a thinker, a reader, and a perpetual investigator. He constantly watches others, that he may know how they do things, but he almost invariably attempts to improve upon the action of others, and generally does. The chances are that he began to make a specialty of something when he was but a mere boy, that he early showed aptitude for some particular thing, and that the bulk of his experiments were in that direction. He may or may not be known as a jack-of-all-trades, that is to say, able to turn his hand to almost anything mechanical. The mere jack-of-all-trades without a specialty is likely to amount to little.

The inventor usually develops from the inventive boy. The boy who cannot invent something, or do something different from what has been done by his associates, will not amount to anything in the line of invention. No boy who does not show some inventive characteristics while at school, and show them to a marked degree, is likely to become a true inventor.

I would advise any boy of an inventive mind who is capable of creating something to graduate from a high-grade institute of technology or other technical school. This school, while it will not teach him how to invent, will give him a fundamental knowledge which will materially aid him in developing his inventive ability. Without this education, this special school-training, he may not have himself sufficiently in hand to accomplish profitable results.

There are comparatively few professional inventors; and by professional inventors I mean those who give their entire time to invention, and who depend upon this for their livelihood.

It is far better for one to take up some scientific or mechanical calling, preferably along the lines of his inclinations, and to use this vocation for a livelihood, inventing as he works.

When in active labor he is more likely to invent something practical, and to succeed, than he is if he gives himself wholly to experiment and invention.

Contact with men and things is necessary to the ripening of the inventor. Alone in his laboratory, away from the world, he has only himself and his books to learn from. As a workman, or as part of a great manufacturing establishment, he is brought into contact with life, and with the necessities of life. In this atmosphere, saturated with the action of experience, he is far more likely to produce something of value or of financial profit than he is alone by himself, away from the world's motion.

I would not advise any boy to think of taking up invention as a profession or trade. If he has inventive qualities, I would advise him to connect with some scientific or mechanical business or trade, depend upon it for his livelihood, and allow invention to be, not a side issue, but a result of practical experience.

Professor Elihu Thomson, A.M., Ph.D., inventor and electrician, and founder of the Thomson-Houston Company, in a letter to the author, says:

"I consider that invention may in most cases be regarded as creative engineering.

"It is unquestionably true that the same factors which lead to success in other lines of effort will help a young man having inventive ability. These are a clear head, good common sense, scientific knowledge, method, and persistency in overcoming obstacles. Good morals, honesty, and integrity are, of course, assumed to be qualities not lacking in the aspirant.

"The absence of these qualities above enumerated, or the possession of their decided opposites, is distinctly conducive to failure in this field as in other walks of life. I desire not to be understood as assuming that success or failure are to be taken in any limited sense. Too often they are written in dollars and cents. But does not that man succeed, in the highest sense, who has been able to enjoy his work, to use his talents, and thereby contribute to the progress of the world?

"A degree of financial success is also very desirable, but it is a deplorable condition when it is the only ideal.

"It is within my knowledge that many of our scientific men, investigators, and discoverers exercise great ingenuity and powers of invention in arranging means and methods for the ascertainment of truth. No patents, no direct financial return need result, yet success is theirs.

"I know little about the 'profession of inventing.' I cannot recall among my friends a sufficient number of such men. I know many men who have made invention a part of their work in various departments of engineering, broadly considered.

" I hardly think that any rules can be laid down as to how, when, or what to invent, invention covers such a wide range.

" When one invents, he pictures to himself, as a sort of mental image, a new thing or a new combination of old things, serving, perhaps, a useful purpose. This conception, if it be clear and definite, may be worked out into practical forms by its originator, or imparted by him to others, whose duty it is to complete the work.

" There is nothing mysterious about the whole matter.

" The inventor is one who recognizes defects in existing means, who looks ahead, who doubts that present conditions are ultimate or best. Authorities are doubted until their conclusions have been amply tested by experience.

" With the inventive mind, obstacles to progress, instead of controlling the situation, often only stimulate to greater effort to pass them.

" It is with inventors as with artists, — there are all grades of ability.

" The obtaining of a patent is often popularly supposed to be indicative of inventive talent. This is a mistake. Neither does the possession of a patent for an invention, otherwise good, necessarily make value. The invention may infringe other existing claims, it may be old or anticipated, it may be ahead of its time, the patent may not adequately claim the real essentials of the invention, and finally the courts may not agree with those versed in the arts as to there being any invention at all or its having merit. Even with the best inventions accidents happen and opinions differ.

" The inventor, therefore, needs to cultivate a judicial temper of mind, enabling him to look at all sides of a subject. Sometimes his enthusiasm, excusable as it may be, dims his vision in certain directions.

" I should say, from what experience I have had, that if any young man thinks of making a profession of inventing, he has launched his boat upon a stormy sea with many rocks and shoals, and extra chances of shipwreck."

Mr. John M. Wakeman, president and general manager of *The Electrical World and Engineer*, in a letter to the author, says :

" I know some inventors, and if they are men of repute who have invented anything of real merit, they are remarkably well-balanced all-round men, and generally their inventions have been made along the lines upon which they work for their daily bread.

" The professional inventor, that is to say, the man who makes his living out of his inventions, without any regular line of work or steady employment, has to be a very exceptional man. He has to take up a field in which there are gaps, and fill in those gaps with some useful invention. The probabilities are that there are scores of men in that same field, thoroughly familiar with it, who have been working upon just those same gaps for years ; and he has to be a very clever man indeed who can step into such a field and fill the gaps. He may waste his whole lifetime in attempting to do so, and never be heard of and never make enough to keep the wolf from the door.

" It seems to me that it would be poor policy to advise a young man to earn his living in so precarious a fashion. It would be better for him to go to work along some line in which he shows an aptitude, and his inventive genius (if he has any) will crop out because of the fact that he will see where the chances of improvement lie in his particular work, and thus there will be suggested to him the ideas which his inventive genius will be able to put into some practical form.

" One of the besetting sins of amateur inventors is that they invent apparatus or machinery to perform a given service in a most complicated manner, in spite of the fact that there are already on the market machines for performing the same work in a more simple and less expensive manner.

"Inventors are born, not made; and while of course it is well both for the individual and the world at large that inventive genius should be cultivated, it would be a serious mistake to advise a whole lot of well-meaning but absolutely inefficient young men to try to develop into inventors."

THE SKILLED MECHANIC

HE term "skilled" or "skilful" may be so broadly defined as to cover all hand-work requiring more than the exercise of automatic action, and it may be so narrowed as to eliminate any work save that of extraordinary, or, at least, of more than ordinary mechanical ability.

For the sake of convenience, I propose to consider in this chapter all hand-workers whose employment demands the use of their brain at the same time that they exercise their muscles. Such men may be classified as brain-and-hand workers, or as hand-and-brain workers; in the one case the brain doing more than the hand; and in the other, the hand accomplishing more than half of the work.

The expert-worker is commercially one grade above the skilled mechanic; by the combination of ability and experience, he does some particular kind of work better than it can be executed by the so-called skilled workman.

Neither the skilled mechanic nor the expert-worker, nor any one who employs both brain and hands, can be classed as a laborer, or as a mechanic in a purely mechanical sense.

While by the false ethics of an artificial society the skilled mechanic and the majority of expert workmen are not considered the social equals of successful workers in some other callings, they are recognized at their full worth by the representatives of civilized society. And this recognition is advancing in mighty strides, and sooner or later the combination of brain-and-hand-work will rank so high that society will dare file no exceptions to it.

The formation of gigantic monopolies, the consolidations of capital, and the fearful increase of business upon paper, cannot but produce a reaction which will appraise work at work's value, and render unto intelligent workmen the appreciation of high progress.

The skilled workman is a product of civilization, and progress in no small measure depends upon the work of his brain and of his hand. He is a builder of something, a maker of the tangible.

The institute of technology and the technical school are to-day more vigorously pushing progress than are many of our classical institutions which teach less of the necessities and the realities of life.

The bright, capable workman, with a fair education, does not permanently remain at a standstill in any department of mechanics, unless, in spite of his mechanical ingenuity and capacity, he completely lacks ambition, — a condition which too often exists. Sooner or later he may become a foreman or superintendent, and possibly a manufacturer.

The boy without pronounced business or professional capacity stands a better chance of success, both in the present and for the future, by entering some trade which allows his hand to do his hand's best, than by taking chances with what he is probably unfitted for.

If his mind takes little thought of what his hand is doing, an ordinary mechanic he will remain; but if the work of his hand comes under the intelligent direction of his brain, then he will rise as high as his combination of brain and hand will allow, which may be only a few steps above the ordinary, or to any height, even to that of manufacturer and proprietor.

The ordinary mechanic, above the laborer grade and beyond the apprenticeship step, earns from ten to twelve dollars a week on an average, and up to four dollars a day as a maximum.

The skilled workman, who is able to do something beyond mere hand-work, seldom receives less than three dollars a day, and from that up to seven dollars a day.

The expert workman often earns as much as two thousand dollars a year, and from that up to five thousand a year, although comparatively few receive the latter amount. His average income is probably not in excess of fifteen hundred dollars, although there are by no means a small number earning as much as twenty-five hundred dollars a year.

The foreman and superintendent, who are either skilled workmen or expert workers, and who are disciplinarians as well as mechanics, are seldom paid less than a thousand dollars a year, the maximum being not far from ten thousand dollars, and the average from twelve hundred to fifteen hundred dollars a year.

The terms "foreman" and "superintendent" are, to an extent, analogous, and frequently both offices are vested in one person; but the superintendent outranks the foreman, the latter being usually in charge of a department, while the superintendent is manager of several departments, and has general oversight of the foremen.

Skilled workmen are usually in demand, and are seldom out of work for more than a limited period. They are not so likely to be affected by depressions in business as are those of ordinary capacity.

Expert workmen represent the highest class of hand-working mechanics, and often grade with foremen and superintendents.

The man at the top, no matter what his calling may be, is a man of mark. The best shoemaker in town is not often out of work. The best blacksmith has about all he can do. The well-informed and reliable engineer works on full time. He knows something, and if that something be a commodity, he is likely to be busy year in and year out, and his earnings will give him all of the necessities and many of the comforts of life.

Electricians as a class are well paid, because there some expertness is required, and good electricians must not only be first-class mechanics, but must understand the principles of electricity. To an extent, at least, they are expert-workers.

The railroad engineer is a machinist, but he is classed above the ordinary mechanic. He is a man of nerve, of character, of presence of mind, of discretion, and able to meet emergencies. Without an abundance of qualities beyond those of mechanical ability, he would not be able successfully to hold the throttle of a freight locomotive.

While shrewdness in business pays better than skill in mechanics, and while this business quality undoubtedly wins a greater money-return than does any work of hand or of intellect, yet the skilled workman is not without opportunity for rapid advancement. He is in no sense a second factor in civilization. As a matter of fact, he has a right to be really prouder of his attainment than has the man whose wealth consists only of money.

When civilization advances another peg, the skilled mechanic, the man of brain-and-hand-action, will have the same social recognition as does the rank and file of our business and professional men.

The quality of skilled labor is rapidly growing better, and is progressing by such gigantic strides that it is only a question of time when the intelligent work of the hand will be considered upon the same plane as is the work of the brain, and there will be no such thing as despised labor. There will be little labor that involves muscle alone.

Comparatively few educational authorities, or those who have given educational ways and means intelligent thought, are in favor of a college education for those who propose to enter a mechanical trade; but the educational opinion is almost unanimous in advising, for any one who intends to be more than a common laborer, a course in the technical school or institute of technology, or at least a course in manual-training.

The boy who enters a trade without at least a partial technical education is liable to stay near the bottom or to rise very slowly; while the technical school-trained boy usually makes rapid advances after his first year at work.

Of course experience teaches, but experience is often too far away properly to instruct in the preliminaries.

A few years given to hard technical study in a good trade school or institute of technology will pay better in the end than can any amount of working experience.

But, on the other hand, technical education without experience is well-nigh worthless.

Experience without technical education is worth something. The combination of the two wins success.

A thorough technical education, with experience, never allows its possessor to remain at a standstill. He must rise, and generally rises rapidly.

No boy should begin to learn a trade, unless poverty requires it, until he has received a good common school education; and, if possible, he should enter some technical school to be scientifically trained for his work.

Time spent in a technical school is not wasted; it pays. Perhaps not during the first year of active work, but during the second year, its advantages will permanently appear. The well-educated hand-worker is sure to outstrip the untrained workman. It is a fact that few well-educated and well-trained mechanics remain in the rear ranks, and that most of them are either front-rank workmen or are promoted to command.

Let us take two boys of equal capacity and of equal trade opportunity. One spends, say three years, in the technical school, and the other enters the shop immediately after graduation from the common school. The latter boy has three years trade-start of the other. At the end of three years the first boy, educated and school-trained for his work, enters the same shop. In shop experience he is three years behind the other, and for one or two years the untrained and unskilled boy may be his superior; but at the end of five years the boy especially trained, with a solid technical education back of him, will outstrip the untrained boy two to one, all things being equal.

Education fits for experience. Experience seldom takes the place of education, and when it does, it does so at the expense of the individual.

One's earlier years are, by nature and by convenience,

an absorbent and educational period, in which it is natural and easy for him to enjoy school-study, and to acquire the knowledge which should precede actual experience.

The first few years of technical school-training give a foundation which the actual work in the shop cannot afford.

Experience needs education for its economical development.

The scientific or technical school disciplines the boy's mind, and gives him, in the most economical way, the broad principles of mechanics, — the principles which experience teaches more slowly.

Too much cannot be said to impress the would-be skilled mechanic with the enormous advantage of a technical education, to be obtained in some high-grade institution where the principles of mechanics are broadly taught.

The graduate of the polytechnic institute, or other technical school, will find his diploma the key to a position.

It should be clearly understood that education, in itself, will not produce the skilled workman or expert hand-worker. Education, to be of any use, must have something to work upon, — some natural ability in the first place. Without this basic material the most liberal education is worthless, and certainly has no commercial value.

The boy of natural capacity, with a willingness to work and an ambition to amount to something, finds that his education makes it much easier for him to market his ability; and, further, it enables him to develop much more rapidly than he could hope to do if he entered the shop directly from the common school.

The man is made from the boy, not the boy from

the man. As the crude boy is shaped, so is the man likely to be. Therefore the boy's educational years will probably be the most important ones of his whole life.

The world needs more skilled workmen and expert hand-workers. There is room for many more than are now available. These men, far more than the business men, are the pushers of progress. They, with the farmer, are producers of material commodities. They actually do something, — something which contributes to the roundness and wholeness of life.

There is a superficiality to some lines of business, particularly of those done upon paper; and even the professional, expert though he may be, to an extent handles the intangible; but the skilled workman and expert-worker are natural producers of actualities — indispensable necessities in the world at large.

All skilled workmen and expert workmen were ambitious men or boys. If they had not been ambitious, their brains would not have sufficiently co-operated with their hands in making their hand-work more than the result of automatic labor. Every one of them expected to rise, either to become a pronounced success, that he might give his entire time to head-work, or to become a foreman or a superintendent, and to enjoy still further the fruits of prosperity.

A liberal technical education is an asset: first, because it assists in developing ambition; secondly, because it broadens the mind and makes it adaptable to the work of both the mind and the hand; thirdly, it disciplines the mind, that the mind may the more master the muscle; fourthly, it opens opportunity for advancement; fifthly, it is economical, because it enables the boy to accomplish more in a given time, after he is fairly started in his work, than he could possibly effect without this education; sixthly, it fits him for proprietorship.

The blacksmith, unless he is self-taught at an expense far greater in the aggregate than is the cost of being school-taught, is many times more likely to remain a journeyman blacksmith than is his neighbor who has had the advantage of some sort of technical education. This school-trained man will not long remain at the anvil. In time he will be master of many anvils and of anvil men. True, he may rise to proprietorship without the aid of the technical school, but he will be promoted quicker with this school-taught education, and can hold his own better than he can hope to do otherwise. This argument applies to other mechanical departments much more than it does to blacksmithing.

It is simply a question of going to one's work before the mind and hand are economically and practically trained, or of going at it with mind and hand especially trained and disciplined to do that work in the most economical and satisfactory manner.

I am not unfamiliar with the criticism, which is sometimes merited, that the technical school-taught boy leaves the institute with a head out of proportion to his body, and considers himself superior to manual labor. Undoubtedly this is the case in altogether too many instances; but if the boy has the right stuff in him, this big-headedness is only a transient affliction, and will do but temporary harm.

The technical school never made a wise man out of a fool, never made a mechanical genius out of a boy who could not saw a board straight, and never will. It simply gives the boy of parts a better opportunity to use what is in him. That is all it can do, and that is all it should do. It is the boy's business to do the rest.

JOHN MITCHELL

Celebrated labor leader; born in Braidwood, Will Co., Ill., 1870; attended school until 10, then studied nights; worked in coal mines, 1882; connected with organized labor from 16; became an officer in the United Mine Workers of America in 1895; elected national president 1899, and directed strikes of anthracite mine workers, 1900 and 1902; vice-president of American Federation of Labor, and also member of the National Civic Federation

The more thorough the preparation, the greater the chance of success.

The rapid increase in manual-training schools in our cities and larger towns has done much properly to fit our boys, and especially our poor boys, for lucrative positions. School boards all over the country, and even in some of the smaller towns, are beginning to appreciate the usefulness of the technical school, and are establishing manual-training schools or classes. Not a few of our manufacturing establishments are supporting training schools where the sons of workmen are educated free of charge, or at nominal cost.

The future of American manufactures is, to a large extent, vested in the manual-training and technical school of to-day.

America cannot hold the position she has worked so hard to obtain unless she does more than she ever has done before to educate the young in technical matters.

Within the next few years I expect to see a technical or manual-training school located in every country centre as a part of the educational system.

What we have to do, we must do; but let us prepare for what we have to do, so that what we have to do may be accomplished at the minimum of exhaustion and at the maximum of effectiveness.

There's economy in preparation.

Charles W. Parmenter, Ph.D., head-master of the Mechanic Arts High School, of Boston, in a letter to the author, says:

" You have asked me to reply to the following questions:
" ' If you advised a boy to become a skilled mechanic, why would you do so? What are the principal advantages to this calling?'

" 'If you advised a boy not to become a skilled mechanic, why would you do so? What are the principal disadvantages to this calling?'

" At the outset, my viewpoint should be clearly understood. Your questions presuppose that I have had exceptional opportunities to judge of the relative advantages and disadvantages of the life of a skilled mechanic because I have charge of the Mechanic Arts High School. This presupposition is, in a large measure, erroneous. The school treats the mechanic arts as educational factors just as it deals with algebra, geometry, or French. The training which it gives is not less valuable to a boy who is to become a lawyer or a physician than to one who is to superintend a manufacturing establishment or work at the bench. The systematic study of the elements of the mechanic arts tends not only to develop manual skill, but also most valuable mental traits; for success in the school shops is impossible without forethought, perseverance, industry, and unceasing care. No shams go undetected. The boy who is not absolutely honest in his work is doomed to failure. Although the school does not aim directly to train boys to become skilled mechanics, the education which it gives often proves a stepping-stone to profitable employment in mechanical pursuits.

" Your questions also appear to presuppose that many boys will be aided by advice framed with reference to a typical boy. This is by no means certain. The fact is that the typical boy is a myth. Before helpful advice can be given, it is necessary to discover and take into account the native ability, tastes, aptitudes, and dominant powers and faculties of the particular boy to be aided. If a boy's native aptitudes and tastes incline him to a mechanical pursuit, I do not hesitate to advise him to become a skilled mechanic. Unless exceptionally favored, he cannot expect to acquire a large fortune, but if reliable, temperate, industrious, and really skilful, he will be sure of a fair income and be likely to lead a contented and happy life.

"The conditions under which many skilled mechanics work are far better calculated to preserve health and prolong life than the surroundings of most persons engaged in purely mercantile pursuits. The skilled mechanic escapes in large measure the nervous strain which destroys so many men in business or professional life.

"The fundamental conditions which should determine the career of every boy are his education, native ability, and inclinations.

"That school is best which does most to reveal to boys their dominant powers and lead them to a happy choice of occupation, and that advice is best which does most to encourage them to become earnest, honest, efficient, and reliable men in the field of activity for which they are by nature best fitted.

"The most deplorable failures in life have resulted from the strenuous efforts of parents to fit their sons for careers for which they had no native gifts."

Mr. Joseph W. Phinney, manager of the American Type Founders' Company, of Boston, in a letter to the author, says:

"If I advised a boy to become a skilled mechanic instead of entering business, what would be my reason for so doing?

"I should only so advise when satisfied that the boy's desire to learn a trade was prompted by a natural aptitude and liking for mechanics; understanding this fact, and knowing the trade that he had the most decided leaning towards, I should then urge upon him a thorough theoretical and practical training, a training that ought to make him an expert, a first-class workman, and one that should command the very best consideration in position and wages.

"The same methods would obtain in advising a boy to take up business.

"As to the particular advantages and disadvantages in becoming a skilled mechanic, I do not know of any disadvantages where the boy has a natural and proper desire for mechanics. Under these circumstances he will make a much larger success in the work for which he has an aptitude than if forced into a work toward which he must always feel indifferent or antagonistic.

" It is simply avoiding the misfit of the square peg in the round hole."

Mr. John Mitchell, president of the United Mine Workers of America, and vice-president of the American Federation of Labor, in a letter to the author, speaks of unskilled labor, or of the laborer, rather than of the skilled mechanic. He says:

"Why do young men go into the field of unskilled labor?

"Because the invention and installation of labor-saving machinery has reduced the number of men employed in the skilled trades in proportion to the total number engaged in mechanical pursuits.

"What are the principal obstacles in the way of rising from the ranks?

" Lack of opportunity, owing to the control of industry by a limited and a rapidly decreasing number of men, and the consequent less chance for the workman to evolve into an employer.

"Has the unskilled laborer much opportunity for promotion?

" No. His greatest hope for elevation lies in uniting with his fellow-workers and seeking the general uplifting of the unskilled laborer."

EXPERTS AND SPECIALISTS

DURING the last twenty-five years there has been established a distinct profession, the representatives of which are known as experts or specialists, each one being much more than ordinarily proficient in an art or science which is directly applicable to business.

The demand for these experts continues to be very much ahead of the supply. Practically all extensive manufacturers employ experts or specialists, who are responsible for the quality and standardizing of manufacture, and who frequently conduct experiments, and who usually decide all questions requiring a scientific knowledge.

The packing-house and manufacturer of food, for instance, employ the exclusive time of an expert chemist. The electrical company creates a department of electrical-engineer-in-chief, and the railroad has a chief-mechanical-engineer.

These men, as a rule, have little to do with the business part of their concerns. Their work is usually along scientific lines, and they are in every sense professionals. They receive high salaries, frequently equal to those enjoyed by any of the officers, save the president and those a grade or two below him. A salary of from five thousand to ten thousand dollars is by no means uncommon, and many of these experts are paid considerably larger amounts. Comparatively few receive less than twenty-five hundred dollars a year.

While some of these experts have not enjoyed a liberal education, and have taught themselves into their present efficiency, more than ninety per cent of them are graduates of our higher institutions of learning, and many of them are post-graduates.

With the present number of technical schools, and opportunities for the most thorough education, the brightest boy is not likely to obtain a very high position unless he is a graduate of one of these great institutions. In fact, a diploma appears to be necessary to an important engagement.

I wish to state clearly that the successful expert or specialist possesses extraordinary ability. Unless he does, he is not an expert or a specialist, and will not be so considered, nor can he hold anything more than a subordinate position. Ordinary proficiency in any science or art, or ordinary ability in that direction, is not sufficient for the making of an expert or specialist.

While no one can hope to hold such a position unless he possesses extraordinary capacity, this capacity alone is liable to be of little use to him, unless it has been developed by thorough study in some institution of learning which makes a specialty of the science or art to be practised.

Not only is the expert or specialist thoroughly familiar with the particular thing he has to do, but he has a broad education and experience covering the principles of his practice. For instance, the expert chemist, who is to devote his days to the manufacture of oil, not only understands the chemistry of oil, but he is familiar with chemistry as a science. He is a general chemist as well as a special one. He cannot be a specialist unless he is a regular. His chemical education and experience have covered chemistry in its broadest sense and all the sciences of which chemistry has a part.

I would not advise any boy to consider becoming an expert or specialist unless he had the most positive evidence of natural capacity for the science or art chosen. While he may not be able to diagnose his ability with exactness, unless he has a firm conviction of his natural ability, and can convince others of it, it is very much better for him to enter some business or profession in which ordinary capacity is sufficient for reasonable success.

BUSINESS *vs.* PROFESSION

BUSINESS, commercially considered, consists of every money-making method in which there is a pronounced element of trade or trading.

Professionalism, on the other hand, may be considered as something entirely separated, or as partially removed, from any method of trading, or from that which trading stands for.

It has been said that a professional man is one who carries a stock of brains, and that a business man is one who has a stock of material goods. This distinction is not fair, because, where business deals with material things — actual goods — the business man could not make or sell those goods if he did not have, as a part of his stock in trade, a reasonable amount of brains.

I do not compare the mental quality of the professional with that of the purely business man, but I will say that there is a vast difference, and one which cannot be scientifically or otherwise analyzed. The successful professional man, be he the superior or the inferior of the successful business man, is mentally opposite ; and the successful business man possesses a mental equipment which is foreign to the professional. The professional man lives a different life from that of his business brother. His environment is not the same. The things he cares for most are seldom those enjoyed by the man of business; nor does the latter, as a rule, obtain the greatest pleasure from those things which interest, and sometimes absorb, the professional man.

For convenience' sake, then, let us consider a business man a representative of the making, buying, and selling of material things, or goods, like flour, furniture, or fabrics; and that a professional man is one who does not engage in distributing other than the products of intellect.

Both business and profession have their advantages, and each has its disadvantages. In the first place, ninety-nine per cent of the boys fitted for professional life show natural tendencies for it, and even at an early age develop characteristics which are in favor of profession and opposed to business.

It is therefore obvious that the boy who is fitted to become a successful professionalist is not equally adapted to business, and that the boy who is likely to make a success in business has not those peculiarities, if I may call them by that name, essential to professional success.

But the boy must choose between the two, and how shall he do it? The difficulties in the way of a decision are of more apparent than of real consequence. In the first place, the boy fitted to become a professional man will, in most cases, show a tendency in this direction long before he is out of his teens. Comparatively few boys enter a profession who do not want to go that way, unless they are forced into it by ignorant or conceited parents. Therefore it would seem that it is best to let the boy apparently, at least, choose for himself, after there has been presented to him, if possible, both sides of the problem. If there is in the boy any well-founded desire or ability for some particular thing, he will express a preference. This often gives the key to the first lock in the situation. This preference, in itself, may not mean that the boy is surely fitted for that which he has chosen, but it indicates that there is some reason to suppose that he is adapted to that calling. If he has it in him, if he is destined to succeed, that tendency will grow until it becomes too definite to be mistaken.

The greatest mistake that a parent can make is to attempt to bias or to prejudice the boy before the boy has had opportunity to choose for himself, or rather, to express a choice of his own. The boy has a right to express himself, to present to his parent what he believes to be the best thing for him to do, whether or not what he thinks is really best. It is then the parent's duty, not to pull the boy or to push him, but to stand by his side and help him develop.

It is as unsafe to force a boy against the grain as it is to attempt to throw the mariner's compass out of adjustment. The parent may push or drag the boy from the right way to the wrong way, as the mariner can make the north-pointing needle turn to the south, to the east, or to the west, but at the risk of disaster.

Here let me speak with all the strength that I can throw into written words : It does not make any difference what the parent wants, and it does not make any difference what the boy wants, but it does make all the difference in the world what the boy can do and can do the best; and what he can do the best is the thing for him to do.

Any parent who uses undue influence, and attempts to turn the boy against his ability, is not only a criminal father or mother, but is a breaker of the laws of progress and of civilization.

The boy has every *eminent domain* right to do what he can do the best, a right which is not yet recognized or practised as it should be. The parent has no right, except that of helping the boy into the right. Unless the boy's parents and the boy's friends have conclusive reasons for believing that the boy is adapted to a profession, the boy is safer in the road of business.

The boy who is a natural trader is made for business. The boy who loves money better than anything else is unfitted to a profession. The boy who is unable to get a material grasp of things will probably fail in any professional calling.

The boy who does not have what may be considered a specialty — that is to say, who does not like some one thing much better than he does all others, and who does not necessarily place himself in that environment, if he can do so, probably will not make a successful professional man.

From a financial point of view the professions offer much less than business. The ordinary professional man makes from fifty to seventy-five per cent less than the average business man occupying a similar social position. Unless one is naturally self-sacrificing, or can develop this virtue, he has no business in a profession ; for the life of a professional man, whether he be a doctor, a lawyer, a minister, or an editor, is one continual round of sacrifice, principally the sacrifice of money-income for intellectual achievement. Therefore the lover of money is not naturally adapted to the professions.

Business offers success, or at least moderate success, to any boy of ordinary capacity who is willing to work, who is honest and faithful to himself and to others, and who will harbor his resources and save for future capital; but faithfulness, honesty, and persistency, of themselves, will not produce the successful professionalist.

The professional man of success not only has more than ordinary capacity and ability, but he has adaptability to his work.

True, the top of the professions pays better, financially, than does the bottom, or even the middle, of business; but business, grade by grade, class by class, degree by degree, gives more financial return than do any of the professions.

The first thing to be considered is, does the boy want to become a professional man? If he does, he should be given opportunity to prove to himself and to others that he is fitted for the profession of his choice. If he cannot present this proof, not only to his parents, but to unbiased friends and acquaintances, business is the place for him.

When in doubt, choose business.

Colonel Albert A. Pope, president of the Pope Manufacturing Company, and founder of the "Good Roads Movement," in a letter to the author, says:

"If I advised a boy to enter professional life, I would do so because I had thoroughly studied his personality and had become convinced that his desire to master a profession was backed by a studious character, and that he either had the necessary means to help him through his education, or, if poor, had courage and determination enough to work his way and win success. Judging from my own experience, I would say that he must, indeed, be a superior boy who, in the face of poverty and other impediments, can shoulder the work which it is necessary to accomplish in order to place himself in a successful professional career. But the right boys should be encouraged.

"Perhaps more boys are fitted for business than for professional life. At all events, a young man starting out in this world should be careful to select the occupation for which he is best suited. He ought certainly to seek the advice of the best business men and others with whom he can get into contact.

"Of course the first thing is to learn how to provide one's self, and those depending upon him, with food, clothing, and shelter.

"To win in either walk of life means a willingness to make sacrifices, to be economical and prudent, and to harbor resources in a rational fashion. This, however, should not be done in such a way as to make the individual selfish, because all along it is necessary for him to give something for the good of others. That helps materially in the development of his own character, and if done wisely, will not be a detriment to the accumulation of funds.

"The school of deprivation is a wonderful training for after life. He who can give up in manhood the luxuries which most young fellows delight in possessing can go through the difficulties which are sure to come in a career which ends in success.

"If a boy has such traits of character as are indicated above, he can win; and he can win in a way that will not injure his own manly character if he will follow the spirit of such a motto as I have long kept near me: 'I will wish to do good to all men; I will do good to many men; I will do wilful injury to no man.'"

Mr. Paul Walton, of the New York Bar, in a letter to the author, says :

" I believe that eighty per cent of boys are much better fitted, by brains and temperament, for a business rather than for a professional life, and would be more successful and contented in the former.

" I would not advise a boy to consider a professional career unless he is conscious of a strong leaning toward, and taste for, the particular calling, and unless he is prepared to wait for years for the material and other returns.

" So far as the 'material returns' are concerned, they are undoubtedly smaller in the profession than in business."

WHOLESALE *vs.* RETAIL

THE selling side of business may be divided into two somewhat distinct parts, — wholesale and retail. The wholesaler sells in large quantities. The majority of his customers are not known as consumers, but as retailers or tradesmen. The wholesaler may or may not be a manufacturer. In most cases he is not, but acts as the distributing medium between the manufacturer and the retailer. As a rule, he carries a large stock of goods, either at his warerooms or in conveniently located store-houses, or in both. These goods are not displayed as are the goods upon the counters and shelves of the retail store, the majority of sales being made by sample; that is to say, the purchaser — the retailer — seldom seeing the goods he buys, except in sample, until after they have been delivered to his store.

The terms "jobber" and "distributer" are analogous to that of wholesaler. All the jobbers and so-called distributers are wholesalers, because they sell at wholesale and depend upon the retailer for patronage.

The retailer, whether he deals in meat, groceries, dry goods, or crockery, buys directly of the wholesaler, the jobber, or distributer, and occasionally from the mill or factory, and sells these goods to the consumer or people at large.

Merchandise business, then, is divided into three distinct classes : first, the manufacturer, who from the raw material produces a finished product; secondly, the wholesaler, jobber, or distributer, who purchases this product in large quantities, and sells it to the retailer; and thirdly, the retailer, who buys of the wholesaler, jobber, or distributer, and sells directly to the people.

If the boy proposes to be a tradesman, to go into mercantile business, he must either be a wholesaler or a retailer, or both. Since comparatively few wholesale houses do any considerable amount of retailing and few retail houses are wholesalers, it is hardly necessary to consider these two classes of trade in combination.

Ninety per cent of our wholesalers are located in large cities. Occasionally one finds a wholesale house at some country centre. Therefore the boy who desires to enter the wholesale business may make up his mind to live in the city, not necessarily at a metropolis, but in a town of considerable size and which is a centre of trade. The retailer is everywhere, in the large city, in the small city, in the country town, in the country village, and at the cross-roads.

Many merchants and other business men thoroughly believe that the wholesale business offers the boy many advantages over those presented by the retail trade. I feel that if a vote were taken among fair-minded men, whether wholesalers or retailers, considerably more than the majority of the ballots would be cast in favor of the wholesale business as presenting more advantages to the boy about to begin his life's work; but even with the majority against it, the retail business is not without its opportunities, and in many instances it presents more advantages than the wholesale trade.

Perhaps the most serious obstacle against which the retail employee has to contend is the fact that he is not permitted to go out into the open and to force trade into the store. He cannot, as a rule, become a travelling salesman. Most of the trade he obtains may be through those who come to him first. In other words, the retail salesman cannot take the initiative, as can the drummer or travelling man, who almost invariably is connected with the wholesale house. The retail salesman must, to an extent, wait for trade. His place is behind the counter, and he cannot readily reach farther for trade than the counter's width; but for all that, he is in a position to hold trade.

Many buyers, and I am not referring to " shoppers," those will-o'-the-wisp women who shop without buying and whose trade is too small to be worth catering to, discriminate between salesmen. These people are the buyers. Their trade is worth cultivating and developing. The retail salesman, although he may not go after this trade, has an opportunity to show his proficiency in holding it. He has it in his power, not only to hold this trade, but to develop it. Comparatively few people, even the most experienced buyers, know exactly what they want to buy. They can be made to change their ideas and to purchase something similar to what they thought they wanted, something better, or more than they originally intended. Here is the retail salesman's opportunity. If he understands his goods, knows how they are made, how they will wear, and what they will do; if he knows how to fit the goods to the customer, not the customer to the goods; if he can give advice of intrinsic value, and thereby assist the customer in selecting, he will build up a patronage which will be his principal asset.

It has been said that the majority of people come to the store on account of the store's reputation, and not because of the salesmen. This is true, but it would not be so if the quality of salesmen was equal to the quality of the store or of the goods on sale. Because ninety per cent of our retail salesmen neither know nor care about what they sell, because ninety per cent are without ambition, are indifferent, and would rather spend their time finding fault than in improving their opportunities, the buyer depends upon the character of the store to the sacrifice of the salesman.

The wholesale salesman is usually a travelling man or drummer. After he has become familiar with the goods, as a boy and as a stock-clerk, he is sent out on the road, and upon the road he will travel for from five to twenty-five or more years, leading the hardest kind of life and being subjected to the fiercest temptations, without a home, and almost without a country. True, he may have greater opportunity than has a retail employee; but he works harder, not necessarily more hours, but the strain upon him is greater.

The manager of the selling department of a great wholesale house, a man who has spent twenty-five years upon the road, told me that he did not know of one salesman who had been upon the road ten years who was not dyspeptic or suffering from some other physical ailment. Investigations and conversations with other salesmen indicate that my friend undoubtedly exaggerated; but it is a fact that the life upon the road is not conducive to good health, to comfort, or to those things which make men better citizens.

I am not advising the boy against the wholesale business, nor would I advise him to consider unfavorably
the retail business.   My advice would depend somewhat
upon his opportunity and capacity.   I think a boy stands
a better chance of success with a good opportunity in
the retail business than with a poorer opportunity in the
wholesale business; and, conversely, he is more likely to
reach fame and fortune, or to do fairly well, with a good
opportunity in the wholesale business as compared with a
poorer opportunity in the retail business.   If he has the
right kind of stuff in him he will succeed either way, all
things being equal.

However, I would advise the city boy, who intends to
remain in the city, to enter the wholesale rather than the
retail business, provided he is energetic, aggressive, and
willing to work hard, and the kind of boy who is not
easily discouraged.   But I would not advise the country boy to go to the great city, and to begin his life in
a wholesale house, unless he has exhausted country
opportunity.

The average country boy, even of ability, though he
may be aggressive and strong in every business trait, is
better off in the country, in the retail store, than he is
likely to be in the city, — a fighter against the fiercest
competition.   I do not mean to say that the country boy
of character and capacity will fail in the city, because he
will succeed if he has the stuff in him that success is
made off; but I do say that I believe that, all things
being equal, he will succeed far better by remaining in
the country and growing up with it.   This, probably,
means the retail business, because this is the country's
business.

One reason why the retail salesman is considered inferior to the wholesale seller is because the rank and file

of inferior boys, boys without ambition and without the capacity for development, naturally gravitate toward the counter. They take little thought of the morrow, and since the counter offers them rather more at the start, and they do not seem to care which way they go, they go retail-counterward.

True, the retail salesman comes in competition with the retail saleswoman, to his disadvantage. But these conditions are not necessarily a handicap to the progressive boy of capacity, ambition, and a willingness to work, and who does not expect to be an easy winner.

Certainly the man behind the counter does not meet the same aggressive competition as does the salesman on the road. Therefore if he is possessed of more than ordinary capacity, he may rise more rapidly than will his wholesale brother, who, on the road, runs a virtual hurdle race, with more chance of tripping than of spurting.

Perhaps the chief advantage of the wholesale business over that of the retail is in that the wholesaler deals in larger units, covers a larger territory, and comes in contact with a greater diversity of active business minds, each one a representative of a distinct section.

This induces a mental expansion, which is not as readily enjoyed by the retail dealer, whose field, as a rule, is limited to his city or town and to nearby territory. The wholesaler comes in direct and constant contact with broad conditions, while the retailer is somewhat limited to local environments.

This broader life, which is the wholesaler's privilege, of course means larger wants and a much greater living expense. The successful wholesaler, particularly if he be located at the metropolis, although he enjoys contact with the entire country and even with representatives from abroad, may have little time to meet or to associate intimately with conditions outside of his business. Therefore his broadness is liable to be confined to business broadness; while the retailer at a country centre, although he is living within a local environment, has opportunities for study and for outside development.

It is very difficult to assist a boy in his choice between the wholesale and the retail. To a considerable extent I would leave it to the boy; but I would try to place before him the advantages of both branches, and the disadvantages as well. I would attempt to let him have an advance view of these two kinds of trading, and then to let the decision rest with him.

Mr. Samuel T. Morgan, president of the Virginia-Carolina Chemical Company, of Richmond, Va., and president of the Southern Cotton Oil Company, of New York City, in a letter to the author, says:

" Answering your inquiry as to why I would advise a boy to enter the wholesale instead of the retail business: I beg to say that the first feature which commends itself in the wholesale trade to a young man is that the business is of very much greater magnitude. Business in this line is not done in a small way. It therefore compels a young man to use every faculty of good judgment and discretion. He cannot afford to make mistakes, for a mistake made in the wholesale trade necessarily means pecuniary loss of greater or less magnitude.

" A young man entering this branch of business must recognize that it is not pennies he is dealing in, and usually it is men of brains and business knowledge that he comes in contact with. He therefore soon understands that the best thought and endeavor he is capable of must be constantly exercised if he would hold his position and work his way to prominence.

" The promises of reward in the wholesale trade, to the

right boy, who is willing to give the business the proper thought and attention, are great; and what he lacks in experience and knowledge when he first enters the wholesale trade must be made up by good judgment and great diligence. Unless a boy is possessed of both of these qualities he should think long before entering this branch of trade, which, in a general sense, is a most profitable and prosperous branch, and is full of promises in all features to the right boy.

" Answering your inquiry as to why a boy should go into the retail rather than the wholesale trade : I beg to suggest a few thoughts that strike me as making this branch of trade more desirable — certainly to the young man beginning work — than the wholesale trade.

" In the first place, there is no education and no knowledge that is worth so much to a man in trade and business as the knowledge of his fellow-men; and in my opinion there is no way in the world that this knowledge can be gained so rapidly and so thoroughly as in a retail store, where a salesman comes in contact with all classes and kinds of people. The right kind of boy, after a little experience, if he is a close student of human nature, will soon learn to ' size-up,' so to speak, his customer when he comes in; then the balance is comparatively easy.

" It teaches also a young man not to ' despise the day of small things,' and teaches him that if he would be successful he must treat the small buyer with the same consideration that he gives the larger one.

" It should instil in a boy a spirit of economy, both as to time and money, and at the same time give him a broad and liberal mind — fitting him for almost any duties that require knowledge of trade and knowledge of people ; and there are but few duties that I have found in this world in which a knowledge of these two is not the keynote of success.

" For a boy to be successful, either in wholesale or retail trade, he must love his business.

" A love of the occupation that a boy is engaged in is as essential to success as intelligence and industry.

" I hardly know a case of a boy who was in love with his business, whether it was wholesale or retail, who did not make a success of it and find rapid promotion."

Mr. Daniel P. Morse, president of the Morse and Rogers Company, of New York City, in a letter to the author, says:

" I would advise a boy, after a few years' apprenticeship in either the retail or wholesale business, to reason with himself as to which form of trading he wishes to make his life work, and then to put his whole soul into that, whether it be a wholesale or retail business, my observation being that some boys are much better fitted for one than the other, and that it takes a few years of apprenticeship in one or both to bring out the qualities which make for success. It is seldom that one succeeds well in a business which he does not fully like."

Mr. Fred L. Howard, of the firm of C. A. Browning and Company, of Boston, in a letter to the author, says:

" A young man in making a choice between a wholesale and retail business career has first his natural qualifications to take into account, with almost as much careful thought as if considering two entirely different professions; for it is well known that many successful ' wholesale ' men have made marked failures in attempts to conduct a retail business, and vice versa.

" It certainly may be said that at the present time the retail business has some advantages over the wholesale. Both are merely distributers of goods which the producers or manufacturers cannot conveniently distribute themselves.

"Originally the producer was the vender of his own product. The first necessity, as the demand for goods increased, was the retailer, and the last necessity the wholesaler.

"While the retail business was done by many small dealers, the position of the wholesaler was a very important one, really indispensable; but as the population increased, and prosperous retailers adopted methods to attract trade to fewer centres, the retailers became able to handle greater and greater quantities of goods, until many of them became larger purchasers than the wholesale dealers themselves, and consequently more desirable customers of the producers. In some branches of business, such as the boot and shoe, grocery, and dry goods business, this has taken place to such an extent that the wholesaler has now most decidedly taken second place to many retailers in the amount of goods handled. The immense quantity of goods that now pass direct from the producer to the retailer once passed first through the hands of the wholesaler.

"So far as I can see, this difference is to be even greater in the future; the larger a retail business, the more direct dealings with first hands and the less use for the middle man.

"Also, where the needs of the retailer are too small to warrant buying at first hand, the combination of a number of smaller dealers, who are not in competition with each other, enables them to obtain the [advantages of large buyers by purchasing together, and dividing their purchases according to their needs. Hence the numerous syndicates.

"In this age of trusts and combinations the necessity for the wholesaler becomes less and less, consequently that field for the young man is diminishing.

"Yet for all this, the opportunities in the wholesale line are greater for a larger percentage of those engaged in it than for those engaged in the retail business.

"In the first place, the salaries of wholesale salesmen, after the first few years, average more; the work to be per-

formed affords the opportunity of travel and larger association with men, and demands a versatility of ability, tact,
and self-reliance not required of the clerk behind the
counter.

" If a man is sure of an opportunity to become a manager
or owner of a business, in most lines of trade, retail is to
be preferred.

" If he can see nothing before him but the life of the
employee, he will get more salary and more business experience, and lead a freer life in most kinds of wholesale business.

" Whichever his choice may be, the hope of the young
man must be in himself, in his own pluck and perseverance.

" The lower ranks of all pursuits have ever been, and
probably always will be, crowded ; but every branch of business is now suffering from the need of upright, persevering,
and efficient young men, and such are bound to succeed,
whether in the wholesale or retail business. The young man
who applies such qualities to his pursuit will always believe
his choice was correct at the beginning. The young man
who does not, will probably attribute his failure to his
choice and not to his own shortcomings."

Mr. William Horlick, president of Horlick's Food
Company, of Racine, Wis., in a letter to the author,
says:

" Should a boy choose the retail or the wholesale line of
business? is the question in brief. A boy who expects to
be successful in the retail line should possess a capacity for
detail. Nothing, however minute, should escape observation, and, if possible, co-ordination. Numberless petty
details will arise every day, which must be decided promptly
and rightly ; and to do this, their full bearing in every direction must be grasped. This will mean, evidently, close attention to work, the use of one's brains, cultivation of the habit

of close observation, systematic reasoning, and a solid substratum of perseverance and determination to succeed. If the business is one that involves the art of selling, it is evident that other factors must be taken into consideration. The boy must cultivate urbanity, cheerfulness of disposition, and be somewhat of a student of human nature.

" On the other hand, the boy who has the opportunity to start in wholesale work evidently needs the same qualities, since success in selling on the larger scale will depend also upon the thorough knowledge of the details of the retail business. A lack in any one of the above requirements would, it seems to me, impede very greatly the success of an aspirant in the wholesale line. To this there must be added such additional knowledge as is helpful in the direction of the particular work. A thorough acquaintance with the materials sold, their sources in the crude and manufactured state, and the needs and peculiarities of the people to whom they are to be sold, should be gradually obtained.

" In both the retail and wholesale lines, therefore, very largely the same qualities will be needed for business success. Without what has been called ' an infinite capacity for work ' no lad may expect to make a large success. Every faculty of the mind must receive proper training to develop that acuteness of business vision which will supply prompt decision, initiative enterprise, and caution. Of course, without proper ambition no boy can expect to succeed. At the same time, it appears to be difficult to imbue into the minds of the youth of the present day a determination to succeed which is not linked with a belief that this may be done rapidly. The idea that with sufficient energy one is sure to acquire a fortune very rapidly — to get rich quickly — is unfortunately an evil of our times. The old Latin motto, ' Festina lente ' — Make haste slowly — is one that I would recommend to all ambitious young men in any line of business; and beneath that, as a basis for real success and real happiness, and especially for that solid business integrity which will command respect and the affection of his fellow-citizens, there should be a thorough acquaintance with, and a determination to adhere to, the Ten Commandments. The last few years have furnished many woful examples of men, supposed to be large-minded, princes of finance, whose down-fall have furnished lessons of business degradation which should prove warning beacons to the ambitious young man who hopes to achieve a solid success."

THE EDUCATION OF BOYS

ASKED several of our representative professional and business men to answer the following pertinent questions:

(1) Why would you advise a boy who intends to enter a profession to graduate from college?

(2) Why would you advise a boy who intends to enter business to graduate from college?

(3) Why would you advise a boy who intends to enter some mechanical trade or business to graduate from an institute of technology or other high scientific school?

The following counsels and opinions were the result:

Jacob Gould Schurman, A.M., LL.D., president of Cornell University:

"In my judgment, the chief reason why a boy should take a college course is that it will expand his horizon, multiply his interests, enable him to take his bearings in the world, and, in general, make a larger man of him."

The Hon. Curtis Guild, Jr., Governor of Massachusetts, and editor of the *Boston Commercial Bulletin:*

GEORGE WESTINGHOUSE

Inventor and manufacturer; born in Central Bridge, Schohaire County,
N. Y., 1846; educated in public and high schools; worked in his father's
machine shop, inventing at 15 a rotary engine. Served in Union Army;
invented Westinghouse air brake in 1868, followed by other inventions in
railway signals, steam and gas engines, steam turbines and electrical
machinery; was the pioneer in introducing alternating current machinery
in America; at the head of corporations employing over 20.000 people

"I think I can answer your questions precisely in the following single paragraph:

"Governor Russell once said, 'It is important that Americans should remember that they have not only to make a living, but to make a life.'

"Technical education is almost a necessity for making a livelihood in the present highly developed condition of all the industrial arts. If the Republic is to succeed, however, American citizens must be something more than cogs that turn easily in a machine. A man with no knowledge of history, literature, or languages is necessarily without knowledge of the governments that have gone before, and of the ideals that lift a nation from mere commercialism.

"To the technical education should be added a liberal education, that the successful business man may also be the valuable citizen."

The Rev. O. P. Gifford, D.D., pastor of the Delaware Avenue Baptist Church, of Buffalo, N. Y.:

"(1) Because the training widens his horizon, teaches concentration and self-control, and puts the young man in touch with the thoughts of the centuries.

"(2) Because the association with men teaches how to meet men, know men, and manage men. The four years reveals him to himself, and other men to him.

"(3) Because the training gives him the use of his powers and knowledge of what has been done."

Arthur T. Hadley, LL.D., president of Yale University:

"I think that every boy, no matter what his trade, ought to be technically trained, even at great pecuniary sacrifice. I think that the majority of boys who can afford a college course are better off for it, whether they intend to enter professional life or business life; but I should not make the answer to this question by any means so general and un-reserved as that to the other."

Joseph Alden Shaw, A.M., principal of the Highland Military Academy, of Worcester, Mass.:

" (1) Nowhere else save in a first-class college or university can the best foundations be laid for preparation for ' the learned profession.' The associations there gained, and the friendships formed, are invaluable for success in after life.

" (2) Habits of close study and observation, so necessary to success in business life, are awakened and fostered by collegiate training. No man need ever think that time spent in the study of the so-called dead languages is ever wasted."

The Rev. Amory H. Bradford, D.D., of Montclair, N. J., associate editor of *The Outlook:*

" (1) I would advise every boy entering a profession to graduate if possible from a classical college, because he needs that kind of culture to prepare him for his work.

" (2) In order that his manhood may be broadened, his sympathies widened, and his ideals elevated, all of which business men especially need.

" (3) I believe the best training along mechanical lines is furnished by the schools of technology, and every man ought to get the best possible preparation for his work."

Mr. Josephus N. Larned, ex-president of the American Library Association and late superintendent of education at Buffalo:

" The undisputed axiom in this country, that our public schools are the nurseries of good citizenship, rests generally, I believe, upon the broad and true conception of what good citizenship means and is. Up to a certain point it represents a full recognition of the plasticity of youth, and the supreme need of care and skilful workmanship upon it to insure the making of a useful good man. But that important recognition halts commonly at the most critical period of youth. It is attentive to the plasticity of the boy and unmindful of the plasticity of the young man. It assumes that a school which dismisses its student from pupilage at just the age when he begins to have the capabilities and feelings of a man, has done enough for the making of the desired good citizen. In reality, that dismissal puts all that has been done for the half-formed youth to the gravest possible risk. The ripening of manhood in him is still to come; which means the whole conversion of boyish dreams and fancies, boyish thinking, boyish caprices of impulse and will, into determined tendencies of thought, aspiration, and purpose in the man. And in that, the very crisis of human growth, the maturing young man is ordinarily sent forth to be exposed to all the hazards of influence encountered in what we describe as business life.

" Consider for a moment what those hazards are. Consider them with reference to our public interest as a community in the formation of the young man. We want him to become a good citizen, useful in promoting and helpful in defending the common weal. This calls for intelligence, and he may be very usefully intelligent with no training beyond that of the common school. But it calls furthermore for a large liberation and elevation of mind, above sordidly selfish aims, above narrowing habits of thought and belief, above all dishonesties, all servilities, all meannesses of every kind. Where the needed moral largeness has been given by Nature to a youth with some depth of fixity in his being, he may be proof against the pressures and strains of that arena of competition that he enters when his life work begins. On the other hand, if Nature shrank him to a poor pattern, there may be nothing that can expand him in heart and mind. But those are exceptions to the natural making of character in mankind. As a rule, the youth who goes early into the world of work and commerce is more or less pliant to the forces that play upon him there. And they are forces very trying and very dangerous to most of the higher motives in life. In many ways they act powerfully for good; but there is an unceasing pull in them toward selfishness, toward egoism in all forms, toward hardness, toward aggressiveness, toward small interests and small thoughts — against public spirit and public service, against fellow service, against everything, indeed, that goes to the making of the good citizen of our desire. And the evil strain is so insidious that even religion — not religion in its purity and perfection, perhaps, but religion that believes itself to be pure — can be cheated into solemn consecrations of it, with blessing and prayer.

"Now, what is there — aside from the mortal strength that may be native in him — what is there that will best protect a young man from those narrowing and hardening tendencies in our competitive organization of life? What will do most to withhold him from the sordid careers that make useless and mischievous citizens? What will do most to keep social and civic and patriotic and altruistic feeling alive in him? Why, assuredly, it is a full-fed mind, left with no leanness and scantness in its growth. Assuredly it is an early armoring of the man with fine tastes, high thoughts, large views; too fine, too high, too large to be reconcilable with an ignoble course in life. That, as I conceive it, is what a liberal education — liberal culture — means to our democracy. It holds the vitalizing leaven of an influence which democracy can spare no more than it can spare the elementary under-culture of its common schools."

The Hon. Carroll Curtis Boggs, Justice of the Supreme Court of Illinois:

"I do not think that either in professional or business life the fact that one is a graduate, or has a degree, will be found of any practical benefit. A classical education is desirable (all learning and knowledge is so), and if a young man can complete a classical course and his professional studies by the time he has reached his twenty-fifth year, he should do so; but I think every man should enter upon his life work not later than at that age, and that it would not be advisable to remain longer in the schools in order to graduate in a classical course. This I believe to be true of either a professional or a business life.

"The knowledge to be obtained in an institute of technology would be useful to every mechanic and every business man, and would probably be almost a necessity in some of the mechanical trades."

Henry T. Byford, M.D., of Chicago:

"Answers to questions Nos. 1 and 2: Because a man cannot know too much, and because it will better develop the man as well as the professional or business worker.

"Answer to Question No. 3: Because it puts him in a better position to rise rapidly to the most important positions."

The Hon. Charles D. Hine, secretary of the Connecticut State Board of Education:

"From considerable experience with boys, including one of my own, I should say that advice with reference to college would depend mainly upon my knowledge of the boy. The individual aptitudes of each person must be considered.

"Answering in detail:

"1. Classical education is not necessary to a profession.

"2. A classical education is not so good from a business point of view as a scientific or technical education.

"3. Probably you have in mind in your third question whether practice in a trade or theoretical education is better. My view is that the technical education of a boy who is to enter upon a mechanical trade should begin before he leaves the common school. His fitness for a particular trade or business ought to be tentatively ascertained. A thorough training in a technical school will then be valuable, but he will not succeed without practice.

"These brief answers do not precisely express my views."

William E. Huntington, Ph.D., president of Boston University:

"A young man who is expecting to succeed in any one of the 'professions' in the coming time should have the liberal training of a good college, both for his own sake and for the benefit of the community he is to serve.

"The same may be said to a boy who is to go into business. If he has a good mind and wants to make himself of most possible use *in the world* (not simply in his business), he should go into life with that mind well-furnished and disciplined.

"Even for a mechanical trade a boy should have as broad a training as possible. Technical schools are doing fine work to train eye and hand, as well as mental faculties, for high-grade work in the trades."

Mr. John Thomson, librarian of the Free Library of Philadelphia:

"I have never met any man who regretted having spent the years necessary to complete his classical or technical education before entering a profession or business. I also believe that the best educated men are not only the best equipped for the competition which they will meet in professional life or business, but that in the event of failure, or in the event of merely moderate success, they will not regret having acquired tastes which will enable them to endure either fate with philosophy."

Harry Pratt Judson, A.M., LL.D., head-professor of political science, and dean of the faculties of arts, literature, and science, University of Chicago:

"In answer to your questions:

"1. I would advise a boy who intends to enter a profession to graduate from a classical college, because in my opinion the mental and moral developments derived from such a course are of value entirely aside from the specific knowledge needed for the given profession.

"2. The same considerations, I think, apply to the young man who desires to enter business. Business means much more than the successful conduct of a specific occupation. The business man who has wide sympathies and who comes into contact with life at many points is qualified to be a business man of the highest type. Moreover, success in business means more than success in making money. It should mean also success in using it, so as to get the largest satisfaction out of life, and so as to be a most efficient member of society. A thorough college education, I believe, will conduce toward these ends.

"3. An institution of technology will enable a boy who intends to enter some mechanical trade to be far more efficient in his work, and better fitted to cope with the higher lines of his employment, than would otherwise be the case."

Professor William Libbey, Sc.D., of Princeton University:

"First, I should advise a boy who intends to enter a profession to graduate from college before taking up his professional studies, because of the broader view of life that he will receive, and also clearer light as to the relations of his own professional work to the other branches of knowledge.

"Secondly, I should advise a boy who intends to enter business to graduate from college before doing so, because

of the more concise habits of application he will acquire if
he attends to his duties faithfully.

" Thirdly, I should advise a boy who intends to enter a
mechanical trade to graduate from an institute of technology, or even a classical college, before doing so, because of
the maturity he would gain by such a course, which would
enable him to rise faster than he would otherwise."

Mr. Philip E. Howard, of Philadelphia, president of
the *Sunday School Times* Company:

" If the way were clear for the boy to take a classical
course, or if it should be his duty to clear the way, then I
should congratulate him on the opportunity he would have
for rigid mental training, and for contact during adolescence
with his fellows in the little world of the college. A professional man is not so much of a man as he ought to be if
he is merely professional. Because the college can train
a boy to think and to live as the professional school does
not, he needs that training in order to acquire and to use the
set of facts that the professional school can give.

" So that he may learn to get the utmost possible work
out of his brain and body in a systematic way, and under
severe strain, whether he feels like it or not at the moment.
So that he may learn to do team-work on the athletic field,
and also learn the give-and-take of contest in an aggressive
partnership, the subordination of self to the common good,
and not to run and cry when he is hurt. So that he may
have his moral fibre toughened against the tough problems
that will charge at him with a rush in business. So that he
may have the outlook and the uplift of ideals that have
governed real men in bygone days, ideals without which
he will become dwarfed and warped and shrivelled in business, when he might become a giant in power and service.
Because he would do well to get knowledge of his specialty
from masters in his chosen field, the theory linked with the

practice, the know-what and the know-how tied fast together. He can get along, perhaps, without the school of technology, but why should he, when every hour of right preparation there saves hours of blundering performance thereafter ? If a boy wishes to be, and knows he ought to be, an engineer, then why not be the engineer?"

Professor Joseph W. Richards, A.M., M.S., Ph.D., of Lehigh University:

"In answer to your queries:
" 1. If the boy intends to be
" (a) a clergyman — because the classical college teaches him the best thoughts of men of all times.
" (b) a lawyer — because the classical college teaches him the historical development of law in the broadest way.
" (c) a doctor — I don't advise it. A course in chemistry and biology in a technical school is his best preparation for his special training in medicine.
"2. I would not advise it. His best preparation is a course in business and commerce in a scientific college, where he meets technical students.
"3. Because no other sort of institution can give him half so good a preparation."

The Hon. Carroll D. Wright. Ph.D., president of Clark University:

" I should advise a boy who intends to enter a profession to graduate from college, — because in a profession he will need all that he can gain in such a college. His college training will broaden him, teach him to appreciate and weigh knowledge, and to utilize it to the best advantage. He will gain much also from the college associations, which will be of great benefit in his profession. I am not speaking from a commercial point of view, but from an appreciation of scholarship in any line of work which a man may undertake.

"And this applies also to your second question, whether a boy who intends to enter business should enter college. I do not care what career a man chooses, — the more he knows the happier he will be, and his usefulness will be all the greater from the knowledge he gains in college. Every man should know the art of his business. He should know what the world has taught in the past, and that systematic training acquired in college will be of the greatest benefit to him in any line of business.

"To your third question, I would say that it seems to me that a man to-day, in these times of mental competition, is thoroughly handicapped if he does not take a course in some technological institution. Of course, practice and experience are necessary in order to make a perfect worker in any mechanical business, trade, or calling, but the application of scientific principles is necessary to success, and such training will enable a graduate from a technological institution immediately to take a higher rank than in any other way. Assuming that a young man has the brain-power to carry on college or technological work, he should by all means obtain a college training. The trouble is that a large proportion of those who enter college or an institute of technology ought never to have entered, but those who are competent will be greatly benefited by their course, not only from a commercial point of view, but from that higher point of view — their ability to render the very best service to the community at large."

Mr. Charles Gallaudet Trumbull, editor of the *Sunday School Times:*

"1. Because the classical course trains the mind more rigorously than does any other in processes of thought. What the student learns there is of far less importance than the art of learning how to learn. That art is taught in the college.

" 2. First, because of the mental discipline referred to in 1. Further, because the business man needs just as much as he can possibly accumulate of the knowledge which is not strictly commercial. He will get the latter quickly enough, if he is the right kind of business man, after he has entered upon business. If he does not begin to learn something of what thought and literature have to teach before he gets into business, he may never come to it later. And he will be a less able business man without it.

" 3. In view of the reasons cited under 1 and 2, let him first take a full classical college course if possible ; then let him study in the best technical school he has access to ; for any man who stops short of the highest possible equipment is throwing opportunity away."

Charles Franklin Thwing, D.D., LL.D., president of Western Reserve University :

" In general, I think a boy who intends to enter a profession or business should go to college. For business, as well as a profession, demands a trained mind. The college is the best condition and force for training the mind.

" I am also inclined to think that a boy who intends to enter a mechanical calling, as well as business, would in many cases gain as large an advantage from graduation from a college of liberal learning as from a scientific school ; for the chief value of training lies, not in knowledge, but in method.

" The gaining of the power to think, to think with comprehensiveness, accuracy, and thoroughness, represents the chief element needed in life, and the securing of this force is most directly and efficiently gained in and through the college."

THE END